Art & Sole

Contents

5	**Foreword**	302	**Index**
6	**Preface**		
8	**Introduction**		
10	**Sneakers & Art**		
12	Intercity	96	Tom Luedecke
14	Shantell Martin	98	Nike Laser Project
16	Peter Saville	102	Katsuya Terada
18	The Haçienda	103	LX One
19	IRAK NY	104	Jeff Staple
20	Gasius	108	Mister Cartoon
21	UNKLE	110	Mike Giant
22	Daniel Arsham	111	Dondi White
24	Nicole McLaughlin	112	Vaughn Bodé
28	Helen Kirkum	114	Haze
32	Steven Harrington	115	Claw Money
33	Ruohan Wang	116	Jeremyville
34	Shigeki Fujishiro	117	MÖTUG
35	Ryan Gander	118	FUTURA
36	Ben Drury	124	Stash
38	Kevin Lyons	130	Vans and The Simpsons
39	Hitomi Yokoyama	134	Mark Ward
40	James Jarvis	135	Experimental Jetset
41	Krink	136	Damien Hirst
42	Geoff McFetridge	137	Shaniqwa Jarvis
48	Taka Hayashi	138	Hiroshi Fujiwara
50	Neckface	142	Kenzo Minami
52	Robert Williams	143	John Maeda
54	Mr Sabotage	144	Jun Watanabe
56	DC Shoes Artist Projects™	146	Kidrobot
58	KAWS	150	Sean Cliver
64	Chris Law	154	Dave Kinsey
66	Crooked Tongues	155	Evan Hecox
70	adidas adicolor	156	adidas Superstar 35th Anniversary
76	Mark Gonzales	160	Blondey McCoy
78	Also Known As	161	Goldie
80	Weiden + Kennedy	162	Transport for London
82	Tom Sachs	164	Jean-Michel Basquiat
88	Virgil Abloh	165	André Saraiva
92	Steve ESPO Powers	166	Gravis Art Collective
94	CLOT	168	Nike SB The Vault

176	**Art & Sneakers**
178	Haroshi
180	I Have Pop™
186	90x90
192	+41
198	//DIY
200	Dave White
208	INSA
212	John Baldwin
216	Steph Morris
222	Toby Neilan
224	Parra
232	Julien Rademaker
236	LORENZ.OG
242	Studio Hagel
246	MSCHF
250	Nash Money
252	Cemal Okten & Martin Price
253	Lady Brown
254	Coolrain Lee
258	Michael Lau
264	Mark James
265	Nike SB Three Be@rbrick Project
266	Nike Transformers
268	Vinti Andrews
270	.SWOOSH
274	RTFKT
278	Freedom of Creation
282	Jethro Haynes
284	Rosie Lee
286	White Dunk: Evolution of an Icon
294	Nick Glackin
298	Gary Baseman
300	Art & Sole Screenprint Series

Foreword
by Nicole McLaughlin

Sneakers are more than just footwear. They're a canvas, a cultural artefact and a statement of identity for many. Originally published in 2008, *Art & Sole* has long been a reference point for those who appreciate the intersection of creativity and footwear – including myself.

In the 17 years since its initial publication, the footwear landscape has evolved dramatically, driven by technological innovations, sustainability efforts and cultural movements. Independent creatives have more platforms than ever to showcase their work, thanks to social media and brands embracing collaboration. Meanwhile, in-house designers continue to push legacy brands forward, by incorporating their own identity and reimagining archival designs. Footwear has even made its way into the fine art world, with some pieces being exhibited, sold and collected as high-value art.

Yet, through all of these changes, one thing has stayed the same: sneakers continue to be a powerful medium for artistic expression.

This updated edition picks up where the first left off, celebrating the designers and artists who have shaped footwear culture over the years and showcasing some of their most interesting ideas. The creatives featured in *Art & Sole* have put their fingerprints on the footwear industry in various ways, from starting trends to experimenting with new materials.

As someone who has long admired many of these designers – some of whom I'm now lucky enough to call friends – I continue to find endless inspiration in their work. This book offers a rare glimpse into their creative processes, showing how they tackled challenging briefs and found inspiration. Whether you're looking for your own inspiration, an archive of culturally significant collaborations or a visual journey of sneaker culture's evolution, this book has something for you.

A special thank you to Intercity's Nathan Gale, who has dedicated so much time and effort to sharing these stories. *Art & Sole* captures an important period of time that will continue to inspire for years to come.

Preface
by Intercity

A lot has changed in the sneaker industry since *Art & Sole* was first published back in 2008 – and that's without mentioning the proliferation of sneakers books published since. When we first came up with the concept for *Art & Sole*, collecting sneakers was a relatively niche pursuit, and sneaker culture was still a somewhat hidden world that had to be searched out and discovered. That has changed dramatically in recent years and the sneaker industry is booming – thanks in no small part to the resale market. Reselling, or 'flipping', was a frowned-upon act in the world of sneakers (buying a pair to flip essentially prevents those who really want the shoes from getting them at retail price), but resale marketplaces such as StockX and GOAT have helped to shift this stigma. Flipping sneakers, sometimes for an instant and very healthy profit, is now commonplace, and the figures are staggering. In 2020, London's Design Museum hosted Sneakers Unboxed: Studio to Street, an exhibition sponsored by StockX. The exhibition disclosed that in 2020 alone, more than one billion pairs of sneakers were sold worldwide, with the associated resale market valued at US$6billion. Even large-scale auction houses such as Sotheby's and Christie's have got in on the action – selling the rarest of the rare, including many of the shoes featured in this book.

The high resale value of limited releases has long been an issue for sneaker brands to contend with. Around the time the first edition of *Art & Sole* came out, sneaker drops would likely take place at specific stores that exclusively released pairs of limited edition sneakers on a first-come-first-served basis. But after a few near-riot situations with huge queues and complaints from neighbours and police, sneaker brands wondered if there was a better and fairer way to issue super limited edition shoes. Raffles were the solution: entrants got the chance to bag a pair of hype sneakers without risking a run-in with fellow die-hard sneaker fans. However, with pairs of limited edition sneakers having such high resale values, it wasn't long before online 'raffle bots' appeared – algorithms designed to automatically snatch up raffle entries in huge numbers and at lightning speed. In 2023, Nike reported that bots make up between 10 and 50 per cent of all entries to their raffles – and the brand removes up to a staggering 12 billion bot attempts monthly, conceding a small number of bot entries may be successful for any given launch.

The scale of the sneaker industry today, and the sheer volume of sneakers produced each year, is now leading to much-needed consideration when it comes to sustainability – something that has become evident when researching this revised edition. Environmental factors are now major drivers in product development for sneaker brands, and a number of shoes in this book feature recycled materials in a bid to try and address the issue of waste. Artists and designers are also taking it upon themselves to address problems of sustainability – like Helen Kirkum (see page 28) who uses discarded sneakers to create her own 'consciously crafted' footwear, and Nicole McLaughlin (see page 24) who repurposes single-use products into multi-functional objects – a concept she also applies to her sneaker collaborations with brands, including Reebok, Vans and Puma.

- Sneakers
- Projects
- Art
- Publications
- Exhibitions
- Toys

Related to its substantial growth, the sneaker market has also become a far more globalized industry, and it's now much harder to find product variation in sneaker stores country-to-country. Jeff Staple's Navigation Pack from 2004 (also mentioned on the following page) was created to celebrate the sneaker hunters willing to cross land, air and sea to find their holy grail. However, the days of having to fly half way around the world to hunt down a pair of sneakers that could only be found in a particular region have all but disappeared – a good thing for the environment, of course. Now sneaker stores across the world have largely the same products on their shelves. Even the myriad reseller consignment stores favour, understandably, the same hype choices.

One thing we could not have predicted when working on the original *Art & Sole*, was the development of digital collectibles, and the creative potential of Web3 technology. Nike's 2021 acquisition of RTFKT – a company specializing in the creation of digital and physical products that combine the worlds of fashion and gaming – signalled a new and experimental direction for the sportswear giant. The RTFKT Nike Air Force 1 Collection (see page 274) was a digital as well as physical ten-shoe project where eligible NFT holders were able to redeem their digital Air Force 1s for limited made-to-order physical versions at a special 'forging' event. And Nike's own .SWOOSH project released the Our Force 1 collection (see page 270), a series of digital-only Air Force 1 sneakers, some of which included attached utilities for special access to physical products or experiences. At the time of going to print, Nike was winding down its RTFKT activities – possibly in response to dwindling interest in NFTs – and .SWOOSH was concentrating more on collaborating with brands and companies that look to fuse the worlds of branded apparel with gaming where digital items such as sneakers can be bought, collected and actually worn by players' avatars.

And so to this revised edition of *Art & Sole*. The original introduction – shown on the following page, with some minor tweaks – still holds true today, and the art of sneaker collaboration is more prevalent than ever (a fact underlined by the amount of new content in this book). The original idea for this edition was to append a section of new content to the back of the book, however it soon became clear that a comprehensive overhaul was required. This new edition sees much of the old content updated and a host of new projects and artists added. As a general rule, we've decided not to include sneaker collaborations when they are with artist's estates – although there are a few such artist projects from the previous edition, including Andy Warhol (page 157), Keith Haring (page 72) and Jean-Michel Basquiat (page 164). The book is still split into two sections – the first displaying artist and designer sneaker collaborations, and the second showing sneaker-inspired art. Within these sections there is also a loose categorization, indicated by coloured dots as per the key shown above. We hope you enjoy the various art and sneaker projects included on the following pages.

Introduction

It all started with sport; and the sport that's done most to propel the humble sneaker to its current celebrity status is basketball. In the 1970s, the only basketball shoes available to the US public came in relatively standard colours such as white, black or navy blue. This made the team-coloured sneakers worn on professional basketball courts, which were often produced to match team strips, very sought after. In those days, colour was just as important as brand name, if not more so. For some, sneakers defined who you were and, much the same as today, wearing sneakers that no one else had was the primary objective.

The mid-1970s saw the dawning of hip-hop culture, and with it a new-found attitude to the wearing of sneakers. Previously, sneakers were worn on basketball courts for both style and function (the more beat-up the shoe, the better the basketball player), but the advent of b-boy culture saw them being worn purely for style. Sneakers were now being preserved in pristine condition for that all-important fresh-out-of-the-box look – and rising prices also ensured that looking after your sneakers guaranteed getting your money's worth. This trend was seen the world over; whether sneakers were initially worn for skateboarding, playing football or just wandering the streets, it was hip-hop culture that turned them into objects of desire. Just think back to Run-DMC's *Walk This Way* promo; it's a much-cited example, but those box-fresh adidas Superstars, famously laceless, had a lasting impact on the youth culture of the day.

Permanently associated with creative subcultures such as hip-hop and skateboarding (both of which have a strong history of customizing shoes), the sneaker scene has always been connected with creativity and this book sets out to document the current state of this relationship. The book is split into two halves: the first half displays the collaborative and limited edition sneakers produced by a wide range of artists and designers; and the second documents the burgeoning art scene connected with this phenomenon. The work featured in the second section of the book emphasizes the iconic nature of the sneaker; from Dave White's expressionist oil paintings (see page 200) to Coolrain Lee's intricate miniature sneakers (see page 254), and even sculptures made from the shoes themselves, the work draws inspiration from a type of footwear now fetishized by millions.

The creative side of the sneaker scene has made the artist or designer collaboration an obvious alliance, creating a phenomenon that has grown rapidly since the beginning of the 21st century. The results are often limited edition, highly collectable sneakers featuring premium fabrics, unique colourways and bespoke packaging. These are not always shoes you can find in your local sneaker store; if you want to acquire them you have to be knowledgeable, dedicated (overnight queuing is sometimes required) and sometimes well connected. The limited nature of some of these releases can create sneakers that garner near mythical status, like the Nike SB 'DUNKLE' Friends & Family shown on page 21. The rarest and most sought-after shoes can skyrocket in value (sometimes within the space of a few weeks) and they frequently crop up in online auctions with generously inflated price tags. Of course, not all artist and designer collaborations are produced in limited numbers; for great examples of mass-produced sneaker art just look at Jeff Staple's Navigation Pack (production run of 10,000) or Tattoo Series (production run of 30,000) on pages 106–107.

Researching this book wasn't easy. Apart from the rarity of the sneakers themselves, there are so many sneaker collaborations to choose from. Collaborations are currently everywhere, and not just in the world of sneakers – even corporate brands with more traditional marketing strategies are getting in on the act. Perhaps unsurprisingly, this has led to 'collaboration' becoming something of a dirty word (along with the term 'limited edition', which applies to almost all products currently). But the fact is, even though the (sneaker) marketplace has become saturated with collaborations, the phenomenon is not going away. Where sports brands once looked to athletes to add credibility and desirability to their products, they now look to artists and designers.

A particularly creative development in the scene has witnessed artists and designers actually influencing the design of sneakers themselves. Just look at +41's hybrid art pieces (combining elements of various sneaker models), which seemed to have spawned a whole new craze in sneaker production (see page 194), or Hiroshi Fujiwara's radical woven creations (see page 138). It could be said that there are currently too many releases of retro shoe models, and even the collaborative limited edition shoes tend to be based on the safety of the manufacturers' best-selling models – a policy that creates obvious limitations. The future of the artist and designer collaboration could well lie in the construction of the actual shoe as well as the choice of artwork, material and colour. Whatever direction the culture takes us in, it seems that the relationship between art, design and the sneaker will continue to evolve and blossom.

Sneak & Art

Art & Makers

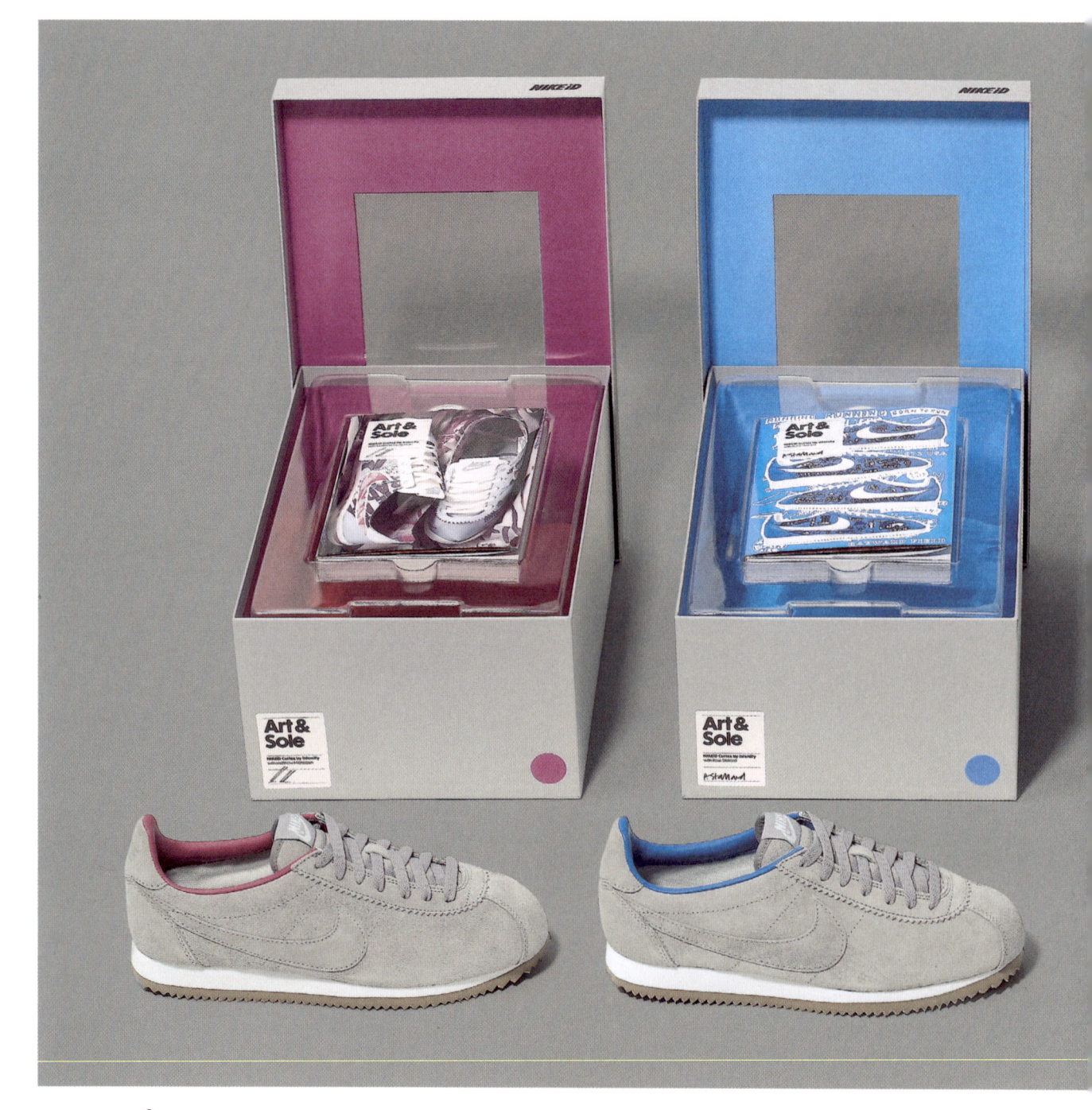

Intercity

To celebrate the release of the mini-edition *Art & Sole* book in 2012, Intercity worked with Nike to design the Art & Sole Cortez iD sneaker collection. As part of the project, Intercity commissioned four artists – Matthew Nicholson, Rose Stallard, Shantell Martin (see page 14) and Jiro Bevis – to create artwork for one of four limited edition book covers. Working with different media; sculpture, sneaker-art, moving image and print respectively, the artists' brief was simply to interpret the Cortez using a specifically assigned colour which correlated to the category-signifying contents dots of *Art & Sole*. A book featuring each artist's artwork was then packaged in a bespoke box alongside a pair of the sneakers, and a moving image piece created by Shantell Martin was also included within the packs on a Cortez-shaped flash-drive.

The sneakers themselves were tonal grey and had a gum outsole that paid homage to the first ever Cortez. There was also an embroidered ampersand on the heel and a colour-coded accent in the lining of the shoe. Each colourway of the collection was produced in a limited run of 40 and was available only through Nike's Boxpark store, London.

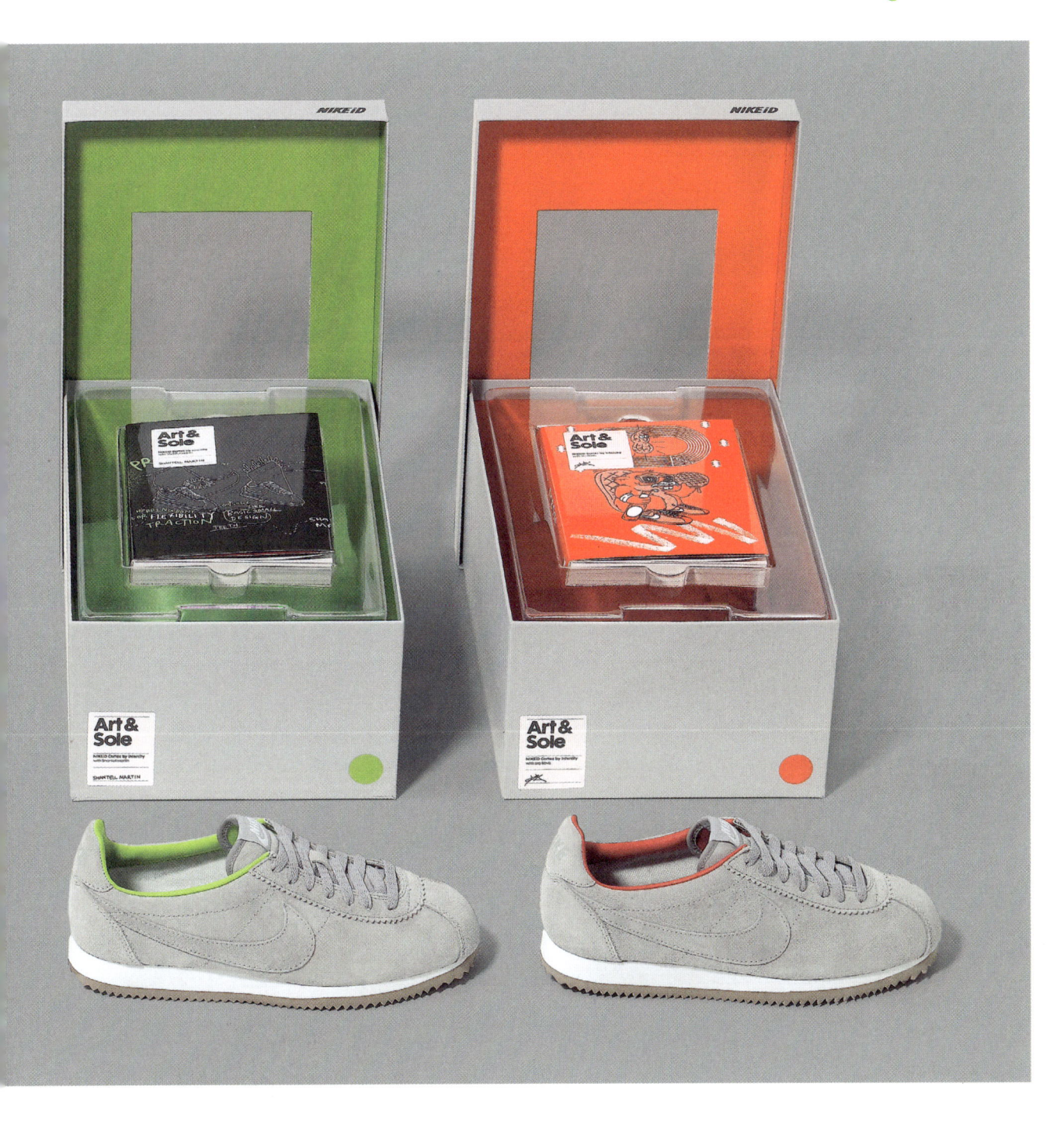

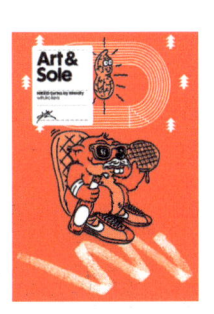

Sneakers

Shantell Martin

Known for her stream-of-consciousness drawings and light projections, Shantell Martin combines the whimsical and autobiographical, bridging the gap between fine art, performance art and everyday life. A multifaceted artist, Martin's work often explores themes such as intersectionality, identity and play.

In 2018, Martin collaborated with Puma on a collection of apparel and footwear, including hero silhouettes such as the Clyde (below and opposite top), Suede (opposite middle) and women's court-inspired Platform Strap (opposite bottom). Drawing inspiration from her signature style and passion for self-discovery, the collection combined premium materials, monochromatic looks and intricate details. 'It was cool being able to apply my artistic DNA to iconic Puma silhouettes,' says Martin, 'but what I particularly loved about the project was hiding little messages throughout the product, offering to make something truly unique.'

Sneakers 15

Peter Saville

As one of the founding members and art director of the legendary Manchester-based Factory Records, Peter Saville is perhaps best known for designing the record sleeves of Joy Division and New Order from the late 1970s to the early 1990s. Since then, Saville has remained a pivotal figure within the UK design scene, with a major retrospective of his work held at London's Design Museum in 2003.

In 2022, Saville worked with adidas and Manchester United Football Club (MUFC) on a capsule collection that included the adidas Spezial Pulsebeat SPZL (an updated version of the adidas Blackburn SPZL). Taking its inspiration from Saville's artwork for the 1979 Joy Division album, *Unknown Pleasures*, the iconic wave graphic featured on the tongue was reworked using biometric data gathered from the men's and women's teams of MUFC. The two-tone black colourway featured 3M reflective material within the serrated three-stripes, heel tab and laces. The shoes were also packaged in a bespoke box with leather swingtag and additional insoles featuring the Pulsebeat artwork.

Sneakers   17

In 2006, Saville worked with adidas to create this adicolor High G2, the second shoe in the adicolor Green Series. Saville's concept was to show the consumer the brief from adidas, displaying selected elements from it across the shoe – including the laces, lace jewels (left), shoe label and wrapping paper (printed with the full brief). The idea was to provide transparency to the design process, and also to allow the consumer the ability to create their own interpretation of the message. Virgil Abloh described Peter Saville as his 'personal mentor' and maybe this concept played a part in that. See the full adidas adicolor project on page 70.

CONCEPT
RELEVANCE
FOR
LIFESTYLE
CONSUMER

RESERVE
THE RIGHT
TO ADJUST
THE
DESIGN

The Haçienda

In 2007, to celebrate the 25th anniversary of the opening of legendary Manchester nightclub The Haçienda, Factory Records teamed up with Y-3 (the brand created by adidas and fashion designer Yohji Yamamoto) to create FAC51-Y3. The project is a collaboration between Peter Saville (the co-founder and art director for Factory Records, and occasional collaborator with Yohji Yamamoto), Ben Kelly (architect for The Haçienda) and Peter Hook (bass player for Joy Division/New Order).

Based on the classic Y-3 Sprint, the shoes were enclosed in a unique six-sided maple-bottomed shoebox inspired by the shape of the club's dance floor. Within the box, the shoes came wrapped in four sheets of tissue paper; two featuring Kevin Cummins' photography of the club in its 1980s heyday, one showing Ben Kelly's original sketches for the club's interior and one reflecting how the space looked at the time of release.

A DVD was also included in the box, featuring original footage from the club and a discussion between Saville, Kelly and Hook about the project and their memories of The Haçienda. Retailing at UK£345, the shoes were limited to just 250 pairs worldwide. Every release from Factory Records was given an FAC number; the name FAC51-Y3 expresses the co-operation between The Haçienda (FAC51) and Y-3. Shown left is a pair of FAC51-Y3s sitting on an original metal plate from the Haçienda's pillars, with pieces of wood from the original dance floor.

IRAK NY

IRAK NY began as a graffiti crew in New York City in the mid-1990s – the name comes from 'I rack', referencing the street slang term 'racking', which describes shoplifiting expensive items. The brand has since established itself as a (legitimate) creative outlet for its members – including footwear collaborations with both adidas and Converse.

In 2007, IRAK NY joined forces with adidas for their first collaboration, using the RMX EQT Support Runner as the canvas for their design. The sneaker featured a fresh retro colourway, using a grey upper with black, blue, neon yellow and hot red accents. The RMX EQT Support Runner was the model of choice again in 2008 for a second collaboration, this time featuring orange suede, a purple tongue and green accents. Both sneakers feature the word 'IRAK' with the year date on the toe, and only 300 pairs of each model were produced.

Twelve years later, IRAK NY and adidas again reunited to release a pair of ZX8000 sneakers, with the design mimicking the 2007/2008 releases shown here. Both pairs featured 'IRAK 2020' on the toe.

Gasius

Released as part of a set of shoes bearing the unofficial title of the Capital Series, this Nike Vengeance was designed by London-based Gasius (aka Russell Maurice) in 2005. There were five shoes in the series, one from each of five European capital cities and each designed by a local creative. The design of this shoe, the 'GasrNike', is based on the repetition of graffiti and the artist's fascination with the diamond and triangle shapes that are a recurring theme in much of his work. The shoe was issued in a limited edition of 240 pairs.

UNKLE

The Nike Dunk High Pro SB 'DUNKLE', was one of the biggest releases of 2004. The project was a collaboration between UK-based DJ, James Lavelle, founder of record label Mo' Wax and recording act UNKLE, New York graffiti legend FUTURA (see page 118) and art director/designer Ben Drury (see page 36). Each had previously produced artwork for a number of Mo' Wax record sleeves and had been instrumental in defining the imagery of UNKLE's unique aesthetic.

Featuring FUTURA's famous Pointman and Atom artwork, the shoes use a combination of leather and nubuck, with a patent leather Swoosh. A total of 11 different screens were used to achieve the print effect. It is rumoured that there are only five pairs of the low-top version in existence. They were made for Lavelle's friends and family only.

Daniel Arsham

New York artist Daniel Arsham straddles the line between art, architecture and performance. Best known for distorting recognizable forms (including sneakers) into corroded and glitched-out artefacts, his work has also included footwear collaborations with Dior, as well as one-off custom sneaker projects. Shown here is a three-shoe collaboration with adidas from 2017. Each shoe related to a chapter in a three-part film entitled *Hourglass*, which explored Arsham's life and creative work through the lens of the past, present and future.

The first release, Past (below), was a chalk-white New York silhouette (interestingly, Arsham often uses all-white colour palettes in his work in reference to his colour blindness). Featuring a deteriorated canvas construction, the frayed edges on the shoe represent Arsham's fascination with archeology and 20th century cultural artefacts. When placed under an ultraviolet light, the shoes reveal a secret message on the mesh midsole that says 'the past is present'. The shoes also feature co-branded graphics on the tongue and a hand-scrawled phone number on the heeltab (linking to a related work entitled *#calldaniel*).

The second release, the New York Present (opposite top), focused on adidas Boost technology and featured a matte grey neoprene upper, with canvas and nubuck overlays. Detailing was created through stamping, which saw the neoprene moulded to make different shapes and textures, and the shoe again featured a co-branded tongue.

The third and final collaboration, Future (opposite bottom), was released in 2018. The Aero Green Futurecraft 4D shoe featured a Primeknit upper with three-stripe and 'Future' branding that is only seen under ultraviolet light.

Sneakers 23

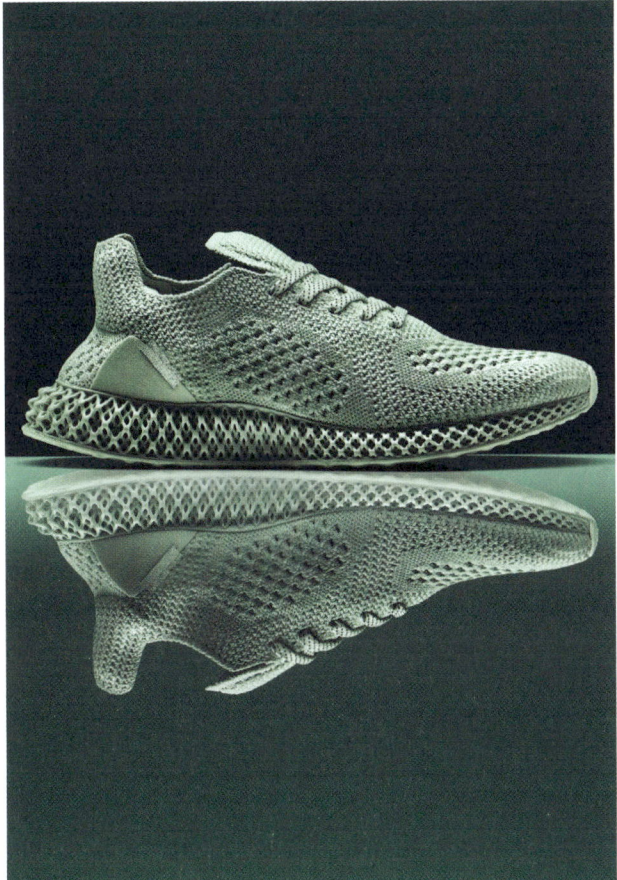

Nicole McLaughlin

New York-based designer Nicole McLaughlin has managed the impressive feat of turning a side-project into a full-time career. With a focus on upcycling and sustainable fashion, McLaughlin's creative exploration unlocks the potential of turning single-use products into multifunctional objects. Often humorous, McLaughlin's approach and creative process has seen her transform anything from beanie hats, sports bags, camera straps and even old tennis balls, into footwear. This unexpected translation of materials allows her to highlight the important message of sustainability and help to change perceptions around waste and sustainable design – she also holds global workshops to help people realize the possibilities of pre-existing objects.

McLaughlin's creative explorations, two of which are shown below, have led to a slew of brand collaborations which started with the Crocs Campsite Classic Clog in 2020. Since then, collaborative projects with Reebok, Vans, Merrell Hoka and Puma have followed, all of which showcase the designer's innovative approach.

McLaughlin began her career as a graphic designer at Reebok and, in 2022, the two reunited on the outdoor-styled Reebok Club C Geo Mid, shown opposite. With multifunctionality and sustainability at its core, the shoe featured recycled materials and Nicole McLaughlin-branded mesh pockets for additional utility.

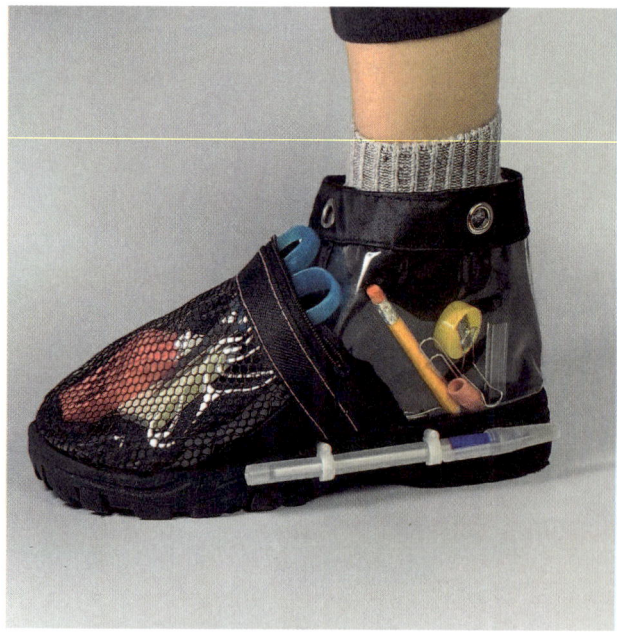

Sneakers   25

Sneakers

In 2024, McLaughlin collaborated with Hoka on the Hoka Mafate Three2. The extremely cushioned running shoe (above) featured a full-coverage, four-in-one gaiter system and was finished with five pockets and co-branded labels. McLaughlin's footwear collaboration streak continued into 2024 with the Puma Suede (below). The collaboration was crafted from leftover production materials, meaning each pair is unique, and also featured a detachable bag/wallet. The uppers are made from 57 per cent leftover production cuttings and 14 per cent 'deadstock' material.

In 2023, McLaughlin partnered with Vault by Vans on two shoes inspired by the designer's love for vintage gardening tote bags. The Vault by Vans Slip-On VP VR3 LX (opposite) featured pockets for gardening materials and work tools across the toe vamp. Available in two colourways, the shoes were built using organic cotton canvas uppers and Vans' bio-based insole (made using at least 25 per cent bio-based foam). The outsole also contains 60 per cent natural rubber obtained from sources that follow proven sustainable practices with the intention of reducing impacts on the planet. Both silhouettes were finished with custom Nicole McLaughlin labels and custom ankle collar straps as a functional way to carry and store the shoes.

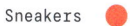

Nicole McLaughlin   Sneakers   27

Helen Kirkum

Helen Kirkum is a London-based artist and designer known for her processes of deconstructing and rebuilding. With a focus on recycling and sustainability, Kirkum's studio creates artisanal and authentic pieces and is known for its pioneering sneaker leather collage technique. This entails patchworking discarded sneakers (see below), reimagining them into 'consciously crafted' footwear and accessories.

Kirkum champions the process of production and the aesthetics of the handmade – challenging us to rethink the meaning of consumption and the way we interact with the products we own. Each pair of sneakers is truly unique and, as well as the signature sneaker – Palimpsest – Kirkum also offers a bespoke build service. Offering the opportunity to reignite the love for those forgotten beaters, or even to elevate a prized pair to a truly unique level, Kirkum's creative process facilitates the creation of something inherently personal and unique. With so many sneaker buyers focused on keeping their shoes box-fresh, Kirkum's 'wearing is caring' attitude is an inspiring one. 'We believe that, from paint splatters to skating scuffs, you have been building your history into your shoes ever since you first got them out of the box.'

Sneakers 29

30   ● Sneakers

Helen Kirkum Sneakers 31

Sneakers

Steven Harrington

Los Angeles-based artist and designer Steven Harrington is best known for his bright, iconic style – which often incorporates his signature Mello the dog character. Described as having a contemporary Californian psychedelic-pop aesthetic, his work is largely inspired by life in California – from the diverse landscape to the thriving mix of cultures.

In 2019, Harrington worked with Nike on the Earth Day Collection, a Quickstrike release that utilized Nike's Flyleather (a performance material made with at least 50 per cent recycled leather fibre, resulting in a lower impact on climate change compared to traditional leather). The collection included an Air Force 1, Blazer and Cortez, all featuring artwork overprinted on the sustainable material. For Harrington, sustainability is simply about making better choices for the planet in our everyday lives: 'I think Earth Day Every Day, to me, is really just a friendly reminder. It's a reminder that every little bit counts.'

Ruohan Wang

To celebrate Earth Day in 2020, Nike collaborated with Ruohan Wang, a Chinese-born, Berlin-based female artist and illustrator whose work focuses on painting, illustration and fashion design. The collection included an Air Force 1, Air Max 90 and a Blazer Mid '77 – all featuring uppers made from Nike's Flyleather material (made from at least 50 per cent recycled leather fibre). Wang's multi-coloured illustrations covered the majority of the sustainable uppers, utilizing an asymmetrical construction and included re-imagined tongue tags, heel tabs and insoles. Each pair was also housed in a special-edition colourfully illustrated box that included alternative, accented laces.

Sneakers

Shigeki Fujishiro

This collaboration between adidas Consortium and Japanese product designer Shigeki Fujishiro used the blank canvas of the Stan Smith in a very alternative way. Although a product/furniture designer, Fujishiro's collaboration (entitled Play) had a distinctly art-like aesthetic, and the simplicity of the idea is what made it stand out. 'I really liked the shoe without any modification,' explains Fujishiro, 'so I came up with the idea of threading the perforations, allowing you to bring the shoe back to its original condition if you remove the thread.' It's certainly a more interesting and unusual take on the art of the collaboration – and one that builds on the fundamental design elements of the silhouette.

Released in 2014, the shoe was part of a wider Consortium pack that saw designers from the Far East making their mark on the Stan Smith. Other designers in the series included renowned streetwear labels Neighbourhood, CLOT and Mastermind.

Ryan Gander

London-based conceptual artist Ryan Gander collaborated with Kazuki Kuraishi of fragment design fame and adidas Originals Tokyo (under the A.Four label) on the art-themed ZX750 'Pencil' and ZX750 'Mud'. Blending Tokyo style with playful creativity, the pencil-themed shoe (*Yo-yo Criticism*, 2014) features an all-over penciled graphic that follows the forms of the all-white premium leather upper, while the mud-themed shoe (*And everyone will see through it*, 2014) features a hand-painted mud effect on the base of the shoe – to appear as if the owner has walked through mud.

Ben Drury

UK-based art director and designer Ben Drury has a body of work which includes collaborations with the likes of Mo' Wax, Nike, FUTURA, Dizzee Rascal, 3D (Massive Attack), All Tomorrow's Parties and Mark Gonzales. One of Drury's earliest footwear projects was working on the Nike 'DUNKLE' shoe (see page 21). 'It was around the time of the second UNKLE album, *Never, Never, Land* and we really went to town on cross collaboration. The design of the shoe was really a case of applying the artwork elements we already had in place for the album – as we (myself, Will Bankhead and James Lavelle) had gone to Brooklyn to actively art-direct the cover painting with FUTURA. The prototype designs were actually more subtle and less character-based than the final shoe. We also had a Vans collaboration lined up, but it never happened.'

Shown below are the Nike Air Max 1 and Nike Air Max 90 Current from the respective 2006 and 2008 Air U Breathe packs. At the bottom of the page is a two-shoe project from 2009 which celebrated the long-term collaboration between Drury, Dizzee Rascal and Nike. The Air Max 90 'Tongue N' Cheek' (bottom left) focused on Dizzee Rascal's upcoming album of the same name (with cover artwork also by Drury) and featured Drury's signature combination of experimental materials – premium leather and suede with embroidered 'Tongue N' Cheek' tongue details, transparent Swoosh, 3M reflective heel tab and transparent outsole revealing the Dirtee Stank Recordings fly logo. The Air Max 90 Current 'Silent Listener' (bottom right) was inspired by London at night. Designed as a counterpoint to the Dizzee Rascal shoe, Drury's design referenced his experience at the time of living between city and countryside, and his love for walking through both environments – influences clearly visible in details such as the D-ring eyelets and 3M lace detailing.

Released in 2006, the 15th anniversary of Nike Air, the Air U Breathe pack from Nike was a Quickstrike artist collaboration that Drury was also involved in. The theme of the project was simply 'air', and the pack included three different shoes: an Air Max 1 by Drury, an Air Max 360 by Kevin Lyons (see page 38) and an Air Stab by Hitomi Yokoyama (see page 39). Drury took his inspiration from the pirate radio scene in London. The shoe features some beautiful detailing, including the phrase 'Hold Tight' (a reference to the language of pirate radio) embroidered on the tongue, and a stitched radio wave graphic on the heel, while the mudguard of the shoe is made from a 3M Scotchlite reflective material. 'The black and 3M elements represented the undercover nature of the whole thing,' says Drury, 'I'm always looking for balance and tension in my work.'

Shown on this page are two versions of Drury's shoe: a sample version and the final production version. The sample features black stitched 'Hold Tight' lettering on the tongue instead of silver. 'In the context of pirate radio,' explains Drury, "Hold Tight" is a statement of intent – get ready, prepare yourself. I love the way the atmosphere and excitement of the listener's communion with pirate radio can be distilled into a literal shorthand. The words contain great power and resonance for me as a silent listener.' Other differences between the sample and production models are that the aerial graphic on the insole is gloss black on black instead of silver on black, the heel piece is plain black premium leather instead of perforated leather and the top lace eyelets are 3M Scotchlite instead of black suede.

Kevin Lyons

Kevin Lyons is a New York-based creative director, illustrator and artist who has worked with Nike, Converse, adidas, Huf, Stüssy, SSUR, Vans, Uniqlo, CLOT and Girl Skateboards, among others. He also finds the time to run his own experimental studio, Natural Born.

In 2006, Lyons worked with Nike on the Air U Breathe pack – alongside Ben Drury (see page 36) and Hitomi Yokoyama (see opposite page). The artwork on the laser-etched Air Max 360 (above) was influenced by three things: Peter Saville's cover art for Joy Division, Fillmore poster art and the flyers of DJ Kool Herc.

In 2012, Lyons created an in-store installation for the now-closed Parisian boutique, Colette. As part of the project, Lyons also worked on a limited edition Chuck Taylor All Star (left), fusing his signature monster characters with Colette's blue and white brand palette. Released as part of the Converse First String initiative (a limited edition collection created to celebrate craftsmanship, authenticity and collaboration at the highest level), only 125 pairs were made available for purchase exclusively through Colette.

Hitomi Yokoyama

Japanese-born Hitomi Yokoyama has designed for streetwear brands Gimme 5 and GoodEnough UK, as well as collaborating with brands such as Undercover, Mad Hectic, Let it Ride, aNYthing and A Bathing Ape.

This Air Stab was part of the 2006 three-shoe Nike Air U Breathe pack, with Yokoyama taking her inspiration from the lightness and agility of animals such as cats and rabbits – hence the cartoon graphic on the heel. 'The idea behind my design is that Nike Air is so light that it feels as if you are running barefoot. I was thinking of some agile, bouncing animal like a cat or a rabbit, which is where the idea of the paws with shoe laces comes from.'

James Jarvis

Based in London, James Jarvis is an artist and illustrator whose work encompasses cartoons, objects, comics, graphic design, printmaking and moving image. His practice is heavily inspired by skateboarding and Jarvis' first commissioned work was for influential skate shop Slam City Skates. He has since worked as a commercial artist for clients worldwide, including adidas, Coca-Cola, Ikea and Uniqlo.

In 2014, Jarvis was commissioned by Nike SB to work on two T-shirt graphics – drawings that looked at skateboarding through Jarvis' philosophical eye. The project also involved the creation of a repeat pattern – an element that was eventually used on this two-shoe Nike SB Free release. 'I wanted something abstract for the pattern,' explains Jarvis, 'without any heavily figurative elements. I used some of the simple, gestural marks I make in my drawings. Perhaps the marks give a sense of the physical traces left by skateboarding.' The complete capsule collection was finally released in 2015, with the shoe insoles featuring the character illustrations from the T-shirt designs. 'This is the character I've been drawing for the past few years – a character that has no 'character'. Rather than being distracted by the character as a decorative element, you hopefully look beyond its appearance to what it is saying or doing.'

For the release of the Nike and Stüssy Court Force Low collaboration in 2006, Jarvis was asked to create a vinyl figure based on Stüssy's UK store manager Leon Dixon Goulden. Inspired by fresh summer colours, the design of the corresponding shoes (left) was the responsibility of Dixon Goulden, Steve Bryden and Mark Ward.

Sneakers 41

Krink

Craig Costello, also known as KR, is a New York-based artist whose practice encompasses painting, installations and photography. He is also the founder and creative director of Krink, an artist materials brand and creative studio. Krink began life as the first ink and paint marker company for graffiti writers and has since grown into a global brand with collections of specialty tools, apparel and accessories.

In 2008, Krink was invited to create an Air Force 1 Low Supreme as part of Nike's 1World project, which saw 18 global designers, artists and influencers create their own AF1s. The Krink shoe featured a 3M reflective metallic silver upper with signature dripping paint detailing, a silver midsole and a gum rubber outsole. Released in an edition of 500, the shoe also came in a custom silver box, with a K-70 ink marker.

Geoff McFetridge

Los Angeles-based artist and graphic designer Geoff McFetridge started his career making artwork for various skateboard companies, as well as art directing the Beastie Boys magazine, *Grand Royal*. 'I have always been interested in how different ways of working affect what I'm capable of as an artist,' says McFetridge, 'so I like to work on projects that are commercial, and also projects that are purely art-based.' This approach has led to McFetridge working on a huge array of projects, encompassing painting, animation, sculpture, ceramics, title sequences and even wallpaper. 'Making a wide variety of work challenges me creatively and has come to inform what sort of artist I am.'

McFetridge first collaborated with Nike in 2003, on the 'Tear Away' Vandal Supreme above (McFetridge originally wanted to call it the Champion Vandal, referencing his studio). Interpreting the word 'vandal' literally, McFetridge created a shoe with a secret underlayer pattern. When new, the pinstripe upper appears flawless, but once the cotton canvas upper starts to wear away (or is vandalized), McFetridge's hidden silver artwork is revealed – with the words 'I just can't stop destroying' appearing. The shoe was produced in both a blue and green colourway.

2015 saw McFetridge work with the classic silhouette of a Nike SB Blazer (bottom right). With off-white suede and accents of orange throughout, the shoes feature various hand-rendered typographic elements, including a hand-drawn Nike Swoosh. Also shown here are a selection of initial proposal sketches for the project, and one of the final illustrations created for the project's promotional campaign.

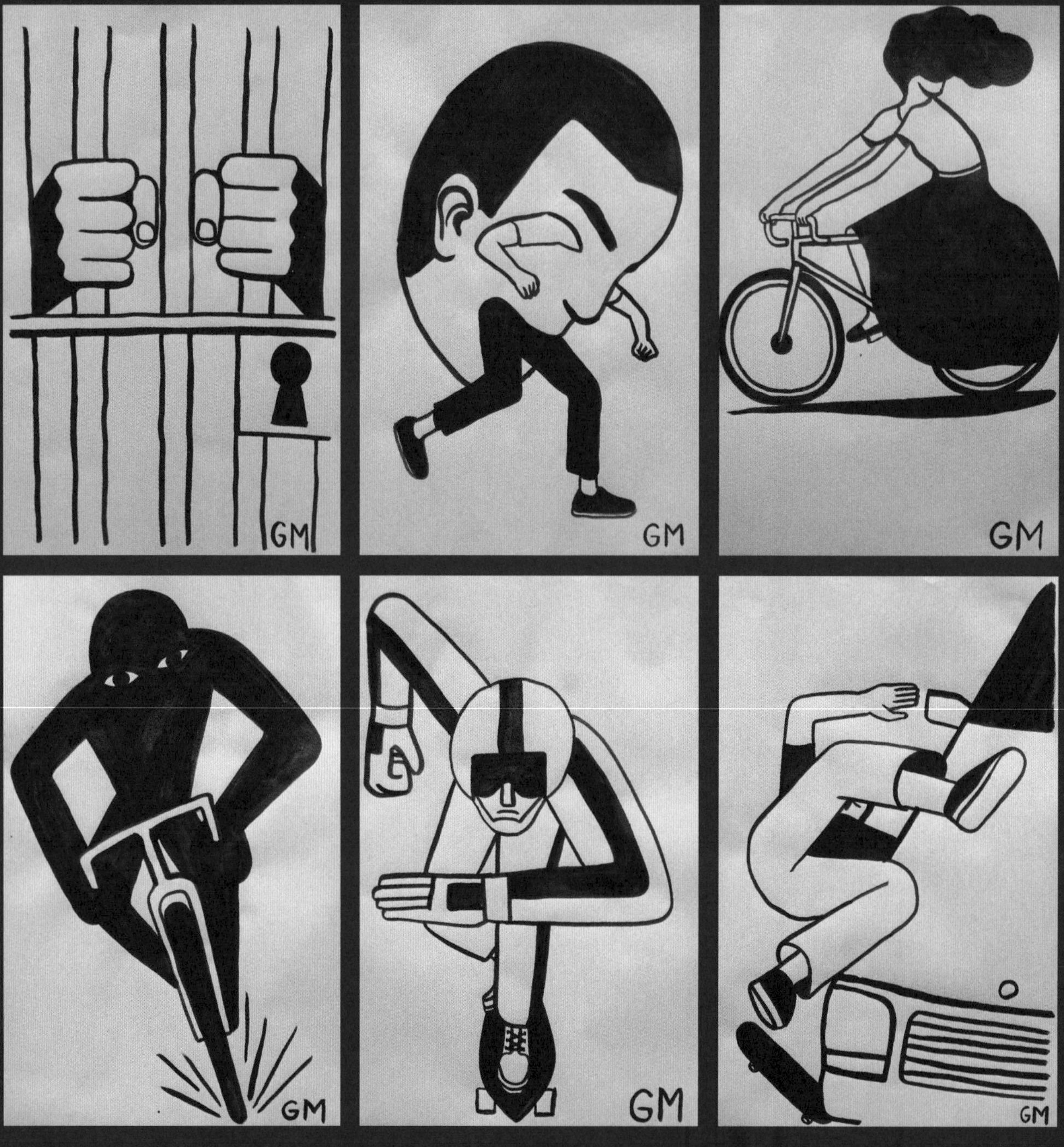
GM
GM
GM
GM
GM
GM

Released in conjunction with the Art in the Streets exhibition at the Museum of Contemporary Art (MOCA) in Los Angeles, 2011, these (wearable) Nike SB Paper Dunks feature abstracted artwork created by McFetridge. Limited to just 24 pairs, each Paper Dunk is unique as it features a section of a larger illustration. Available in sizes 9, 10 and 11 (US), the shoes were auctioned with a starting price of US$100, and all proceeds benefited the MOCA foundation. 'I wasn't really interested in making a normal shoe,' explains McFetridge, 'so I proposed the paper shoe to Aaron Rose as a challenge to Nike. I knew it would be a lot of work at their end, but having worked on the two-layer 'Tear Away' Vandal from 2003, I knew that they were capable of rising to technical challenges. I liked the idea of destroying a piece of art in order to make a pair of shoes. The challenge for me was to make drawings that were special enough for me to be sad about cutting up. Needless to say, I think most people value shoes more than art.'

Each drawing was created on the floor of McFetridge's studio on recycled brown paper, with each sheet being big enough to cut out two shoes. 'There are a lot of skateboard images and some characters that might be doing graffiti. There is a lot of other stuff in there as well – it's my take on stuff from the street, or maybe just an overview of things that interest me: super competitive skateboard racing, cycling, dancing, people being run over by cars.' Each pair came with a miniature version of the particular drawing that was cut up to make the shoes. The box also featured McFetridge's artwork.

46 　● Sneakers

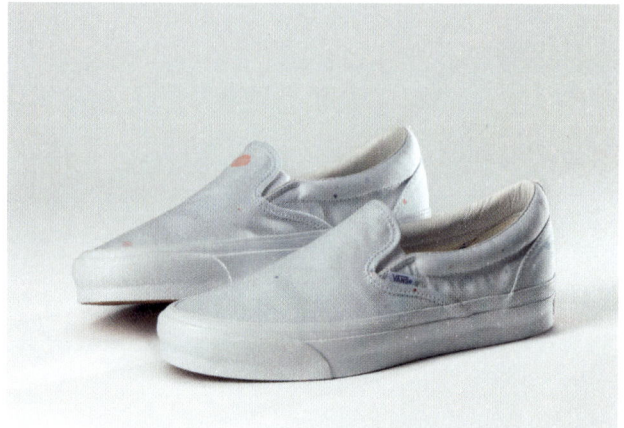

Geoff McFetridge · Sneakers · 47

In 2021, McFetridge collaborated with Vault by Vans on a vibrant capsule of footwear and apparel. 'As a skater, I have a close personal history with Vans,' says McFetridge. 'I have worked with them on a number of projects over the years, but this collection was an opportunity to create a microcosm of my personal history with the brand.' Shown on the opposite page, from top to bottom, the collection led with the OG Authentic LX and OG Slip-On LX silhouettes, featuring recreations of fabrics pulled from McFetridge's favourite items – including a shirt he wears for painting and a trusted 20-year-old tote bag.

The OG Style 38 NS features artwork in the form of a label of McFetridge's 'Jump' graphic, while the OG Lampin LX and OG Old Skool LX are decorated with minimalist forms and figures. Shown on this page are three of the process sketches from the collection. 'The project was about telling my own history through objects and icons,' explains McFetridge. 'It was an experiment to see how much personal meaning the shoes could hold.'

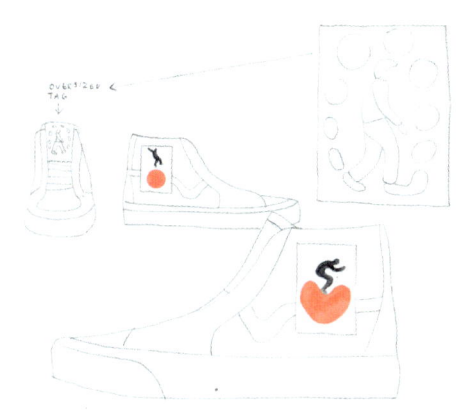

Taka Hayashi

Self-taught painter, illustrator and graphic designer Taka Hayashi was born in Japan in 1971 and moved to the US in 1981. He grew up in Santa Monica where the early 1980s skateboarding scene had a huge impact on his life. He began drawing at a very early age and spent most of his time either skating or experimenting with art.

Building upon his longstanding (and prolific) partnership with Vans, in 2021 Hayashi looked to the early days of Formula 1 racing as inspiration for two Vault by Vans archival silhouettes – the OG Style 24 LX and OG Style 47 LX. Released in both black-on-white and white-on-white colourways, the high-top OG Style 24 LX featured Hayashi's interpretation of the classic checkerboard finish line pattern on the uppers, with detailing inspired by Formula 1 team jackets. The OG Style 47 LX featured a quilted vamp with contrasting heel stripes, inspired by car racing suits of the 1970s. Released in both a blue and a black colourway, the midsoles were also printed with the classic Vans checkerboard pattern, again referencing finish line flags.

Sneakers

The design of this Vans Taka Hayashi DIY pack (above), partly inspired by the Mr. Potato Head toy, allows for endless customization options using Velcro-style panels that feature multi-coloured heritage Vans prints. Released in 2020, each shoe effectively contains two Vans silhouettes in one – with colour coded guideline stitching throughout the uppers to indicate where to place the components. The DIY Hi VLT LX features pieces from both a SK8-Hi (blue stitch line) and a Half Cab (red stitch line), while the DIY Lo VLT LX features pieces from a Classic Slip-On (blue stitch line) and an Old Skool (red stitch line).

According to Hayashi: 'This design concept was a tribute to Paul Van Doren's days of customization at the Vans store in the 80s. You were able to bring in your own textiles or go through binder books full of prints, canvas and suede swatches to create your own unique design.' A blacked-out colourway was also released in 2020 (below), featuring a mix of animal print and camouflage panels.

Neckface

California-based Neckface is a skateboarder and artist whose graffiti has assaulted urban landscapes around the world. Best known for his uniquely scratchy and violent drawing style, Neckface made his name on the streets of San Francisco and later New York, stickering and scrawling his art on to various buildings and street signs.

Neckface has collaborated twice with Nike SB – firstly on a Blazer in 2013 (below) that featured the names of the SB team in display lettering inspired by horror B-movies to form a web-like pattern. His second collaboration with the brand, released in 2023, was a Dunk Low, shown opposite, that paid homage to black metal 'battle vests'. The artist's drawings were rendered with embroidered patches, completely covering both shoes. The release even included bonus patches as an added custom feature.

Sneakers 51

Robert Williams

The controversial painter Robert Williams is probably best known for his depiction of robot to human rape and brutality on the album cover of *Appetite For Destruction* by Guns N' Roses (controversy later forced Geffen Records to move the artwork to the inside cover). The founder of *Juxtapoz Art & Culture Magazine*, Williams began his career as a part of the innovative and groundbreaking Zap Collective, alongside underground cartoonist revolutionaries like Robert Crumb, and his art can be described as a mix of Californian hot rod culture, film noir and psychedelic imagery.

In 2007, Williams' artwork featured on this series of shoes from Vault by Vans. Launched in 2003, the Vault by Vans line was created to give designers the ability to experiment with fabrics and prints, while maintaining Vans' classic design. Williams' series includes two Slip-On LX, a Sk8-Hi and a Chukka 69 LX.

Sneakers 53

Mr Sabotage

It would be hard to produce a book about sneakers and art without mentioning Singaporean sneaker customizer Mark Ong, aka Mr Sabotage, or SBTG (a contraction of Sabotage). What initially started as a hobby for Ong quickly turned into a full-time business after he won a custom competition on sneaker community website niketalk.com.

Originally known for customizing (or sabotaging) only Nike shoes, it wasn't long before SBTG collaborated with Nike on a legitimate sneaker release. In 2006, the (Asia exclusive) Nike SB Dunk Low Premium 'SBTG' was released (right). The collaboration had the look and feel of a custom shoe; it even included one of SBTG's trademark custom features, the lace cover. In 2007, a special version of the shoe was issued (below), this time to a worldwide audience. The rerelease featured the inclusion of new laces, a special lace lock and a specially designed slide shoebox.

Sneakers   55

From his early days working only with Nike silhouettes, Ong has now worked with a multitude of sports brands including Vans, ASICS and New Balance. Shown this page, top left to bottom left, are the Vans Old Skool 'SBTG' (customized version shown, 2024), the Limited Edt and ASICS Gel Kyano 14 'Monsoon Patrol' (custom-dyed versions shown, 2024), the Staple Air Force 1 Low 'Pigeon Fury' customs (2016) and the Infinte Objects Air Force 1 'Nautical Fury' customs in white (2015).

DC Shoes
Artist Projects™

One of the earliest sneaker brand and artist collaboration initiatives of its kind, DC's Artist Projects™ was created in 2001 to recognize the creativity inherent in skateboarding. Working on the basis that skateboarders have always customized their shoes – either by drawing or painting on them, changing the laces or even cutting or modifying the shoe – the Artist Projects™ programme gave selected artists the opportunity to express themselves through the creation of special-edition DC shoes. Artists who have taken part in the project include Shepard Fairey, KAWS, Dave Kinsey, Eric So, Phil Frost, Thomas Campbell, Evan Hecox, Andy Howell, Michael Leon, André Saraiva, SSUR, Johanna Jackson, Methamphibian and Natas Kaupas.

KAWS
2002

Sneakers   57

Shepard Fairey
2001

Dave Kinsey
2003

André Saraiva & Arkitip
2005

Methamphibian
2007

Natas Kaupas
2007

SSUR
2007

KAWS

Brooklyn-based artist KAWS, real name Brian Donnelly, traverses the worlds of product design, painting and large-scale sculpture. His journey to becoming one of today's biggest contemporary artists started in the early 1990s, with a graffiti-based body of work referred to as 'ad interventions' – essentially appropriating fashion and product advertising billboards and poster sites around the world.

KAWS has since collaborated with the likes of Vans (see page 130), DC Shoes (see page 56), Visvim, MTV and Nike – and his collaborative work with iconic Japanese streetwear label A Bathing Ape has given him a huge following in Japan. Over the years, KAWS has worked on various incarnations of the Bape Sta sneaker, with his 'XX' and 'Chompers' iconography being applied to the silhouette using a huge variety of materials and colourways (2006's 'Chompers Grey' shown below).

The shoes that seem to have reached 'grail' status for many collectors are the three pairs KAWS produced for Nike in 2008 – an Air Force 1 (part of Nike's 1World collaboration series that involved 18 different creatives from around the world), an Air Max 90 and an Air Max 90 Current. The colour theme across the series was a minimal black, white and Volt (Nike's signature high visibility neon yellow/green), and the shoes also featured a variety of materials including suede, nubuck and mesh. In addition to the custom tongue labels and lace jewels, KAWS' signature 'XX' was incorporated into the design by way of cross-stitch detailing around the toe box area.

Sneakers

Sneakers

The KAWS Air Jordan 4 Retro was one of the most anticipated releases of 2017 – a London raffle for the grey shoes even had to be shut down by police over fears of safety. The shoes feature premium grey suede, as well as the artist's signature 'XX' symbol on both the heel tab and hangtag (above the word 'AIR') – not to mention the glow-in-the-dark outsole. The all-black version of the shoe was originally limited to family and friends, but Cyber Monday saw a limited release via the KAWS website.

Sneakers

In celebration of Dover Street Market New York's 10th Anniversary, Sky High Farm Universe (a brand created in support of New York-based non-profit Sky High Farm) partnered with KAWS on a 10-piece capsule that customized existing Nike Life workwear silhouettes. Released in 2023, the collection also included the Sky High Farm 'Cloud Force 1s' (opposite) – a sneaker concept created by Matty Friedman from SHFU and reimagined by KAWS. 250 pairs were made between both colourways (black and white).

Part of a wider partnership between Nike and Chitose Abe's fashion label Sacai, the Nike Blazer Low (above) features double-layered details including the Swoosh, shoelaces and tongue. In 2021, Sacai pushed the design of this silhouette further by collaborating with KAWS on a four-shoe collection (above). The four colourways – Neptune Blue, Reed, Purple Dusk and Team Red – were inspired by a series of works by KAWS entitled URGE. Each pair also had his 'XX' motif lasered onto the midsole.

Chris Law

Chris Law began his obsession with sneakers in 1983, during the football terrace style heyday and hip-hop's global boom. In the late 1990s, while working at the seminal London street-wear store, Bond International, Law met his future business partner, Russell Williamson. Williamson had an idea for an online project (later named *Spine Magazine*) and was also keen to start a small design firm that could focus its work on more street-based projects – a vision that later came to pass under the name Unorthodox Styles (now U Dox).

A feature on the topic of sneaker culture, part of the early incarnation of the *Spine Magazine* website, generated sufficient positive feedback to incite the next key in-house project for the Unorthodox Styles team: Crooked Tongues (see page 66), a sneaker-related website named after the aesthetically displeasing phenomenon in which a shoe's tongue doesn't sit straight.

After more than six years at Unorthodox Styles/Crooked Tongues, where he worked with multiple brands on various footwear design collaborations, Law joined adidas as a colour and materials design manager. Since then, and now with more than 20 years experience in the footwear industry, Law has also worked with a multitude of other brands, including Axel Arigato, New Balance, Clarks, Converse and Jordan – as well as with artists and collaborators including Mark Gonzales (see page 76), Donald Glover, the Beastie Boys, and Kenny Scharf. At the time of writing, he is the head of footwear at Cole Buxton.

During his time at adidas, Law worked with Ad-Rock and Mike D of the Beastie Boys on this adidas Campus silhouette (above). Created in 2019 to coincide with the Beyond The Streets exhibition, the design referenced vintage American sportswear, and featured a canvas upper with the three stripes appearing as a terrycloth underlay. The iconic tag-inspired logo (originally by Eric Haze) from the *Check Your Head* album was playfully applied over the traditional tongue label, and the shoes also featured a soft rubber gum sole and toe bumper.

Sneakers   65

During his time with Axel Arigato, in 2024, Law worked on the Area Typo sneaker (above) with playful typographic lettering inspired by graffiti 'bombing' and 'throw-up' styling. The double layered, leather letters were held in place by extra eyelets and stitch detailing. Law also worked with designers Jess Dalton and Matty McMorran on the Maybe Pack (left) in 2024. Inspired by Berlin-based artist Illya Goldman Gubin, the pack was created around the raw beauty of foam.

66 • Sneakers

Crooked Tongues

Online sneaker resource (and store) Crooked Tongues was the public face of London-based creative agency Unorthodox Styles, and was founded in 2000 to address the lack of qualitative information about the sneaker scene. Crooked Tongues' goal was to gather the elements of value to the sneaker community and create a single online resource. The website (which closed in 2015) included news, interviews with key players and in-depth information on upcoming and current releases. There was also the opportunity for users to upload and display their collections, or just show off what they're wearing each day (which always provoked lively debate). As ardent sneaker enthusiasts, the team at Crooked Tongues worked on numerous sneaker collaborations with the likes of Nike, adidas, New Balance and Puma. Their attention to detail and knowledge of the culture helped create some of the most beautiful, informed and creative releases on the scene.

Released in 2006, Crooked Tongues' third collaboration with New Balance saw a collection of four different sneakers, each themed after a particular historical villain. Named the Confederation of Villainy, the pack consisted of an NB 1500 (themed on the pirate Blackbeard), an NB 577 (themed on Chinese outlaw Song Jiang, aka Black Sword), an NB 575 (themed around a crook of the Old West, Black Bart) and an NB 991 (themed on Bedfordshire highwayman Black Tom). Bored with the generic boxes stacked in their closets, Crooked Tongues worked with tattoo artist BJ Betts to produce themed premium packaging featuring Betts' obsessively detailed art. All four shoes in the edition featured a white metal top eyelet and unique Confederation of Villainy tongue label. Retailing at UK£150 and available only through the Crooked Tongues online store, 99 pairs of each colourway were made.

Sneakers

Created as a tribute to the most basic form of customization, the lace switch, Crooked Tongues decided to take things one step further with this adidas adicolor BK3 from 2006. This classic adidas silhouette features a choice of six sets of laces and six removable tongues in different colours: red, yellow, black, white, purple and green. Third in the adicolor Black Series (hence the BK3), the various colour combinations allow the whole look of the shoe to change against the solid, neutral black background. As Crooked Tongues put it: 'Co-ordination is a problem, and we're fairly obsessive about colour matching, because nothing screams 'no effort' more than a mismatch between sneakers and garments. Consider this our donation to the shoe world – a trainer that's adaptable to your entire wardrobe.' See the rest of the adidas adicolor project on page 70.

Crooked Tongues teamed up with Puma in 2006 to launch the CT Clyde pack, a trilogy of releases that took inspiration from the early days of hip-hop and B-Boy style. 'We were trying to cater to the heads still hunting the rust-coloured pair from a misspent youth, as well as some kid fiending for something bright, wearable and different from the rest,' explains Crooked Tongues. To coincide with the project, and as part of the Crooked Tongues website's Clyde retrospective, users were given the opportunity to design and submit their ideas for the third CT Clyde. Out of more than 700 online entries, Crooked Tongues member albellisimo's yellow and orange creation was chosen. Each colourway was limited to just 300 pairs worldwide and dropped exclusively to Crooked Tongues online store (each with a matching T-shirt and keyring) before becoming available at select retailers.

adidas adicolor

Ahead of its time, the original adicolor concept was launched back in 1983; adidas offered pure white footwear models with specially created quick-drying and weatherproof pens. This innovative approach allowed consumers to produce their very own customized pair of sneakers.

The concept was relaunched in 2006 by adidas Originals, enhanced by a set of comprehensive, sophisticated customization tools ranging from felt-tip pens to spray paints and more. In addition, adidas expanded the project into a collection of 42 pairs of adicolor shoes. The collection was divided into two major parts, the White Series (featuring six sneakers that referred back to the original customization concept) and the innovative colour-themed series (divided into Red, Blue, Yellow, Green, Pink and Black), which featured a number of collaborations with icons from the worlds of fashion, design and art.

Each colour (including the White Series) featured six shoes: an adidas adicolor Low, an adicolor High, a Century Low, a Stan Smith and two versions of the Superstar II. The different models were available through various distribution channels, with each sneaker being coded according to the colour series and level of release. For example, R1 was the most limited release of the Red series, and B6 was the most widely available release of the Blue series. A range of apparel and accessories was also created for each of the series.

White Series

W1
adicolor Low

W2
adicolor High

Blue Series

BL1
Black Tiger Studio for Styles
adicolor Low

BL2
Cey Adams
adicolor High

Sneakers 71

W3
Century Low

W4
Stan Smith

W5
Superstar II

W6
Bill McMullen for
Foot Locker - New York
Superstar II

BL3
Toy2R
Century Low

BL4
Tron
Stan Smith

BL5
Denim
Superstar II

BL6
Bill McMullen for
Foot Locker - Bronx
Superstar II

Sneakers

Green Series

G1
Jim Lambie for The Hideout
adicolor Low

G2
Peter Saville
adicolor High

Pink Series

P1
Wood Wood
adicolor Low

P2
Fafi
adicolor High

Black Series

BK1
Claude Closky for Colette
adicolor Low

BK2
Keith Haring and Jeremy Scott
adicolor High

adidas adicolor | Sneakers | 73

G3
Emilio Pucci
Century Low

G4
Kermit
Stan Smith

G5
Camo
Superstar II

G6
Bill McMullen for Foot Locker - Staten Island
Superstar II

P3
Vice
Century Low

P4
Miss Piggy
Stan Smith

P5
Satin
Superstar II

P6
Bill McMullen for Foot Locker - Brooklyn
Superstar II

BK3
Crooked Tongues
Century Low

BK4
Trimmy
Stan Smith

BK5
Leather
Superstar II

BK6
Bill McMullen for Foot Locker - New York
Superstar II

Sneakers

Red Series

R1
J-Money for
Dave's Quality Meat
adicolor Low

R2
Surface To Air
adicolor High

Yellow Series

Y1
HUF
adicolor Low

Y2
Taro Okamoto
adicolor High

As part of the adicolor project, adidas ran a competition in which anybody could submit a customized design of an adicolor White Series collection piece. Adicolor partners Cey Adams, Fafi and Crooked Tongues narrowed the entries down to 20 finalists, who were then put to a public vote. The winner was New York-based Ari Lankin, whose Hokusai design received 20 per cent of the vote. The design was produced in a limited production run of 50, with 25 pairs allocated to Lankin and 25 pairs going on sale to the public.

adidas adicolor Sneakers 75

R3
Dark Horse Comics
Century Low

R4
Betty Boop
Stan Smith

R5
Suede
Superstar II

R6
Bill McMullen for
Foot Locker - Manhattan
Superstar II

Y3
Panini
Century Low

Y4
Mr Happy
Stan Smith

Y5
Monogram
Superstar II

Y6
Bill McMullen for
Foot Locker - Queens
Superstar II

Mark Gonzales

Mark Gonzales (aka Gonz) is an artist and professional skateboarder, best known as a pioneer of street skateboarding. Originally sponsored by skateboarding company Vision, Gonzales founded Blind skateboards in 1989 (the name was an intentional slight to Vision). He is currently sponsored by a host of companies, including adidas and Krooked Skateboarding (a company he also runs). Known for his canvas paintings and customized priest characters, Gonzales has also established a parallel career as an artist, having shown at various galleries worldwide, and he is also a published author and poet.

When adidas originally approached Gonzales to design a signature skateboarding shoe, he wanted it to be made of wood, 'so you have wood on the board and wood inside your shoe. It would be more natural; you could almost feel the soul of the tree.' Unfortunately, the project never materialized, but Gonzales has since worked on a multitude of footwear collaborations with the brand, including the adidas Stan Smith Skate (above left), released in 2006.

Sneakers   77

The pair of Gonzales' adidas Stan Smith Skates (above) were hand painted by the artist during a visit to London in 2007. Gonzales customized the shoes while painting 1,000 of his Megga America Communion Priest characters for an exhibition at the DPMHI gallery. Gonzales also teamed up with adidas in 2007 to promote Skate, a skateboarding computer game from Electronic Arts. The Mark Gonzales High Score Superstar Skate (right) was limited to 500 pieces, and getting your hands on a pair was only possible (via the adidas website) after unlocking secret codes within the game. Professional skateboarder Dennis Busenitz also produced a sneaker (the High Score Gazelle Skate) as part of the project.

Also Known As

Inspired by vintage spray paint colours, Also Known As (AKA) created this collection of seven patent leather Nike Dunk Lows in collaboration with Nike iD (now Nike By You). Five sets of the shoes were produced, none of which were made available at retail. One of the five sets, however, was auctioned via eBay, with all proceeds going to the Free Arts NYC, a non-profit organization dedicated to bringing the healing and therapeutic powers of the arts into the lives of abused and neglected children and their families. The final bid was placed at US$14,900, making the price of each Dunk US$2,128.57.

AKA also created the limited edition laser-etched Nike Air Force 1s (opposite, bottom right) for the release of the *Also Known As* book by 12ozProphet in 2005. The shoes were designed by Allen Benedikt of AKA, with handstyles by Crude Oil and hand lasering by Tom Luedecke at Nike's fabled Innovation Kitchen in Beaverton, Oregon. There were just under 50 pairs produced, and all were given away to a carefully crafted list of friends, collaborators and celebrities. Each pair came with the extra-rare, gold-covered edition of *Also Known As, Volume 1*.

Sneakers 79

Wieden + Kennedy

In 2007, Wieden + Kennedy, then the world's largest private advertising agency, marked its 25th anniversary and 25-year-long agency relationship with Nike by producing this set of six Dunk Trainer Lows. The concept is the result of a collaboration between Nike designers and W+K employees, and the shoes are a hybrid of the Nike Free Trail, the Air Trainer 1, and the Dunk. The six different colourways represent the different W+K offices around the world; green for Portland, orange for Amsterdam, yellow for New York, red for Shanghai, white for Tokyo and blue for London. The upper of the shoe is made from dark grey denim, grey suede and grey leather, and the forefoot strap features the lettering 'XXV'. Quotes on the insoles read:

"Everything can be reduced to math or emotion. For Nike and Wieden & Kennedy, 1+1 = can you #*&%ing believe it? Quite a run and we've just begun!" Mark Parker'

"This shoe sits empty while you think back on all the two of you have accomplished – all you have laid witness to – and yet this shoe can't help wondering how long before you stop the reminiscence, before you take new roads to new places. This shoe sits empty" Dan Wieden'

Sneakers

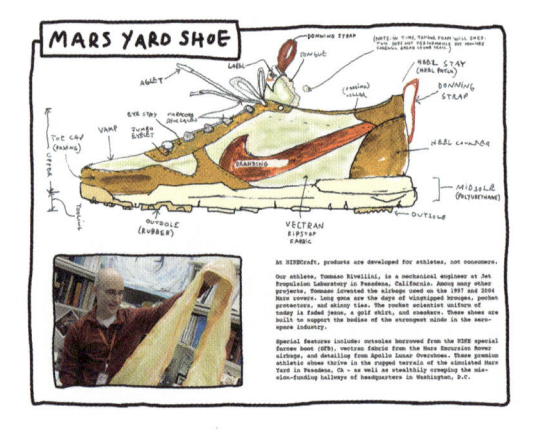

Sneakers

Tom Sachs

New York-based Tom Sachs is a sculptor best known for his elaborate recreations of modern icons – from Knoll office furniture made out of phone books and duct tape, to Cold War masterpieces like the Apollo 11 Lunar Excursion Module. In 2012, as part of his Space Program 2.0: Mars art exhibition at Park Avenue Armory in New York, Sachs collaborated with Nike to release the NikeCraft capsule collection. The collection included the Mars Yard 1.0 sneakers (left), as well as a jacket, tote bag and trench coat. Famously, the upper of the shoes is constructed using Vectran fabric, the same material used on Mars Excursion Rover airbags, while other features include outsoles borrowed from Nike's Special Forces Boot (SFB) and detailing from the Apollo Lunar Overshoes.
'At NikeCraft, products are developed for athletes, not consumers,' says Sachs. 'Our athlete, Tommaso Rivellini, is a mechanical engineer at Jet Propulsion Laboratory in Pasadena, California. Among many other projects, Tommaso invented the airbags used on the 1997 and 2004 Mars rovers. Long gone are the days of wing-tipped brogues, pocket protectors and skinny ties. The rocket scientist uniform of today is faded jeans, a golf shirt and sneakers. These shoes are built to support the bodies of the strongest minds in the aerospace industry.'

84   ● Sneakers

Nike and Sachs revisited the Mars Yard project in 2017, announcing the NikeCraft Mars Yard 2.0 (opposite) – an upgraded and more durable version of the original. While the style and colourway of the shoe stayed largely the same, the materials were upgraded based on long-term testing of the original Mars Yard 1.0 by Sachs. The Vectran fabric was replaced with a breathable polyester warp-knit tricot mesh, the 'donning straps' were secured to the upper with a stronger X-shaped box stitch and the tread of the outsole was inverted to better suit the urban environment. Lastly, the shoes came with both cork and mesh insoles.

Following the Mars Yard 2.0, the NikeCraft Overshoe (below) was Sachs' third collaboration with Nike and was released in 2018. Designed as a lightweight winter shoe, and dubbed 'waterproof enough', the design was essentially a weather-proofed version of the Mars Yard 2.0, with additional white overshoe uppers made from Dyneema® – a reinforced nylon material with water-resistant properties. In 2020, using a detailed programme syllabus, Sachs and NikeCraft gave select 'wear testers' the opportunity to put a new Mars Yard prototype through its paces. The resulting Mars Yard 3.0 featured a black TPU toe cap, silkscreen-printed Swoosh and carbon fibre plate.

While the Mars Yard shoes were designed for space-going scientists, the NikeCraft General Purpose Shoe (GPS), was rooted in the everyday. 'I got involved with Nike in the beginning because we wanted to make a sculpture that everyone could wear. It's a tool for everyday life; it's democratic,' says Sachs. The GPS was created to be an understated do-everything shoe, with the design and material choices providing both comfort and support. 'It took a decade to make a shoe this simple, as simple as can be and no simpler. NikeCraft shuns innovation for its own sake, but embraces it as a necessity,' adds Sachs.

The launch version, the 'Studio' colourway (above), was released in 2022 and featured a gum rubber midsole, durable white knitted upper, blue herringbone 'donning straps' and debossed Nike logo in Sachs' handwriting on the heel. Two further colourways were produced before the project took a hiatus: the 2022 'Archive' (opposite left) and the 2023 'Brown' (opposite right).

NiKE
NiKE

NiKECRAFT

BORING.
Your sneakers shouldn't be the most exciting thing about you. They are tools, and what matters about your tools is that they work. They do their job so you can do yours. You put them on and forget about them. You focus on getting a little bit faster, a little bit sharper, on finding the signal in the noise.
It took us 10 years to make a sneaker this simple——as simple as can be and no simpler. A do-more sneaker. An own-less sneaker. A show-up, prove-it, whole-life, be-you sneaker.
"It's not what you do, it's how you do it."
The NikeCraft General Purpose Shoe.
$109.99 available June 10th at nikecraft.com
NiKECRAFT

CREATIVITY IS THE ENEMY.
Just because you can doesn't always mean you should. Resist newness for newness' sake. Build on a proven foundation and innovate incrementally. Study what came before: its shape, its weight, its colors, who it's for and what it does. Use, observe, design, build, test, fail, repeat. True development is the practice of continuous refinement.
This sneaker is a product of our ongoing research into how our bodies meet the ground. We opened up the archive, wore it out, stripped it down, kept what worked and added what was missing in pursuit of a perennial sneaker. An ever-better sneaker. A never-settle sneaker. A round-the-clock, made-to-last, built-to-code sneaker.
"It's not what you do, it's how you do it."
The NikeCraft General Purpose Shoe.
$109.99 available September 1st at nikecraft.com and September 2nd worldwide.
NiKECRAFT

IT TAKES TIME.
Beauty is not limited to youth. Novelty gives way to true character, and things of quality improve with wear. From entropy to repair, you and your tools shape one another. These sneakers can be bought—what you do in them cannot.
We designed these sneakers for extended play. They are made to be scuffed, shredded, patched, glued, scrubbed, and thrashed again. Everything eventually falls apart, so we design to delay the inevitable, to prolong that sublime space between box-fresh and worn-to-pieces. These are pressure-tested sneakers. Built-for-decay sneakers. Full-circle, signs-of-life, tough-to-fake sneakers.
"It's not what you do, it's how you do it."
The NikeCraft General Purpose Shoe.
$109.99 and available February 6th at nikecraft.com and February 7th worldwide.
NiKECRAFT

Virgil Abloh

Virgil Abloh was an artist, architect, engineer, creative director, industrial designer, fashion designer, musician, DJ and philanthropist. Men's Artistic Director at Louis Vuitton and founder of Off-White™, Abloh blurred the lines of creativity, rewriting the rules of fashion and design while injecting elements of humour and DIY into his practice.

As a teenager, living in Rockford, Illinois, Abloh and his friends sketched shoe ideas and mailed them to Nike. 'By the time I made my first trip to Beaverton,' said Abloh, 'I immediately wanted to make something. I didn't wait all those years just to have meetings.' With this in mind, Abloh's first visit to Nike saw him rebuild a pair of triple-black Air Force 1 Low sneakers using a craft knife, drawing on them with markers and creating one-offs for his staff to wear at that year's Design Miami.

Establishing this reconstructed design language ultimately led to The Ten, a collaborative exploration of ten iconic Nike footwear silhouettes released in 2017. The ten shoes included were divided into two themes and the first, Revealing, featured shoes designed to look accessible: hand-cut, open-source and reconstructed. Included in this theme were the Air Jordan 1, Nike Air Max 90, Nike Air Presto, Nike Air VaporMax and Nike Blazer Mid (below and opposite). The shoes in the second theme, Ghosting, were designed with translucent uppers – to further the idea of 'revealing' while also linking the second theme through materials used. Included in this theme were the Converse Chuck Taylor, Nike Zoom Fly SP, Nike Air Force 1 Low, Nike React Hyperdunk 2017 and Nike Air Max 97 (see pages 90–91).

Abloh's quick pace resulted in one of the fastest collaborations Nike had ever completed: ten shoes in close to ten months. 'Most of the creative decisions were made in the first three hours, while actual design and iteration took two to three days,' said Abloh at the time. 'The Jordan 1 was done in one design session.' The Revealing theme was also visualized through tongue-in-cheek text placements, such as 'AIR' on the side of the Nike Air VaporMax, Air Jordan 1 and Air Presto and 'SHOELACES' on the shoelaces.

Although the designs look complex, Abloh said at the time that he wanted the process – of opening up the guts of a shoe to reveal the innovation within – to feel approachable. 'Yes, we're making a desired product, but by making a trip to your local store, and using tools you have at home, you could also make this shoe.'

Sneakers

Sneakers

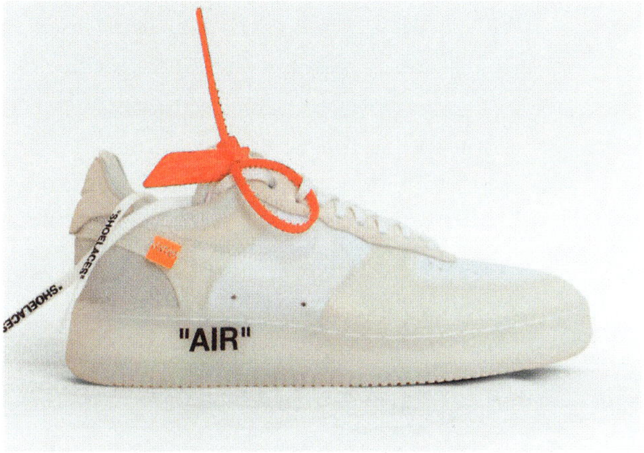
"AIR"
"SHOELACES"

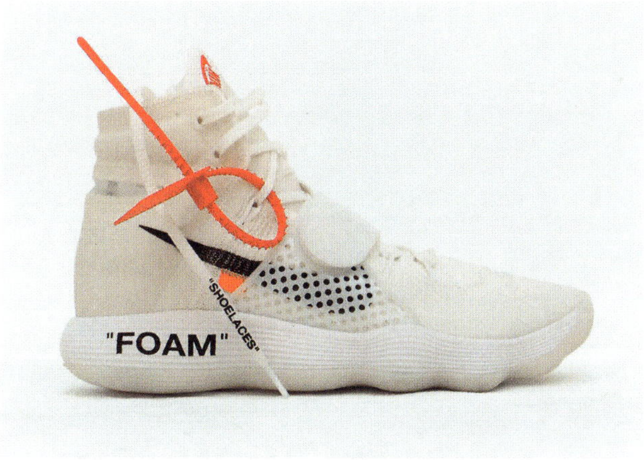
"FOAM"
"SHOELACES"

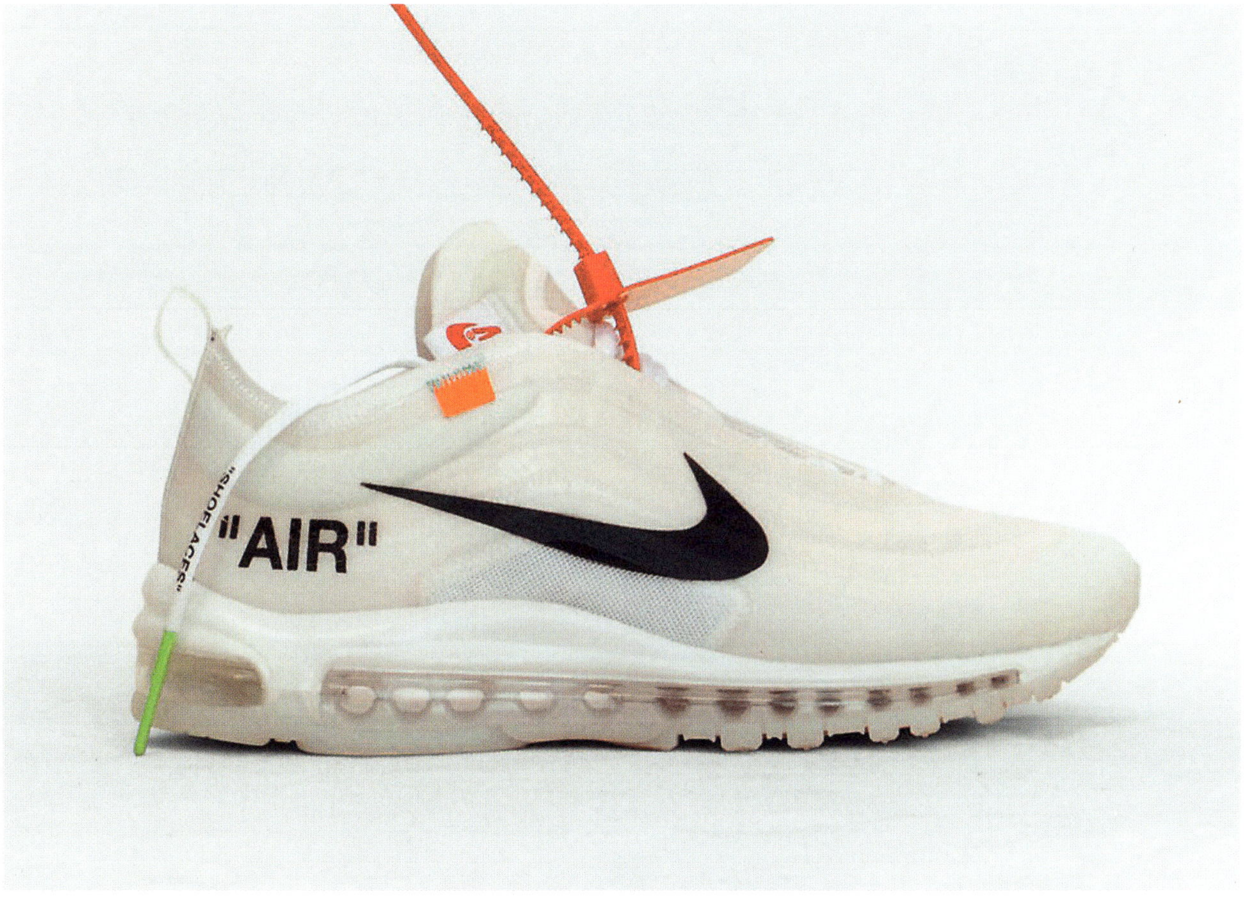
"AIR"
"SHOELACES"

Steve ESPO Powers

Created in 2004 by Philadelphia and New York graffiti writer, Steve Powers, aka ESPO (an acronym for Exterior Surface Painting Outreach), this Nike Air Force 2 Low is a truly unique collaboration that features an innovative clear upper. Originally part of a wider collection (including collaborations from Pharrell Williams and Halle Berry), Powers' approach was to think about the shoes performing as a piece of art, rather than as performance footwear. The result was the first time a Nike shoe had featured a transparent upper – a concept that went on to be used for many other limited releases from the brand. To compliment this innovation, the shoes also came with a pair of blue socks featuring the words 'Wants' and 'Needs'. All of the graphic elements on the shoes reference Powers' signature style and relate to the concepts of 'buying' and 'wanting'. 'Being mostly plastic,' says Powers, 'the shoes self-destruct due to inherent vice. But the first art shoe, and what it asks of the buyers and sellers of culture, will always remain relevant. Stuff gets old, art is always fresh.' The shoes were released in an edition of 1050, with proceeds from the shoes donated to God's Love We Deliver, a charity (chosen by Powers) that distributes meals to those in need.

Sneakers 93

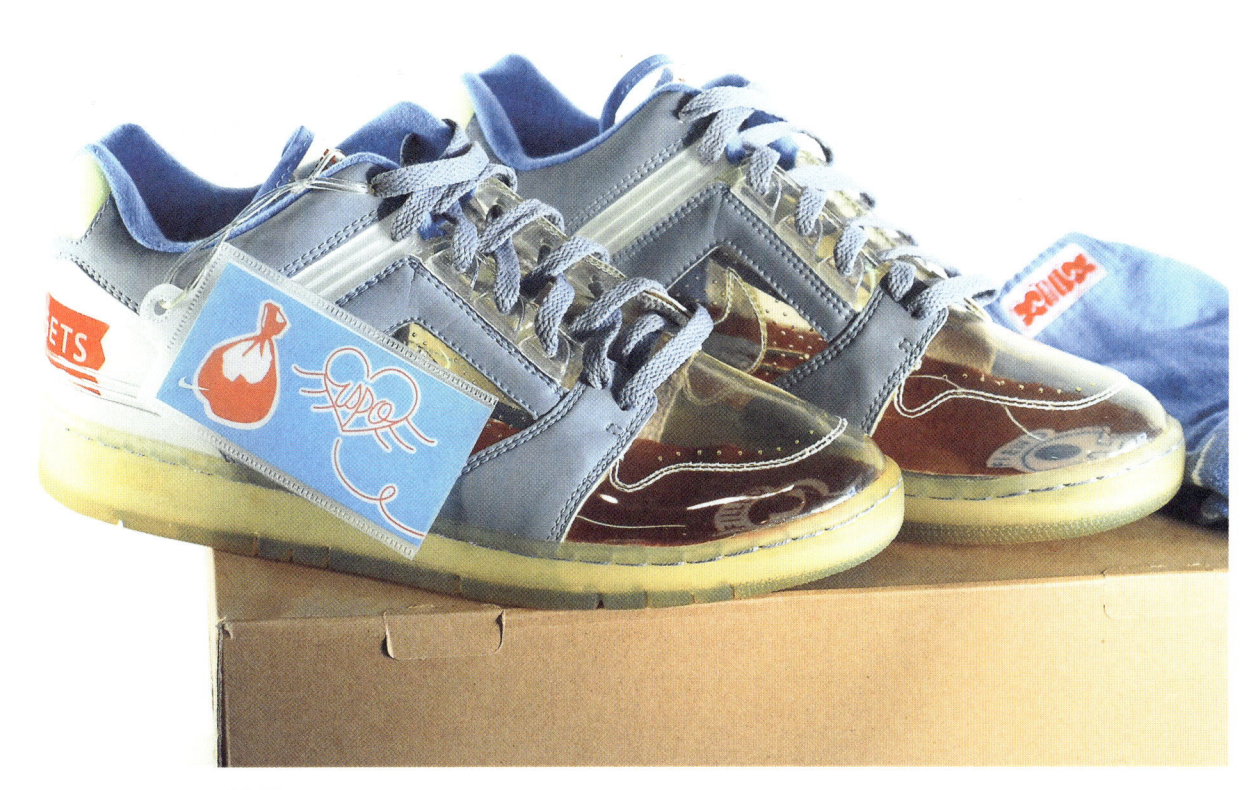

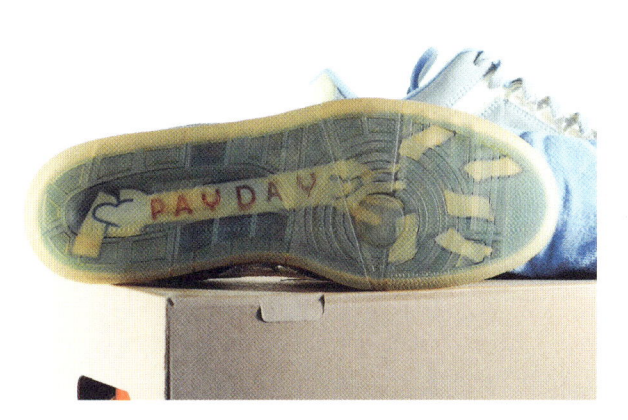

CLOT

Hong Kong-based lifestyle brand CLOT was established in 2003 by Edison Chen, Kevin Poon and Billy Ip. It specializes in almost everything involved in youth culture and was started as a creative outlet and showcase for fashion, music, design and entertainment.

The Air Max 1 'Kiss Of Death' (above and opposite) was CLOT's first sneaker collaboration with Nike. It was inspired by the pressure point (known as Kiss of Death) that is located at the centre of the foot; supposedly the most lethal pressure point in the human body. The original concept came from Hong Kong graffiti artist MC Yan, with the team at CLOT providing the additional design details. Released to purely Tier Zero accounts, the shoes were stocked in only a handful of stores around the world, and the Hong Kong edition came with a unique box and manual, resembling an ancient Chinese book.

Shown below left is a Nike Air Max 1 made to commemorate the collaboration between Edison Chen and Kanye West in the Hong Kong leg of West's Touch the Sky Tour – where Chen performed the opening act. The shoe featured a laser-engraved CLOT logo on the heel, with a calligraphic rendering of 'Clot' on the mudguard. Only four pairs were made, two going to CLOT and two to Kanye West.

Controversially for some, 2021 saw a rerelease of the Air Max 'Kiss of Death', alongside two additional colourways – a tan and brown colourway inspired by cha (tea), and a red and grey colourway referencing the Kanye West shoe.

Sneakers 95

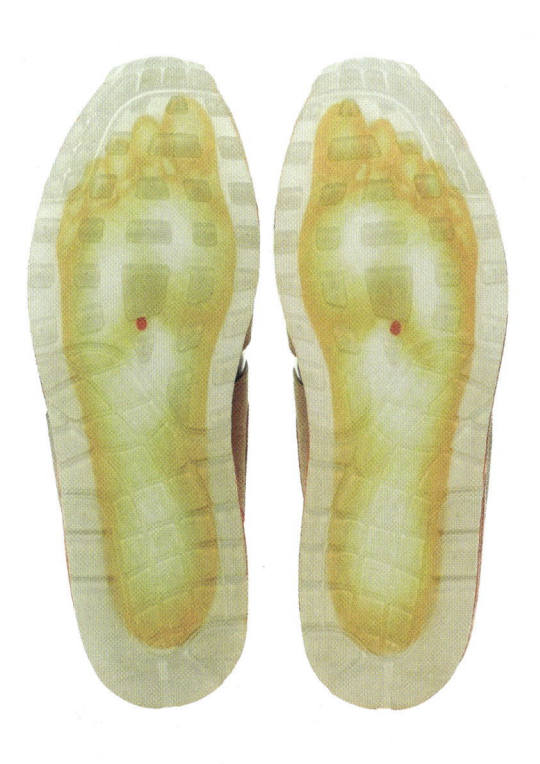

Tom Luedecke

In 1997, Nike released the original Air Talaria sneaker to wide acclaim throughout the running community. The Air Talaria has always been a classic running shoe, loved for both its comfort and unusual use of vibrant colours. In 2006, German-born Nike designer Tom Luedecke (an artist in his own right) and the Innovation Kitchen (Nike's technological development centre) took this iconic running silhouette and fused it with design, technology and street style to create the Talaria Chukka.

The upper has been laser-etched with a design by Luedecke that mimics the anatomical structure of the foot, complete with bones, nerves, blood vessels, tendons, muscles and veins. A similar mapping of the foot's structure is displayed on the outsole, just beneath the cover of clear rubber. The Talaria Chukka also offers a supremely well-crafted fit, with minimal foam padding on the inside of the shoe. This Tier Zero release was available in two colourways, the first using mainly black and dark brown, with the second adding neon yellow and pink highlights for a more traditional Talaria appearance (below). The white version of the shoe (opposite) is a handcrafted sample created by Luedecke.

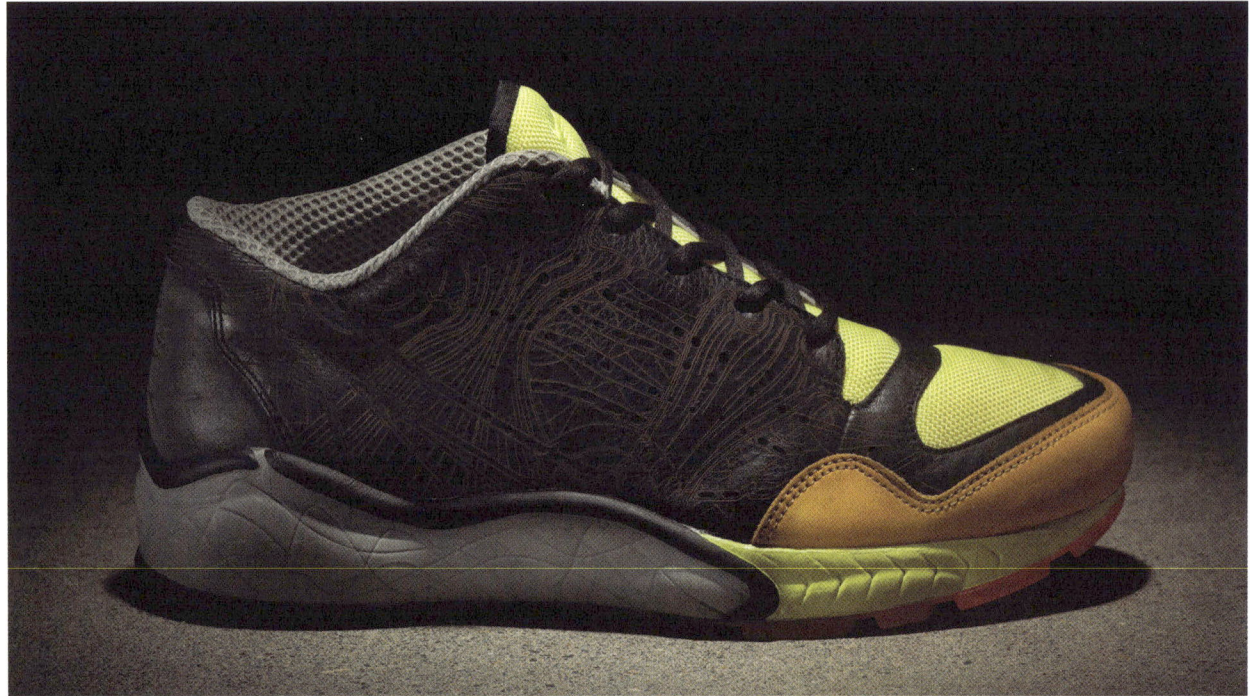

Sneakers 97

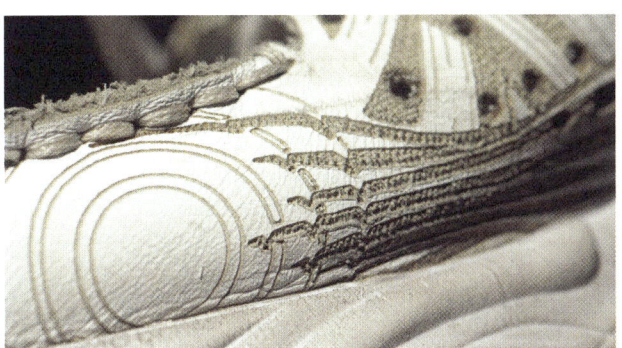

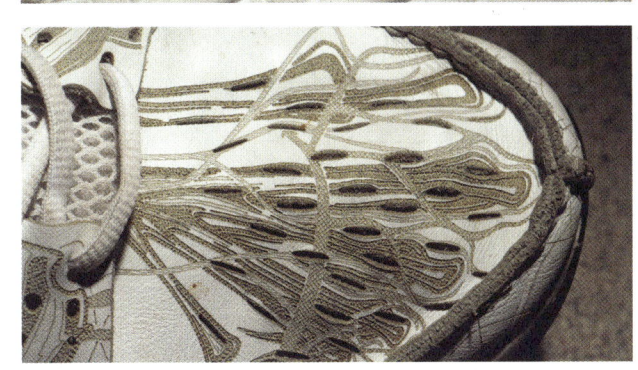

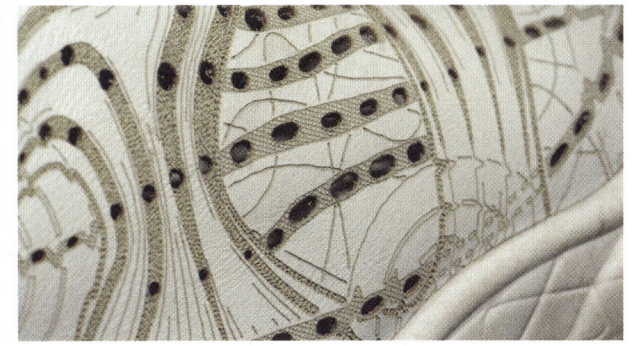

Nike Laser Project

Originally starting life in Nike's Innovation Kitchen, the use of a laser was first developed as a way of accurately cutting material. The laser technology itself is nothing new – working in much the same way as a desktop printer, the laser simply plots a course based on computer instructions, burning a pattern that can be incredibly intricate (similar to the technology used in the creation of electronic circuit boards). It was Nike designer Mark Smith who saw past the industrial applications of the technology and realized the potential the process had as a creative tool. In 2003, the Nike Laser Project was born, with Smith asking four artist friends (Tom Luedecke, Stephan 'Maze' Georges, Mike Desmond and Chris Lundy) to help produce six shoes, all of which were to be lasered with specifically created artwork. Smith himself created an Air Force 1 and a Cortez, Luedecke a Cortez, Georges an Air Force 1, Desmond a Dunk Low and Lundy a one-piece Dunk Low.

Depending on the design, the laser works in much the same way as a tattoo gun, with a 'line burn' setting for detailed line graphics and a 'solid burn' for removing more material and filling in shaded areas. There is also the ability to combine both of these processes, resulting in a more complicated application of the laser. Obviously, the graphic artwork had to be based around the architecture of the shoe elements; but incredibly, the drive for the biggest canvas space possible led Smith and Nike to re-engineer a number of shoes, creating uppers made entirely from one piece of (pigskin) leather. This meant that not only did the laser technology change the aesthetic possibilities of the shoe design, but it also improved performance, as less material aids breathability, and means less weight and greater comfort. The project was launched with an exhibition at the Elizabeth Street Gallery in New York featuring original artwork and developmental shoe models, as well as the final sneakers.

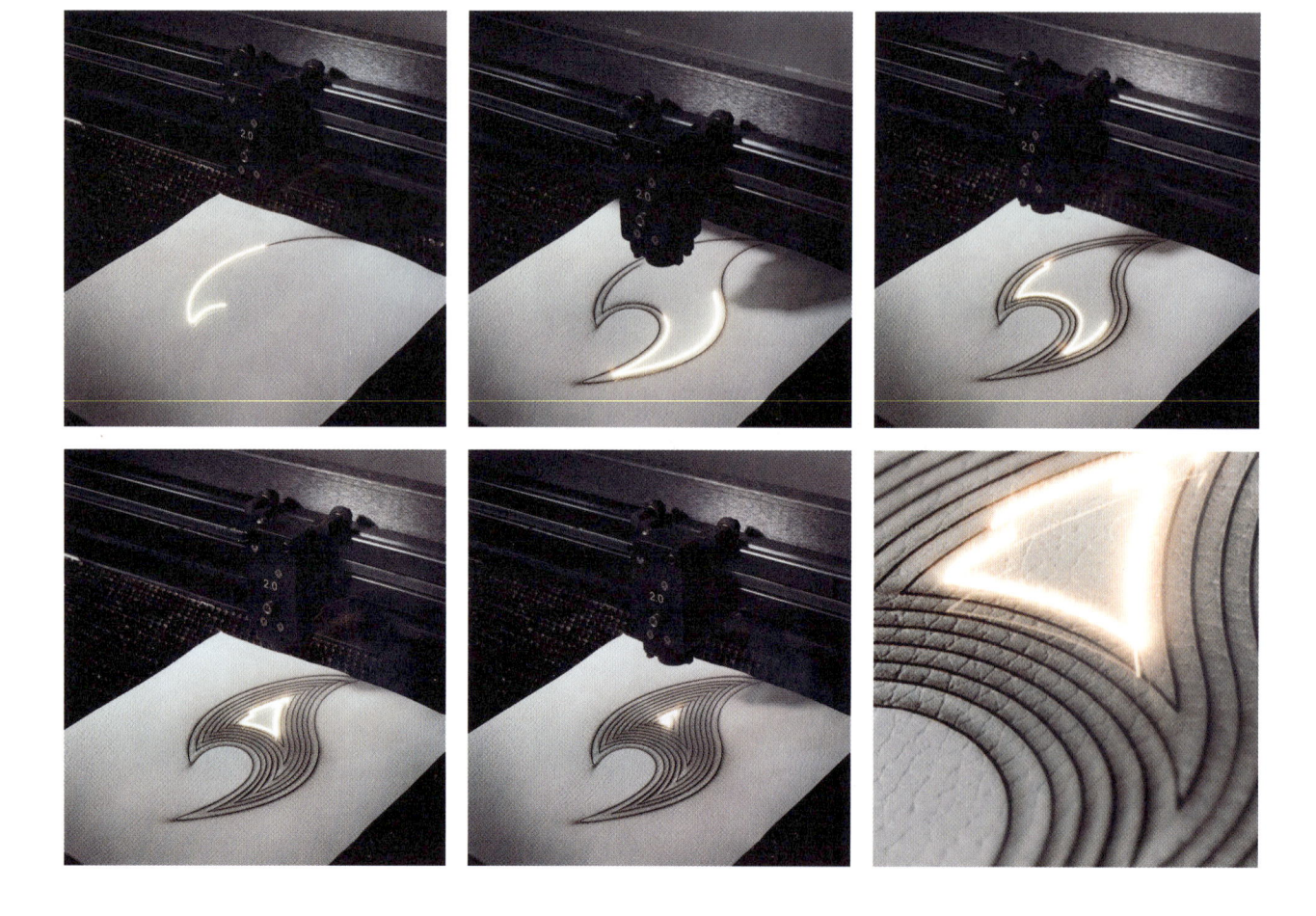

Mark Smith
Nike Air Force 1
Nike designer and project curator Mark Smith designed this tattoo-inspired Air Force 1. Previously working for Vans and DC Shoes, Smith started his career at Nike in the early 1990s as an apprentice to famed Nike designer Tinker Hatfield.

Chris Lundy
Nike Dunk Low (One-Piece)
Surfer and artist (after a serious accident to his knee, he decided to concentrate on painting), Lundy applied this flow-inspired artwork to a one-piece Dunk.

Stephan 'Maze' Georges
Nike Air Force 1
New York graffiti artist Maze (who was also part of Nike's Advanced Concept Team) applied his street art-style to this Air Force 1.

Nike Laser Project | Sneakers | 101

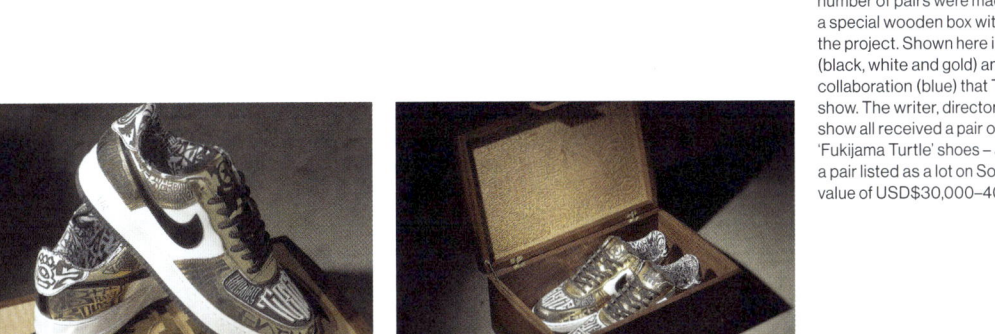

Mark Smith again worked with laser technology on these Nike Air Jordan 3s (above) – a special project for basketball superstar Michael Jordan's 40th birthday. In 2007, Smith also designed these laser etched Nike 'Fukijama Turtle' Air Force 1s (left) for the HBO series, Entourage. Episode 33 of the show featured lead character Turtle hunting for a pair of sneakers at Los Angeles sneaker store Undefeated. Only a very limited number of pairs were made, and Smith also created a special wooden box with lasered details as part of the project. Shown here is the 'Fukijama Turtle' (black, white and gold) and the 'Fukijama Undefeated' collaboration (blue) that Turtle was hunting for in the show. The writer, director and cast members of the show all received a pair of personally customized 'Fukijama Turtle' shoes – at the time of writing, there is a pair listed as a lot on Sotheby's with an estimated value of USD$30,000–40,000.

Katsuya Terada

Prolific Japanese artist Katsuya Terada is probably best known as the character designer for the animated Manga classic, *Blood: The Last Vampire*. Terada defines himself as a rakugaki artist, a Japanese term for a drawing style and philosophy in which the artist draws continuously without too much thought. He has also worked for US comics such as *Iron Man* and *Hellboy*.

In 2005, Terada applied his art to the Nike Air Zoom Terra Tattoo. The graphics were inspired by the elements air, wind, fire and water, with the right shoe differing from the left as the story of the illustration unfolds across both sneakers. Limited to 300 pairs worldwide, the package also contained a wooden shoebox laser-engraved with Terada's artwork.

LX One

This New Balance 1500 was originally created by the (now closed) Strasbourg boutique, RZOstore. Renowned for using artworks as inspiration for shoe collaborations (including a Reebok ERS 5000 inspired by Andy Warhol's iconic *Gold Marilyn Monroe*), this project utilized a painting by French optical artist and founder of RZOstore, LX One – real name Alex Bloc. Released in 2006, the shoe was limited to just 84 pairs, with each pair featuring a unique composition of LX One's artwork. 'The process was simple,' says Bloc, 'we sent the design to the manufacturer for printing and then we randomly cut pieces from the leather so that every pair was different.'

Jeff Staple

Jeff Staple (real name Jeff Ng) is the founder and owner of prolific independent visual communications agency, Reed Art Department (as much a cultural barometer as a business), and the pigeon-themed clothing brand, STAPLE. Multi-talented, Staple is a graphic, web and clothing designer, artist, DJ, writer and entrepreneur. 'I know how long I've been into shoes and it started at an extremely young age,' says Staple. 'But it's hard to explain why. I think since I was young, shoes were sort of a status symbol. They showed how fly you were… or how stylish you were.' Staple has worked with numerous brands, including New Balance, Levi's, Puma, Timberland, Uniqlo, Apple and Sony PlayStation, to name but a few, and has enjoyed repeated collaboration success with Nike. Sneaker fans probably best know Staple for his role in the creation of the New York-themed Dunk Low 'Pigeon', which caused mass hysteria on its release.

Shown on this page is the Nike Dunk Low 'NRF Edition' from 2005. The Nike Recess Federation (NRF) was a basketball league run for Nike under the Staple Design umbrella. It was an exclusive group of New York's most influential creatives playing organized basketball each week, with the finals at Madison Square Garden. With only 12 pairs produced, this super-exclusive sneaker was the trophy for the winning team.

Produced in 2005 as part of the White Dunk exhibition (see page 286), the Nike Dunk Low Pro SB 'Pigeon' shown above is highly regarded as one of the most coveted sneakers of all time. The shoe was themed on the city of New York – with the design based on a pigeon. Only 150 pairs of this sneaker were produced, causing a near-riot when they were released to the public through Staple's Reed Space store.

After the success of the New York-themed 'Pigeon', the pigeon became the driving inspiration behind Staple's extensive apparel range and collaborative projects – including footwear releases with New Balance, Puma and Reebok. Shown below, left to right, are the Nike Dunk Low Pro SB styles 'Black Pigeon' (2017) and 'Panda Pigeon' (2019). The 'Panda Pigeon' was based on a previously rejected sample design, and the graphics on the outsole pay tribute to the newspaper headlines created by the infamous launch of the original 'Pigeon' Dunks.

106 · Sneakers

Staple and Nike created the Navigation Pack (above) in 2004, especially for sneaker hunters willing to cross air, land and sea to find their holy grail. 'Sneakerheads are the navigators of our time,' says Staple. The Air Burst (top) is dedicated to the sea and is laser-etched with graphics of water currents that flow around the country of Japan. The Air Max 90 (middle) is dedicated to the land and has a block-by-block map of Lower Manhattan lasered onto the upper. The Shox NZ (bottom) is dedicated to the air and features jet-stream patterns from around the UK. Shown right, the 2006 Nordic Pack (featuring a Nike Air Force 1 Low, a Dunk Low and an Air Stab) was based on three previous winter Olympic games – at Sapporo, Lillehammer and Salt Lake City. Merino wool and leather inlays were used throughout the pack, with each insole featuring a map of each of the Olympic cities.

Created in 2004, the Nike Tattoo Series was the first commercially available project involving Nike's laser technology and incorporated art based on traditional Japanese tattoo techniques. Staple produced two shoes for the project, the Nike Original Cortez (above) and the Air Rift + (sample version shown below).

Mister Cartoon

Earning his name through his drawing abilities and personality, Mister Cartoon (aka Mark Machado) is one of the world's premier tattoo artists, having inked the likes of Nas, Eminem, Dr. Dre and Pharrell Williams. Famed for his intricate masterpieces, Cartoon uses a technique called fine line tattooing, which originated in US prisons where black ink was watered down to create shadows and depth, as coloured inks just weren't available. As well as being a world-renowned tattoo artist, Mister Cartoon was one of the co-founders of the Joker clothing brand and also finds the time to take part in various artistic collaborations. Finding his calling in hip-hop, Cartoon was originally introduced to art and design through a career in graffiti back in the 1980s. He has since worked on sneaker collaborations with both Nike and Vans, produced album cover artwork (most famously for Cypress Hill) and created backdrops for music promos – he even created graffiti backdrops for Rockstar's cult classic game *Grand Theft Auto: San Andreas*.

Mister Cartoon is synonymous with the city of Los Angeles, and Los Angeles has often been considered the home of the Nike Cortez. In 2017, Cartoon and Nike partnered to release three new iterations of the classic silhouette (below). Each colourway features distinct elements hand drawn by Cartoon, and a tricolour midsole made up of white, black and gum rubber. Composed of premium leather and suede accents, the obsidian black colourway features a custom 'LA' symbol within the Nike Swoosh. For the all-white leather colourway, the Swoosh was replaced completely with custom Cortez lettering. Finally, with quilted denim and suede accents, the blue colourway featured a unique cross stitch pattern. 'These shoes represent what I grew up with on the streets of LA,' explains Cartoon, 'I see kids embracing the Cortez because of the simplicity and classic history.'

Shown top, and created for the 10th anniversary of Vans Syndicate in 2015, is the Vans Syndicate Authentic "S" 'Mister Cartoon'. Paying tribute to the ten-year milestone, Vans returned to several original Syndicate collaborators, such as Cartoon, to represent and reinterpret a decade of style and heritage. The Vans Syndicate Authentic "S" 'Mister Cartoon' (above) was a reinterpretation of the original Vans Mister Cartoon Authentic collection from 2005.

Mike Giant

A graffiti artist, tattooist, designer and illustrator, Mike Giant is a prolific and versatile artist famed for his signature style, which mixes Mexican folk art and Japanese illustration with religious symbolism. Amazingly, Giant is colour-blind and nearsighted, part of the reason he mostly works in high-contrast black and white. Born in New York, Giant initially studied architecture before producing his first design work for Think skateboards. In recent years, Giant has shown his artwork in galleries worldwide, as well as designing for streetwear label REBEL8®.

In 2007, Giant collaborated with adidas on this Superskate Low. The sneakers were made from hemp material and featured Giant's skull artwork and signature graffiti logo on the side.

Dondi White

The graffiti legend Dondi White (who died in 1998) was part of the 1970s New York graffiti scene when the city's Metropolitan Transit Authority eradicated graffiti writing from its trains. White (born Donald J. White) became one of a select group of street artists who began to work above ground and was at the heart of New York's art scene in the 1980s.

In 2007, Converse worked with the White family on this Pro Leather 76 shoe as the first of 100 for the Converse 1HUND(RED) artists project supporting (PRODUCT)RED. Working closely with White's brother Michael, Converse produced a shoe featuring White's artwork on the insole, the outer and through the transparent outer sole.

(PRODUCT)RED is an economic initiative designed to deliver a sustainable flow of private sector money to the Global Fund to invest in African AIDS programs with an emphasis on the health of women and children. Since White's death, the Dondi White Foundation has continued to fundraise for AIDS charities, making this a perfect collaboration.

Vaughn Bodé

An icon to graffiti writers, and an influence on street culture from the mid-1970s to the present day, the late Vaughn Bodé was one of the most influential American cartoonists of our time. In September 1957, Bodé designed Cheech Wizard (below left) a unique character who wore a huge yellow hat covered in red and black stars. The inspiration for the name came from an ordinary can of Cheechy nuts.

In 2007, Puma introduced the Vaughn Bodé Clyde to celebrate the 50th anniversary of the creation of this iconic cartoon character. Released in two colourways, the first instalment stayed true to the Cheech Wizard identity, while the second, all-white version sported a much more wearable look. Limited to only 264 pairs in each colourway and made from nubuck leather with high-gloss printed stars, the sneakers featured three sets of laces for colour customization and a key chain explaining the history of Cheech. Mark Bodé, Vaughn's son (and an artist in his own right) teamed up with Puma to design both the sneakers (see his design sketches below) and a Bodé-style hoodie.

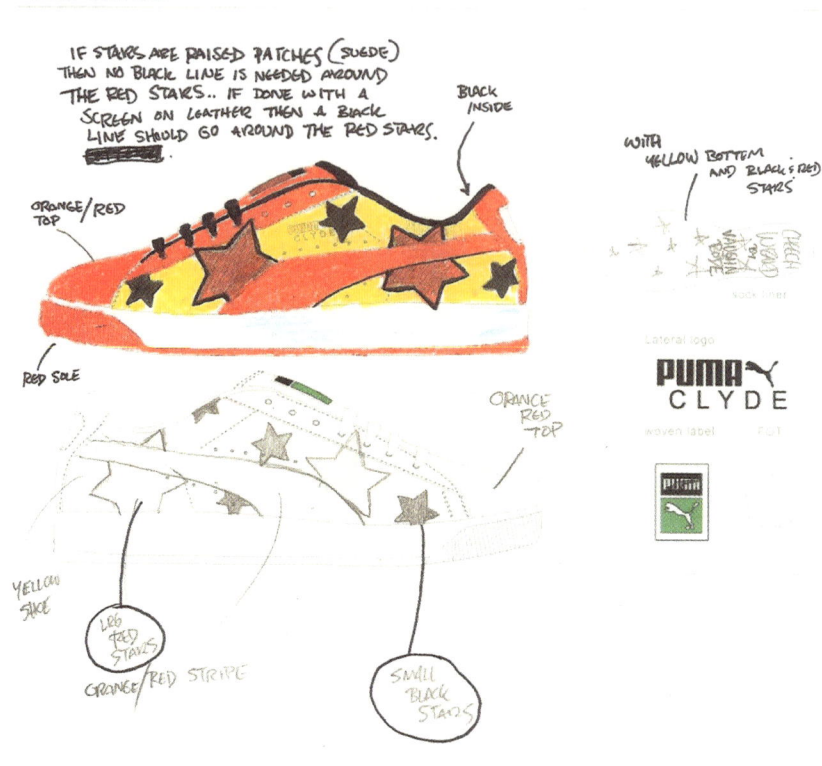

Sneakers   113

Haze

Eric Haze is a now-legendary graffiti artist from New York. Born in 1961, Haze was part of the collective of artists who first brought graffiti into the arena of art galleries – alongside names such as Keith Haring and Jean-Michel Basquiat. Not only a graffiti artist, Haze founded a graphic design studio in 1984, producing logo designs for the likes of Public Enemy and MTV, as well as album covers for The Beastie Boys and Tommy B Records. In 1991, Haze moved to Los Angeles, where alongside his design studio, he founded an independent clothing company and launched a streetwear range featuring the unique drawing and lettering style he had developed as a graffiti writer. In 2005, Haze relocated back to New York, where he continues to work on various art and design projects from around the world, including sneaker collaborations with Nike (an Air Force 1 in 2015) and New Balance (an NB 574 in 2006).

In 2003, working with Nike design director Jesse Leyva, Haze produced these Dunks (High and Low) inspired by his graffiti style. The fades were created with the use of an airbrush, meaning each shoe was one of a kind. Special versions of both the High and the Low, with Haze embroidered tongue labels (shown left), were limited to an edition of 250 and distributed through an online raffle in Los Angeles and New York.

Claw Money

Released in 2007, the limited edition Nike Claw Blazer was the first of a two-part collaboration between Nike and female graffiti legend Claw Money. The sneakers were released in three colourways and featured Claw Money's signature three-nailed claw symbol, which is based on the letter W. Later the same year, the anticipated follow-up to the Blazer, the Nike Vandal High, was released. According to Claw, she has a special connection with this sneaker: 'I wanted to do the Vandal because it's my favourite high-top, and, after all, I'm a vandal, too.' Claw, who also runs her own clothing label and was fashion editor of *Swindle* magazine, added peacock feather illustrations to the body in reflective ink to achieve a more couture look.

Jeremyville

Dividing his time between studios in Sydney and New York, prolific artist, toy designer and animator Jeremyville has collaborated with many clients including Kidrobot, Coca-Cola, MTV and adidas (creating a custom sneaker design for the Australian leg of the adicolor world tour). Jeremyville also collects rare toys, clothing and sneakers.

In 2007, Jeremyville was invited to take part in the Converse 1HUND(RED) artists programme, creating a design for a pair of Chuck Taylor high-tops. As Jeremyville explains, 'I initially painted a blank shoe that was sent to me (below), then I sent it back, and the art directors at Converse adapted the design to take into account production issues.' The finished version of the shoes (above) was released in 2008.

MÖTUG

This shoe from JB Classics was produced, designed and developed in conjunction with MÖTUG (Monsters Of The Unda-Ground) as the world's largest single-shoe artist collaboration. The ten artists involved were FUTURA, NYC Lase, Doze Green, Ghost, Shepard Fairey (Obey), Ewok, Toofly, CES, TKID 170 and Dizmology. The shoes, a JB Country Club Mid model, were limited to just 24 pairs (only seven of which were actually made available to the public) and were released in 2005 via the Showroom NYC Gallery in New York at US$1,500 a pair.

FUTURA (formerly FUTURA 2000, a name inspired by a combination of Stanley Kubrick's film *2001: A Space Odyssey* and the Futura typeface) was born in Brooklyn in 1955 as Lenny McGurr. Known for his highly skilled, uniquely abstract and futuristic style, FUTURA's graffiti was more about shape and textural pattern than lettering. He was a pioneer in elevating graffiti from the street to art galleries, and famously produced record sleeve artwork for punk band The Clash.

FUTURA's involvement in the music industry was revived in the 1990s (with the help of James Lavelle) when he produced artwork (alongside designer Ben Drury) for several of Lavelle's Mo' Wax releases – a collaboration that later defined the imagery of Lavelle's UNKLE project (see page 21). Much of FUTURA's work has been channelled towards the production of collectible toys and his involvement in the clothing industry. In the 1990s, he started the Project Dragon line, and collaborated with the likes of Nike, Phillie Blunt and Zoo York. He currently runs the design studio and experimental lifestyle brand, FUTURA LABORATORIES.

Shown below is the 2005 Nike Dunk High Pro SB 'FLOM' (For Love Or Money). Only 24 pairs of these sneakers were ever made, with just three pairs going to the public as part of a raffle in Hong Kong. Each pair is made up of images of various currencies (meaning no one shoe is the same), with an embroidered 'FL' logo on the heel.

FUTURA

Shown above is FUTURA's subway-inspired suede, leather and mesh Nike Dunk Low Pro SB from 2003. In 2005, Nike and FUTURA collaborated on the Nike Zoom Air FC iD (below left) to commemorate Lance Armstrong's seventh, and last, Tour de France. The 'Flance' sneaker features a series of symbols and icons designed by FUTURA; the symbols were also reproduced on Armstrong's Tour de France time trial bike. As well as Nike's Swoosh, the sneaker features the Lance 'L' logo and the FUTURA LABORATORIES 'FL' logo. As part of the 10/2 clothing line (commemorating the date when Armstrong was diagnosed with testicular cancer), 500 pairs of the sneakers were released to the public. The Paul Rodriquez Zoom Air Elite from 2006 (below right) featured patent leather and a clear Swoosh.

Sneakers

The Converse Chuck Taylor II (below) – a camouflage-inspired collaboration from 2016 that was part of a wider weather-ready Rubber Pack capsule collection. The water-resistant rubber uppers feature FUTURA's artwork, with reflective laces and additional specially designed insoles. The hi-top silhouette also features FUTURA's Atom motif as a removable patch.

Shown opposite, and originally conceived to be shared with Virgil Abloh and FUTURA's creative communities as a celebration of the power of friendship, collaboration and creativity, these shoes were first seen at the Off-White™ c/o Virgil Abloh's Spring/Summer 2020 show in Paris. Three years after their debut, the first and only public release of the Nike Dunk Low 'Virgil Abloh™ x FUTURA LABORATORIES' happened in 2023. The Virgil Abloh Foundation, along with Nike and FUTURA, teamed up with Sotheby's to exclusively auction eight pairs of the limited edition Dunks, with proceeds going to The Virgil Abloh™ Foundation.

FUTURA   Sneakers ●

The Nike SB Dunk Low Pro 'Bleached Aqua' (above) is a 2022 collaboration between Nike SB and FUTURA's product brand, FUTURA LABORATORIES. Using bleached canvas as the background, the shoe features FUTURA's artwork on the overlays, with puff-print details, custom tongue labels, artwork on the insoles and a translucent outsole revealing FUTURA's signature. A very limited 'Sunblush' Friends & Family edition was also issued, featuring artwork from FUTURA's 1984 painting, *Untitled*.

Released in 2024, ahead of the Olympic Games in Paris, the Nike Jam (below) was Nike's first ever footwear (and apparel) collection made specifically for breaking. FUTURA partnered with Nike to design the collection, which included federation kits for the United States, Korea and Japan. The shoe's black and white colourway is inspired by FUTURA's iconic 1980 *Break Train* piece, his studio's floor splatter and his iconic signature, Atoms and characters.

FUTURA & Stash

Made for FUTURA's 50th birthday in Hawaii in 2006, the Nike Dunk High Premium 'F2T.50' sneakers (below) were given to family and friends only and never released to the public. Embroidered with 'F2T.50', FUTURA chose the colour palette, while Stash selected the fabrics. The Nike Dunk Low from 2005 (bottom left) is an incredibly rare shoe, co-designed by Stash and FUTURA. With a brown and olive upper, the design was created through Nike iD (now Nike By You) and utilized premium materials. The lateral heels of each shoe feature a Trenitalia logo, the national Italian train operating organization.

FUTURA again collaborated with Stash and Nike on the Hyperstrike version of the Air Force 1 from Stash's 2006 Blue Pack (see page 125); the left shoe (bottom right) featured an embroidered Stash tag and laser-engraved Stash graphic, and the right shoe featured an embroidered FUTURA tag and laser-engraved FUTURA logo. This edition was never released to the public.

Stash

Born in New York, Stash (aka Josh Franklin) started writing graffiti in the stairway of his building in 1980; he painted his last active subway train in 1987. Another of graffiti's elite artists to have made the crossover into the worlds of art and design, Stash has since established himself as an innovator in the world of clothing design. Founder of legendary clothing studio, Subware Visual Maintenance, Stash also opened Recon clothing stores (in New York, San Francisco and Tokyo), and collaborated with friend and fellow graffiti artist FUTURA on the Project Dragon clothing line. He has also collaborated with many other labels, working as a designer for A Bathing Ape, taking part in the Vans The Simpsons project (see page 130) and working with Nike on numerous sneaker designs.

Released in three cities (New York, London and Tokyo), the 2003 Nike Air Force 1 High (shown above) marked the beginning of Stash's longstanding relationship with Nike. Featuring Stash's Fat Cap pattern, the individually numbered shoes came with a different coloured metal box for each city, and were limited to 1,000 pairs in total (250 for New York, 250 for London, 500 for Tokyo). In 2006, the shoe was voted the best Air Force 1 of all time at Nike's One Night Only event and, to mark the occassion, Nike and Stash remixed the original for a very limited release (shown left). The shoes featured One Night Only branding on the heel tab, and an individually numbered tag (from 001 to 231) on the heel.

Released in 2003 as part of an artist collaboration series with Nike, the Air Classic BW (bottom) was individually numbered and limited to just 1,000 pairs. The shoe is the first application of the iconic tonal blue colourway that has since become a signature style for his sneaker collaborations. The tongue featured an embroidered Stash signature, and his artwork is printed on the custom insole. Stash collaborated again with Nike on the two-shoe Blue Pack in 2006 (below) – featuring a Nike Air Max 95 and an Air Force 1 Low IO Premium. The pack heavily referenced the Air Classic BW, continuing the blue theme and cementing it in sneaker culture history.

126   ●   Sneakers

18 years after the release of the original Blue Pack, Stash worked with Nike in 2024 to give both the Air Max 95 and Air Force 1 a new lease of life (opposite). The concept for the new Blue Pack was simply to amplify the original concept, and colourway, through the use of the latest design processes and construction technologies.

The Nike Air Zoom Spiridon (above), released in 2017, was again inspired by Stash's signature use of blue. The shoe featured a mesh upper, 3M overlays, gloss Swoosh, co-branded heel tabs and an embroidered Stash graffiti arrow on the nubuck mudguard. Shown below left is a mesh sample of Stash's original Air Classic BW, before the nylon was applied. Toddler versions of the Blue Pack, gifted to Stash from Nike, are shown below, to the middle and right.

The unreleased Nike Air Zoom Talaria 'Nort' (top left) was a 2004 Friends & Family edition (rumour has it only 48 pairs of these were made). With bold colour-blocking and graffiti-style detailing, the shoes feature the Nort logo on the heel (Nort was Stash's sneaker store, the name being 'Tron' spelled backwards). In 2005, Stash hosted an art show in Portland, Oregon, where seven pairs of one-piece leather Nike Dunks (top right) were lasered with Stash's Fat Cap pattern and then sold at the event. Released in 2004, and featuring a Recon camouflage pattern, the Nike AF-X Mid QK (middle) was produced in both black and olive colourways, and had a steel toecap, silver strap buckle, laser-engraved Recon logo and Recon logo lace tag. 2010 saw a reissue of the olive pair (shown here) in collaboration with CNCPTS store. Dubbed the 'Re:CNCPTS', the pair featured lasered Recon and CNCPTS logos.

In 2008, to promote Nike snowboarding, Nike invited Stash to work on its Zoom Force 1 snowboarding boot – a design based on the Air Force 1 silhouette – as well as a snowboarding jacket featuring his Fat Cap pattern. The Air Force 1 High (bottom left), made as part of the project, was released in limited numbers and featured Stash's Fat Cap pattern in black. In 2017, and in celebration of the 35th anniversary of the Air Force 1 silhouette, Stash reintepreted his original Air Force 1 High from 2003, using a white on white reflective Fat Cap pattern (bottom right). Fewer than 100 pairs were made available through the ComplexCon festival.

Released as part of the Tools Of The Trade touring exhibition, 50 pairs of this Nike Dunk Low (top) were made available via the Paris concept store Colette in 2003. The shoes feature Stash graffiti tags on the heel and a paint drip motif on the side panels. Each shoebox was also individually numbered by the artist. The Kobe 24 Premium Pack from 2006 (above left) was created to celebrate Kobe Bryant's 24-hour-a-day dedication to basketball, uniting Bryant's passion for basketball with the culture that surrounds the game. Just 100 sets of the sneakers (and jacket) were released worldwide. The Nike Paul Rodriguez Zoom Air Elite 'Stash' (above right) was released in 2006 and featured a laser-engraved Brooklyn skyline.

Neckface
Vans Chukka Boot

Sam Messer
Vans Slip-On

Gary Panter
Vans Era

FUTURA
Vans Sk8-Mid LX

Vans and The Simpsons

For the 2007 release of *The Simpsons Movie*, Vans commissioned 12 urban artists to help create 14 pairs of sneakers. Each artist was invited to give their interpretation of the iconic US cartoon, leading to 14 completely different designs. The artists involved included David Flores, FUTURA, Gary Panter, Geoff McFetridge, KAWS, Mister Cartoon, Neckface, Sam Messer, Stash, Taka Hayashi, Todd James and Tony Munoz. Each shoe was limited to 100 pairs. In return, the creator of *The Simpsons*, Matt Groening, created caricatures of each of the contributing artists. The portraits can be found on shoeboxes created especially for the project.

    To celebrate the release of the shoes, Vans and *The Simpsons* put on a launch party and exhibition. On display at the event were original sketches by the artists, skateboard decks emblazoned with Matt Groening's caricatures of the artists and the shoes themselves.

Sneakers 131

DAVID FLORES	FUTURA	GARY PANTER
KAWS	MR. CARTOON	NECKFACE

VANS **The Simpsons "Off the Wall"** **VANS**

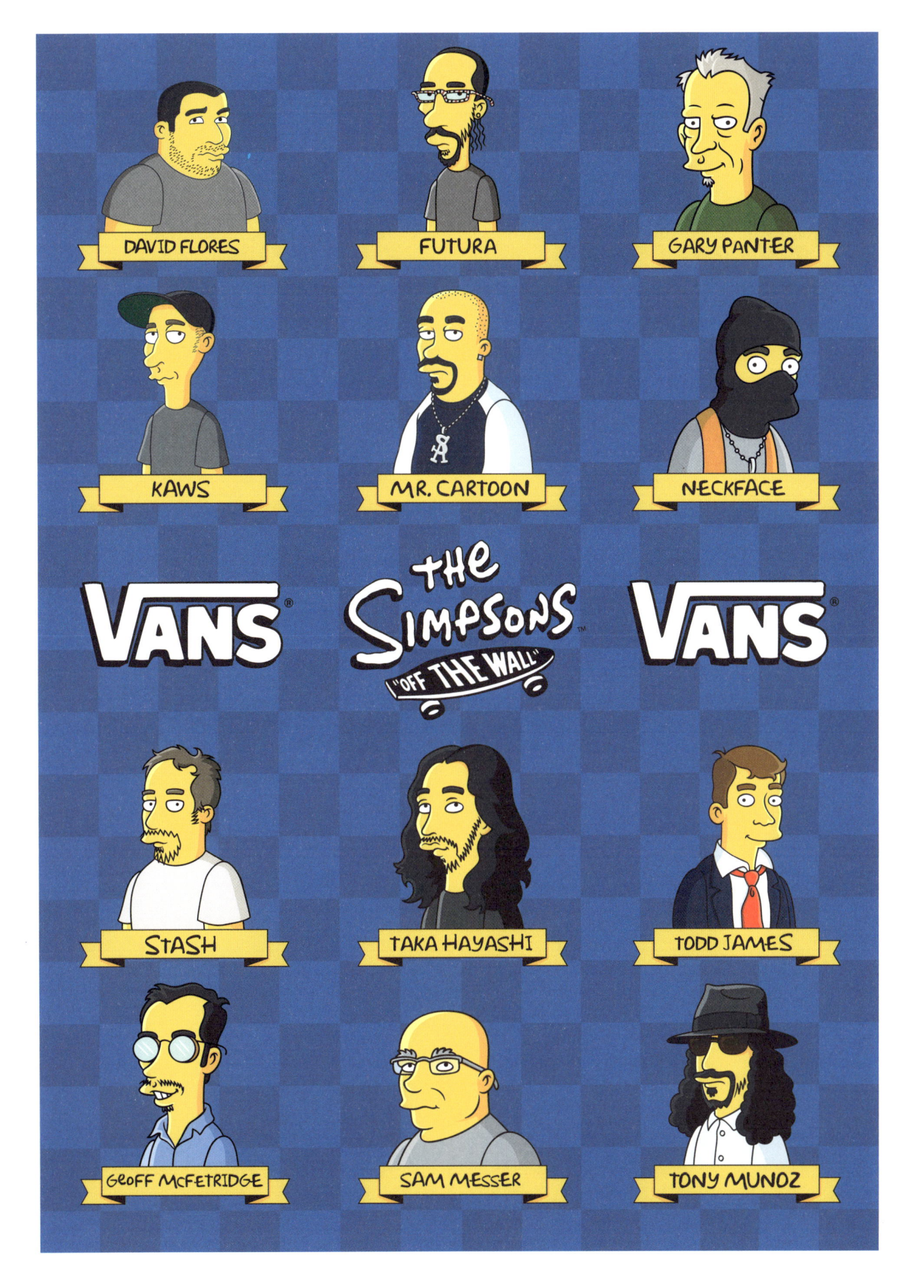

STASH	TAKA HAYASHI	TODD JAMES
GEOFF McFETRIDGE	SAM MESSER	TONY MUNOZ

Sneakers

Taka Hayashi
Vans Sk8-Hi

Geoff McFetridge
Vans Chukka Boot

Stash
Vans Mid Skool

Todd James
Vans Sk8-Hi

KAWS
Vans Chukka Boot

Mister Cartoon
Vans Slip-On

Vans & The Simpsons

Sneakers

133

David Flores
Vans Slip-On

David Flores
Vans Sk8-Hi

Tony Munoz
Vans Sk8-Hi

Tony Munoz
Vans Slip-On

Mark Ward

Mark Ward is a London-based graphic artist and art director whose work is an adoration of Americana filtered through a British perspective. Ward has created images in his distinct style for brands such as Nike, Medicom and Stüssy, with some of his best-known work created for London sneaker boutique Foot Patrol – working on both sneaker collaborations and graphic design for the store.

In 2012, Ward partnered with Nike to create graphics for this special London edition of the Nike LunarGlide+ 3. His artwork adorns the tongue and 'dynamic support' wing areas of the shoe, with a tonal black upper and white Swoosh. The artwork celebrates the dedication that runners display, with insider-jokes such as sweaty sock puppets, breaking walls, Big Ben with legs – plus an extra 'running food' detail on the insole. 'Runners often eat bananas for the carbs and potassium levels,' says Ward, 'and bananas are also objects I identify with – they make me think of Andy Warhol, linking back to the Americana element in my work.'

The project was part of a wider City Pack that included nine styles, highlighting major marathons around the world including New York, Beijing, Chicago, Berlin and the San Francisco Women's Marathon.

Experimental Jetset

With the simple mantra of 'turning language into objects', Experimental Jetset is an Amsterdam-based independent graphic design studio founded by Marieke Stolk, Erwin Brinkers and Danny van den Dungen in 1997. Utilizing its modernist, typography-led aesthetic, the studio teamed up with Converse and renowned sneaker store Patta in 2022 to create this Chuck 70 High, inspired by unexpected city exploration. Referencing metropolitan maps and directional signage, the collaboration focuses on the theme of 'psychogeography' – a playful and inventive way of navigating through a city that defies prescriptive directions. A shoe all about where you take your sneakers, the white canvas uppers feature screenprinted arrow graphics, with co-branded tongues and insoles, different colour graphic outsoles and a bespoke 'Keep on driftin' license plate on each heel.

Damien Hirst

Based on his *All You Need is Love* butterfly print from 2007, controversial British artist Damien Hirst worked with Converse to create this vivid red Chuck Taylor All Star shoe for the Converse (PRODUCT)RED initiative. Hirst's original artwork sold for a huge US$2,420,000 at the Sotheby's (RED) auction in 2008 – in support of The Global Fund to fight AIDS, Tuberculosis and Malaria. Hirst also co-hosted the auction, alongside Bono, and in total the event generated over US$40 million for the cause.

Released in 2010, the collaboration with Converse launched on 5 November in Europe and the UK, and on 1 December (World AIDS Day) in the US, with 100 per cent of the net profit being donated to The Global Fund. High-definition laser printing techniques were used to achieve a carefully colour-matched version of the original piece, and the print also continues to the inside of the shoe, appearing on the insole and lining.

Sneakers 137

Shaniqwa Jarvis

Shaniqwa Jarvis is London-based photographer and artist known for combining a modern fashion aesthetic with sensitive and emotional portraiture. She captures vivid reality across a wide variety of subjects and has executed large-scale portrait projects and exhibits in London, Tokyo, Los Angeles and New York. She also co-created Social Studies, an experiential retail pop-up focusing on connecting the youth to creators through curated programming, and has collaborated with a range of brands including Supreme, adidas and Converse.

In 2020, Jarvis brought her artistry and storytelling to the comfort-focused Converse Chuck Taylor All Star CX, with an accompanying hoodie. Utilizing stretch canvas on the upper of the shoe, Jarvis' floral print is an ode to her father's sharp sartorial aesthetic, and is a means of paying respect, or 'giving the man his flowers'. The image itself is a digital print of one of her favourite photos, a double-exposure image taken on a trip to Mexico. The colourful upper is contrasted with a crisp white corduroy tongue – a nod to the fabric her father often wore – and translucent foxing extends the print to the bright pink sole, exposing the shoe's construction. A floral print lace flip was also included in the co-branded special edition box.

Hiroshi Fujiwara

Japanese artist, designer and musician Hiroshi Fujiwara is a pioneer in collaboration. He has worked with the likes of Converse, Nike, Burton and Levi's, while also developing his own T-shirt brand GOODENOUGH which has since evolved into brand and design agency, fragment design. He was also one-third of Nike HTM, the research and development project consisting of Hiroshi Fujiwara (the 'H'), Tinker Hatfield (the 'T') and Mark Parker (the 'M'). HTM combined heritage with innovation – mining Nike archives for inspiration while utilizing the company's latest technology to explore new concepts and push the possibilities of design.

Fujiwara's sneaker work can be more than just colourway application, developing new shoe design concepts and hybrids like the Nike Air Footscape Woven, shown below. Inspired by the 1995 Nike Air Footscape, the Air Footscape Woven uses an innovative woven design, itself taken from the Air Woven Boot (opposite, bottom left). The version shown here is made from patent leather and was part of Fujiwara's Polka Dot Pack, a Tier Zero release that also included a Dunk Low and an Air Force 1.

The first two shoes on this page are part of the Nike HTM collaborative project. The Nike HTM Air Woven 'Rainbow' (top) was constructed from multi-coloured woven material. Released in 2002, a number of colourways were produced, ranging from classic greyscale to the multi-coloured version shown above. Just 1,500 pairs of each colourway were released. The Nike HTM Air Woven Boot (above left) was also made from woven material. The shoes were individually numbered and limited to 1,500 pairs worldwide. Released in 2002, this silhouette was available in black, brown and khaki.

The Nike Air Footscape Woven Chukka (above right) combined the sole unit from the Air Footscape and the upper from the HTM Air Woven Boot, using a suede-like woven material. Released in 2006, they were available in brown (with a blue outsole), sail (with a yellow outsole) and black (with a black outsole).

Fujiwara and fragment design worked on another three-way collaboration in 2021, teaming up with Jordan Brand and Houston rapper Travis Scott on the Air Jordan 1 Low (below). The shoe features Scott's signature backwards Swoosh, with a Military Blue heel, collar and outsole. fragment design and Cactus Jack (Scott's official brand) logos are embossed on the right and left heels, respectively.

Fujiwara collaborated with Chitose Abe of Sacai in 2021 on the 'LDWaffle' – a fusion of two iconic Nike silhouettes, the Waffle Daybreak and LDV. The shoe mixes signature features from both brands, including fragment design's text labelling across the midsole, and Sacai's double tongues, shoelaces and Swooshes. The release included two colourways – Light Smoke Grey and Blackened Blue, both shown above.

Shown below, and inspired by the CLOT Air Force 1 'White Silk' from 2018, the Dunk Low collaboration between fragment design, Hong Kong-based streetwear brand CLOT (see page 94) and Nike, features an all-white tear-away 'Silk-Royale' upper that can be removed or simply worn away. With the tongue and lace stay rendered in black, the colourway references the pandas that Fujiwara and CLOT's founder Edison Chen saw when visiting China's Chengdu reservation. Released in 2023, the project celebrated CLOT's 20th anniversary (there is a 'CLOT20' logo on the insole) and followed a previous three-way collaboration on an all-black Nike Air Force 1 in 2019, which again featured a tear-away upper.

Kenzo Minami

In 2005, New York-based artist and designer Kenzo Minami was featured in Reebok's I Am What I Am advertising campaign (along with Jay-Z, 50 Cent, Lucy Liu, Christina Ricci, Allen Iverson and Yao Ming). He was one of the few artists selected for the Artist Series, and his campaign was run together with that of Jean-Michel Basquiat (see page 164). As part of the campaign, Minami created his own model of the Reebok Instapump Fury (shown right), which was limited to only 500 pairs worldwide.

Minami revisited the partnership with Reebok in 2020, working on a small capsule for their R58 project – a nod to 1958, the year Joe and Jeff Foster founded Reebok. The collection included an Instapump Fury 'R58' (above) and a Zig Kinetica 'R58'. 'The concept was the abstract interpretation of time and space,' explains Minami, 'breaking through the barrier, going into warp speed, distortion of the space, dimensional jump and so on. I also wanted the silhouette to suggest the abstract impressions of a launching pad and rocket booster, which themselves are made of sound waves, shock waves, signals and patterns.'

John Maeda

A renowned designer, technologist and visual artist, John Maeda continues to push the boundaries of both art and technology. In 2007, Maeda teamed up with Reebok to create this Ventilator Timetanium. Inspired by the personal nature of sneakers, the project explored the mass-produced custom sneaker phenomenon, integrating production technology purely for artistic reasons. Maeda created original mathematic algorithms and computer codes to create the imagery for the shoe; his handwritten code is featured on the insole and lining of the shoe, with the graphic generated from this code displayed on the outer. Limited to only 100 pairs worldwide, the shoes were exclusively available through Reebok's custom sneaker website.

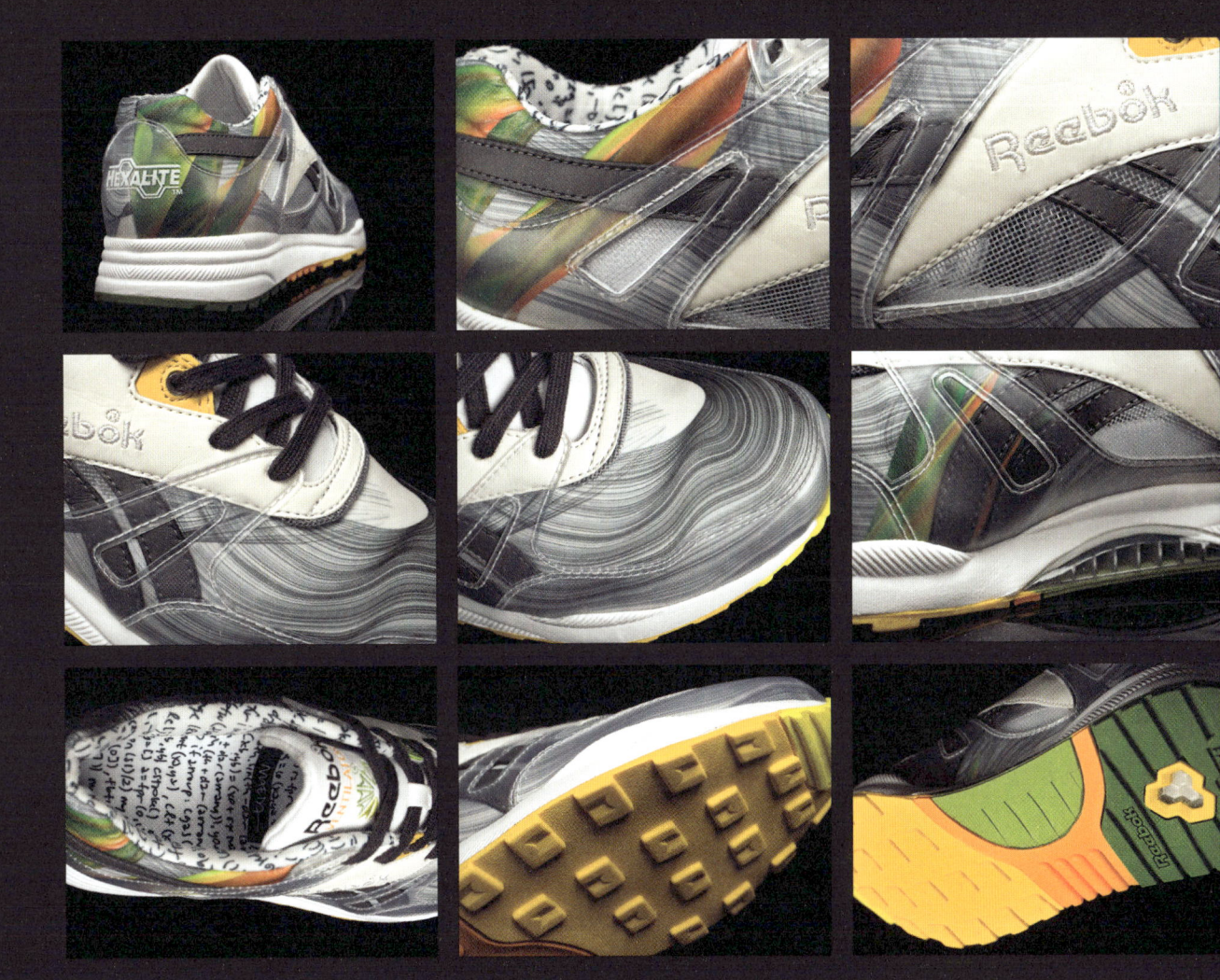

Sneakers

Jun Watanabe

Jun Watanabe is a Japanese designer and art director who works mostly in the fashion and music industries. He's applied his inimitable use of colour to numerous sneaker collaborations, including projects with brands such as Reebok, ASICS, Madfoot!, Le Coq Sportif and Ubiq.

Following on from a three-way collaboration with Reebok and Tokyo-based sneaker store atmos in 2011, Watanabe again worked with the Instapump Fury silhouette in 2012 – this time with the collaboration extending to include a Tamiya The Hornet radio controlled car. Limited to 600 pairs, the shoe itself is an evolution of the 2011 collaboration – with black and white dots and contrasting bright pink and purple gradient.

Watanabe evolved the design concept further still for a third and final Reebok collaboration in 2013. The pull tabs (front and back) on all three shoes are printed with Watanabe's trademark Bottle Head character.

Sneakers   145

Shown clockwise from main image are Watanabe's Reebok Instapump Fury (2012), Reebok Instapump Fury (2011), Reebok Instapump Fury (2013), ASICS Gel-Lyte III (2011), Ubiq eL (2011) and Le Coq Sportif Eureka (2017).

Kidrobot

Since its birth in the late 1990s, the vinyl toy movement exploded into the consciousness of artists and designers worldwide. Founded in 2002 by designer Paul Budnitz, Kidrobot is the world-famous creator and retailer of limited edition art toys and apparel, originally operating three store/gallery spaces in New York, San Francisco and Los Angeles. Many of Kidrobot's toys and clothing feature collaborations with graffiti artists, graphic designers, illustrators and musicians, including the likes of Frank Kozik, Tilt and Dalek.

Its take on Nike's iconic Air Max 1 silhouette (shown below) is probably Kidrobot's most famous foray into the world of sneakers. Produced in 2005 as a collaboration between Kidrobot, Nike and Barneys (the New York department store), the shoe featured a gum rubber outsole and a heat-embossed Kidrobot logo on the heel. Each pair came in a custom gold and pink drawer-style collector's box and included a special limited edition Kidrobot keychain and one of five blind packaged insoles created by artists Gary Baseman, Dalek, David Horvath, Huck Gee and Frank Kozik. Just 250 pairs of the black edition were produced worldwide – with a pink Hyperstrike edition (left) issued to friends and family only.

Sneakers   147

Shuttlemax is a limited edition vinyl space shuttle based on the Nike Air Max 95. Produced in collaboration with art director and designer Bill McMullen, just 100 yellow, 200 red and 300 lime editions were produced.

Sneakers

In 2007, Kidrobot teamed up with Lacoste to launch a collection of three pairs of sneakers. Paul Budnitz and Chad Philips from Kidrobot chose three patterns that matched their toy lines to use on the collection. For the Missouri 85, Kidrobot opted to use their monochrome bones pattern. The Revan 3 featured an eyeball pattern, while the Revan 2 used the Kidrobot head logo. The insole of each sneaker was also printed with the Kidrobot head logo and the shoes featured 3M reflective highlights. Each of the three styles was produced in a limited edition of 500 pairs worldwide and each pair came with its own PEECOL toy (customized to match its respective sneaker) created by eBoy and Kidrobot.

Kidrobot — Sneakers — 149

The blue JB Getlo sneaker marked the beginning of a series of footwear developed by JB Classics Lab in conjunction with Kidrobot and the artist Tilt. Made from nubuck leather, the shoe featured the Tilt bubble design and a gold interior. The shoe was distributed through Kidrobot in 2006. The second collaboration used an all-black JB Peddler model and again featured Tilt's colourful artwork. The shoe also featured Kidrobot lace locks, and material combinations and accent colouring by JB Classics designer Mdot. Limited to 240 pairs globally, the shoe was distributed through Kidrobot in 2007, along with a matching crew neck hoodie. As with all JB Classics releases, both styles were hand-numbered and packaged with an official certificate of ownership.

Sean Cliver

Having launched himself into the world of skateboard graphics in the late 1980s (by creating the artwork for Vans skater Ray Barbee's first signature model with Powell-Peralta), Sean Cliver is now considered a living legend within the world of skateboard art. His inimitable style came to prominence throughout the 90s after working on various board graphics for the likes of Blind, World Industries, 101, Element and Supreme. The appropriateness of Cliver's subject matter (or lack of it) often caused controversy – something that suited the rebellious nature of skateboarding down to the ground.

For the 2014 collaboration with Vans Syndicate, Cliver was given the opportunity to apply his aesthetic to both an Authentic Pro S (shown below) and Mid Skool Pro S. The uppers were adorned with a classic Vans checkerboard pattern, although in this instance each square reveals the striped edge of a seven-ply skateboard deck. The artistic theme followed through to the inside of the shoes, where an illustration of various gnomes 'enjoying themselves' was applied across both sets of insoles. A sticker sheet and miniature skateboard (displaying the complete insole artwork) was also included with the shoes.

Cliver has also collaborated on numerous Nike SB Dunks, as shown on this page and overleaf. The Dunk Low 'Disposable' (top) was a 2014 Quickstrike release that celebrated the 10th anniversary of Cliver's book, *Disposable: A History of Skateboard Art*. The Dunk High 'Krampus' from 2012 (above left), featured pony hair panels and was inspired by the half-goat, half-demon character thought to punish naughty children at Christmas in central and eastern European folklore. The Dunk High 'Gasparilla' (above right), a 2016 collaboration with the Skatepark of Tampa, was inspired by Spanish naval officer turned pirate, José Gaspar, and celebrates the Gasparilla festival that takes place in Tampa, Florida, every year.

152 • Sneakers

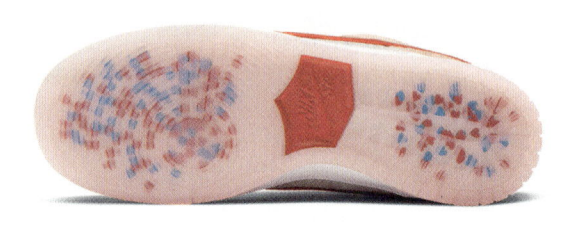

Shown opposite is the Nike SB Dunk Low 'StrangeLove' from 2020, a Valentine's Day-inspired shoe with crushed velvet underlays and a translucent pink outsole with red and blue heart confetti, made for Cliver's skate brand, StangeLove. A limited number of pairs were also released with a special shoebox (bottom).

Shown below is the Nike SB Dunk Low 'Cliver' (also from 2020), a festive holiday-inspired release with ice blue velvet suede overlays, a translucent blue outsole with glitter and a perforated snowflake pattern on the toe box.

Dave Kinsey

World-renowned street and fine artist Dave Kinsey is most famous for his haunting portraits of urban characters. Based in Los Angeles, Kinsey works with a range of media, including wood, canvas, paint, found materials, pen and ink – and sneakers. He also founded creative design agency (and gallery) Blk/Mrkt, working with clients such as Absolut, adidas, Royal Elastics, Heineken, DC Shoes and Nissan.

In 2006, Kinsey, with fellow artist Evan Hecox (see opposite), teamed up with adidas to create a limited edition sneaker (and accompanying advertising campaign) for the launch of adidas Originals Skateboarding. Kinsey produced this Superstar Skate inspired by the city of San Diego, with his graffiti-based graphics laser-etched on to a limited run of 1,000 pairs.

Evan Hecox

Evan Hecox is a Colorado-based illustrator and skateboarder known for his unique style and subtle depictions of urban environments. As well as producing numerous skateboard graphics and T-shirts for skateboarding brands Chocolate and Girl, Hecox has famously produced work for Carhartt clothing and has been a regular contributor to Arkitip magazine.

For the launch of the adidas Originals Skateboarding line in 2006, Hecox (together with Dave Kinsey) created a limited edition sneaker, along with an accompanying advertising campaign. Hecox's creation, a Stan Smith Skate, was beautifully screened with his artwork of the San Francisco cityscape and limited to 1,000 pairs.

adidas Superstar 35th Anniversary

In 2005, adidas celebrated the 35th anniversary of its most iconic shoe, the Superstar. The first Superstar went on sale in 1970 and, within a few years, was worn by more than 75 per cent of all NBA players. It quickly migrated from the basketball court to the street and evolved to become a cultural icon. Since then, the shoe has become a design classic.

To commemorate the anniversary, adidas invited icons from the worlds of music, art and fashion to create five different series of unique Superstars (35 models in total) to honour a special place or time in the Superstar's history. The different styles created tell the shoe's story, from the humble beginnings of the 'shell toe' to its regular fixture in the worlds of fashion, music and film.

The five series – Consortium, Expression, Music, Cities and Anniversary – were made available through various distribution channels and covered a range of price levels. All 35 models were part of an integrated concept with a specially created Superstar 35 logo – each series featuring the logo in a distinguished colourway. The Expression series (shown here) holds particular interest, with leaders from the worlds of art, photography and graffiti contributing designs. Organizations such as Disney and The Andy Warhol Foundation, as well as the clothing company Project Playground and the artist Lee Quinones, created seven individually distinctive limited edition Superstars.

Expression Series
Captain Tsubasa
In 1983, Youichi Takahashi sat down at home in Japan and drew the animated character Tsubasa Ozora, a boy destined to become the world's best football player. In the years since, Captain Tsubasa has become a worldwide phenomenon and is almost single-handedly responsible for turning football into Japan's national obsession.

Sneakers 157

Expression Series
Andy Warhol
Appropriating images from popular culture, Andy Warhol is famed for his paintings of 20th century icons, from Campbell's soup cans to Marilyn Monroe. This Superstar celebrates his Athlete Series from the 1970s, featuring the basketball legend Kareem Abdul-Jabbar.

Expression Series
Lee Quinones
Considered one of the most influential artists of the New York subway graffiti movement, Lee Quinones' career has spanned multiple decades. Today, Lee's paintings are included in some of the most prestigious art collections around the globe.

Expression Series
Upper Playground
Based in San Francisco, California, Upper Playground was founded in 1998. It became a leader in today's progressive art movement with its innovative apparel line and art gallery, FIFTY24SF. This BBQ-themed shoe featured a red gingham pattern synonymous with tablecloths and patterned greaseproof paper used to serve food on at BBQ diners across the US – complete with a knife, fork and spoon appearing on the three stripes. The adidas logo on the heel tab is also encased in a kettle-style barbecue illustration with the letters 'BBQ' running down the heel stripe.

Expression Series
Disney
This shoe celebrates one of the most loved Disney characters, Goofy, who first appeared with a bit part in a Mickey Mouse short in 1932, and celebrated his 90th birthday in 2022.

adidas Superstar 35th Anniversary · Sneakers · 159

Expression Series
adicolor
adidas launched adicolor in 1984, making it one of the first customization projects executed on a global scale. These all-white Superstars were delivered with a set of coloured quick-drying markers, an artwork stencil and seven pairs of coloured laces – allowing the wearer to create their own original look.

Expression Series
Project Playground
Justin Leonard founded Project Playground in 2000 as an independent company that embodies the playground culture of New York – and many of Project Playground's creative design concepts are derived from the proud New York City basketball community. Designed by sneaker connoisseur Bobbito Garcia, this shoe commemorates Project Playground's progressive approach, recognizing and celebrating the close ties between basketball, art, music and fashion.

Anniversary Series
Superstar 35
This was the most sought-after release of the collection. Only 300 pairs were produced, and the only way to obtain one (unless you were very well connected) was through a treasure hunt competition. The shoe is made almost entirely from premium leathers (including the outsole). The white leather box also contained a gold shoehorn, sandalwood lasts and a cleaning kit.

Blondey McCoy

Blondey McCoy, real name Thomas Eblen, is a London-based artist, skateboarder, model and founder of clothing label Thames MMXX. In 2019, McCoy collaborated with adidas on the limited release of a see-through Superstar 80. The (vegan) shoe featured a transparent upper, gum toecap and midsole, gold-foiled 'Blondey' print on the sidewall, and also included three pairs of high socks in red, blue and white.

Four further Superstar colourways followed, including 'Autre' (2020), 'Starlight Blue' (2020), 'Schwarz Tint' (2021) and 'Tourmaline Green' (2021), shown here. 'Making your own stuff from scratch is one thing. But being trusted with another brand's DNA, to build on a tried-and-tested formula – it's a great responsibility,' said McCoy. The Tourmaline Green was produced in a limited quantity of 50 and gifted to friends and family only – until a few pairs were auctioned through the Thames MMXX website in 2024.

Goldie

Well known for his pioneering role as a musician in the UK drum and bass scene, Goldie originally made a name for himself as a graffiti artist – something which helped shape this 2024 collaboration with adidas Spezial. More than a decade in the making, the release of the Goldie SPZL coincided with the 30th anniversary of Metalheadz, the record label co-created by Goldie, and the 10th anniversary of the adidas Spezial line, created by Gary Aspen.

    The collaboration takes the Silverbirch SPZL as its foundation, updating it with matt gold stripes and heel (the colour a reference to both Goldie himself and the adidas Forest Hill silhouette he admired when he was young), faux stingray leather overlays (a subtle nod to his B-Boy roots and transatlantic influences) and a bold pink dual-branded tongue label (inspired by a pink that he used consistently since his early days as a graffiti writer). 'Pink was a colour that really eluded us as graffiti kids,' explains Goldie, 'you could only get it from one brand of paint at the time, which was ridiculously past our paygrade.' Each pair is finished with Goldie and Spezial lace jewels, and special-edition insoles that feature original Goldie artwork, again honouring his favourite shade of pink.

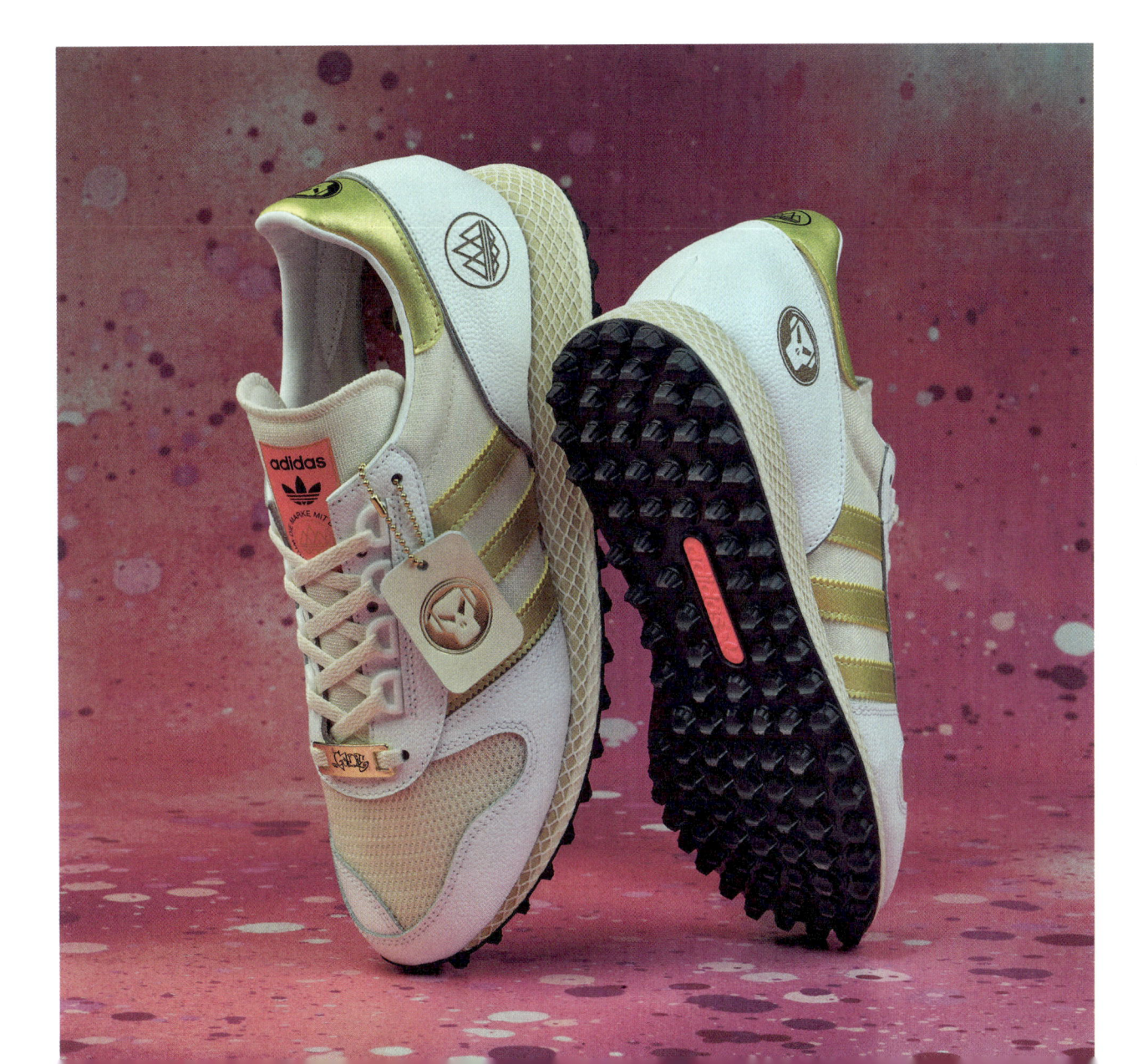

Transport for London

To mark the 150th anniversary of London Underground in 2013, Nike partnered with Transport for London (TfL) on a pair of Air Max silhouettes (below). The pack utilized an engineered woven jacquard pattern made from moquette (a hard-wearing wool and polyester mix) and referenced the seat upholstery of London Underground's District Line – a geometric pattern originally created by designer Misha Black in 1978. The Air Max 90 was made using a one-piece woven upper, while the Air Max 1 kept a traditional cut-and-sew approach to construction. Both shoes feature TfL's classic 'roundel' branding on the tongue, and natural gum rubber outsoles. The first 150 pairs were released via a pop-up kiosk at Piccadilly Circus station.

In 2016, TfL once again partnered with Nike to bring 'the lettering of London' to life (opposite) – marking the 100th anniversary of the iconic Johnston typeface. Edward Johnston's lettering was first introduced by London Transport in 1916, featuring in signs, maps and other customer information. Then, in its centenary year, the typeface was subtly updated to create Johnston100 for the digital age. The Nike partnership revived the cult classic Air Zoom Spiridon silhouette, originally released in 1997, and the release was available in white and navy colourways. The uppers featured the Johnston letterforms, with a contrasting iridescent Swoosh and reflective mudguards.

Shown above, is part of the accompanying creative campaign designed by creative agency Rosie Lee (see page 284) with typographic messaging set in Johnston100 and images inspired by London's 90s garage music subculture – paying tribute to the Nike silhouette's unique heritage.

Jean-Michel Basquiat

First making their appearance in Reebok's I Am What I Am campaign (see page 142), these Reebok Basquiat Reeboppers were designed by Maharishi in conjunction with the Jean-Michel Basquiat estate, who had signed a multi-year contract with Reebok in 2005. Released in three colourways, the shoes included a custom tag on the tongue, embroidered Basquiat artwork on the side of the shoe, and a clear outsole through which more of Basquiat's artwork was visible. Initially launched in 2005 at a Basquiat retrospective at the Museum of Contemporary Art in Los Angeles, a few pieces were also pre-launched at the DPMHI and Maharishi stores in London. Only 500 pairs of each of the three colourways were produced.

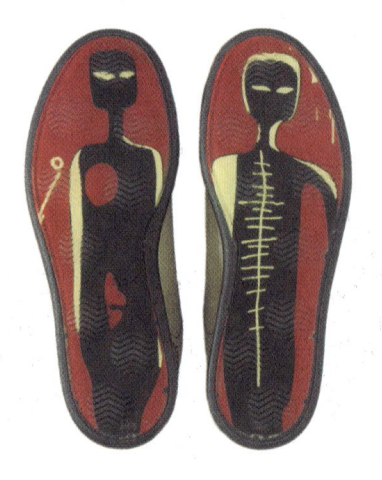

André Saraiva

French artist, hotelier and nightclub owner André Saraiva is known on the street by his graffiti-artist alter ego, Mr. A – a winking, round-faced character with a huge smile. Often working in pink – a colour that is unusual in the graffiti world – Saraiva's Love Graffiti concept is evident in much of his work, including this 2022 collaboration with adidas.

Part of a wider collection that honoured Saraiva's commitment to sustainibilty, the adidas Stan Smith (shown left) and Superstar (shown right) were designed to celebrate the Earth. Both silhouettes feature Saraiva's smiling Mr. A character, various heart motifs, pink insoles and the uppers are made from at least 50 per cent recycled materials.

Gravis Art Collective

Pushing artist collaborations to a whole new level, the 2005 Gravis Art Collective project began life as three original canvas artworks from urban artists Matt Sewell, Marok and Delta. Each artist created a 200 x 200cm canvas panel, which was then skilfully cut up to become part of a collection of Gravis Comet Mid shoes.

The artists not only integrated the fabric of their actual artwork but also decided the style direction of their shoes, colourway and creative detailing. Gravis involved the artists at all stages of the product development, using the Collective as a testing ground for future artist collaborations. Only 36 pairs of shoes were made from each canvas. The project was showcased on a European tour before the shoes were released worldwide at selected outlets.

Matt Sewell

Marok

Sneakers 167

Delta

168 • Sneakers

Nike SB
The Vault

Since its inception in 2002, the Nike SB division (and the Nike SB Dunk silhouette in particular) set the benchmark in the world of sneaker collaboration. Some of best and most sought-after shoes in this book are from Nike SB – with releases from the early 2000s being some of the most highly regarded. FUTURA, Jeff Staple, Mr Sabotage, Parra, Medicom, Michael Lau, Geoff McFetridge, Sean Cliver and Neckface are just some of the artists who have partnered with Nike SB to produce exceptional examples of what can be achieved through the art of collaboration.

In addition to showing SB shoes throughout this book (on the pages of individual artists), we also wanted to delve deeper into 'The Vault'. Nike SB has explored hundreds of collaboration concepts over the years, taking inspiration from subjects as far afield as jewellery, beer and even horror characters (controversially). Shown here are some of the many art-related shoes, including some truly mythical pairs such as the Dunk Low 'Paris'. As Nike SB is also well-known for its iconic sneaker boxes – 2016 even saw a set of four Dunk SB releases based on the black, pink, silver and orange box design – we've listed shoes in chronological order, according to box 'era'.

Orange Box Era
Mar 2002—Dec 2002

Featuring distressed denim, the Dunk Low Pro SB 'Reese Denim' (bottom) was released in 2002 and saw Reese Forbes collaborate with artist, designer and fellow skateboarder Natas Kaupas. From 2002, the Dunk Low 'Chocolate' (below, front) was designed by Richard Mulder and the Chocolate Skateboards art department, with the detailing on the heel chosen to commemorate the legacy of Chocolate team rider Keenan Milton (1974-2001). The typography-heavy Dunk Low 'Zoo York' (below, behind), also from 2002, was the East Coast companion to the Chocolate shoe and was designed by Zoo York co-founder and art director, Eli Morgan Gesner.

Silver Box Era
Jan 2003—Sep 2004

Aligned with the White Dunk: Evolution of an Icon travelling exhibition (see page 286), the White Dunk City Series was a pack of four shoes representing Paris, Tokyo, London and New York. The Dunk Low Pro SB 'Paris' (bottom) utilized the work of French expressionist painter Bernard Buffet, and was originally intended to release exclusively at the Paris leg of the exhibition in 2003. However, the release of the shoe was delayed and limited pairs were later circulated through select stores. The blank canvas-inspired Dunk Low 'Tokyo' from 2004 (shown top right) was created with an all canvas/muslin upper and was devoid of any heel or tongue branding. Although London's 'White Dunk' event was cancelled, the Dunk Low 'London' (middle right) was eventually sold through Foot Patrol in 2004 and featured a simple, embroidered representation of the River Thames on the side heel panel. Also from this box era was the 2003 Dunk Low 'FUTURA' and 2004 Dunk High 'FLOM' (see pages 118-119), the unreleased Friends & Family Dunk High 'Iron Maiden', and the one-of-one Dunk Low 'Charity' that was auctioned to raise money for the Tim Brauch Foundation (with the sample of the shoe being cut up to preserve the auctioned pair's rarity.)

Pink Box Era
Sep 2004—Dec 2005

The pink box era saw the release of a trio of shoes from Japanese collectible toy manufacturer, Medicom. The 2004 Dunk Low Pro SB 'Medicom 1' (below left) was the first Dunk SB to feature a double layered Swoosh. The 2004 Dunk Low 'Medicom 2' (below middle) was inspired by the 'Reese Denim' shoe and utilized contrasting black denim with a more controlled fraying process. The third shoe in the set, the 2005 Dunk Low 'Medicom 3' (below right), featured a monochromatic treatment with minimal white accents and chrome Swoosh. All three shoes were exclusively offered to registered members of the Medicom website.

The 2005 Dunk Low Pro SB 'Pushead' (shown bottom) was the first of two collaborations with American graphic artist Brian Schroeder, better known as Pushead. Alongside skateboard graphics, Schroeder is perhaps best known for his record sleeve artwork, which featured heavily on the covers of punk and heavy metal releases throughout the 80s and 90s. The design of the shoe was based on an artwork originally created by Schroeder on a 35mm film slide. Also released from this box era was the 2004 Dunk High 'DUNKLE' (with artwork by FUTURA, see page 21), the 2005 Dunk Low 'Pigeon' (by Staple Design, see page 105), and the 2005 'De La Soul' Dunk High and Dunk Low.

Black Box Era
Feb 2006—Sep 2007

Designed by skate industry illustrator Todd Bratrud, the Dunk High Pro SB 'Send Help' (below) was devised in the early days of SB's cluttered Beaverton office. Bratrud has been a prolific SB collaborator, and more of his designs are featured on the following spread. Other art-related releases from the Black Box era included the 2006 Dunk Low Pro SB 'SBTG' (see page 54) and the 2006 Goldilocks-themed Dunk Low, Mid and High 'Three Bears Pack' (see page 265).

Gold Box Era
Oct 2007—Mar 2009

A visual celebration of all that had gone before, the 2007 Dunk Low Pro SB 'What the Dunk' (bottom) was imagined by Nike designer James Arizumi and was part of a campaign for the *Nothing But The Truth* skateboarding documentary film. Taking inspiration from 31 separate Nike SB Dunks (some of which were themselves very rare editions), this much-coveted design aimed to be the 'Dunk to end all Dunks'. Only a very small number of shoes were ever offered to the public. The 'What the Dunk' since became an inspiration for a variety of other Nike releases including the 'What the Doernbecher', the Lebron 'What the MVP' and the 'What the CLOT'.

172 Sneakers

Blue Box Era
Apr 2009—Jun 2012

Artist and illustrator Todd Bratrud worked on the Dunk High Pro SB 'Brain Wreck' in 2009 (below left). Combining pinks, blues and 'grey matter', the pair also featured 'brain tissue' stitching around the inner ankle padding. Shown here is an early sample featuring a lighter contrast Swoosh, as opposed to the tonal grey Swoosh on the final production pair. Bratrud collaborated with SB again in 2010 on the Dunk High 'Skunk Dunk' (below right). With obvious connotations, the shoe features a 'fuzzy' suede upper, with various 'strains' of green and a dazed-looking skunk illustration on the insole.

Taped Box Era
Jul 2012—Nov 2013

Nike SB's second collaboration with artist Brian Schroeder (aka Pushead), was the Dunk Low Pro SB 'Pushead II', released in 2012. Shown below, the shoe featured a corrosive-looking black and brown pattern on the canvas upper panels and laces, with the rest of the shoe comprising black suede overlays, black midsole, gum outsole and a skeletal Pushead motif on the heel (Schroeder is well known for featuring depictions of skeletons in his work).

Teal Box Era
Dec 2013—Dec 2019

The Teal Box era saw a huge number of releases, including art/design collaborations such as the 2019 Dunk Low and Blazer Low 'Parra', and the 2017 'Black Pigeon' Dunk Low from Staple Design (see page 105) – and the 2019 Dunk High 'FPAR' (shown top right). An artist and designer whose world view was shaped by skateboarding, Tetsu 'Tet' Nishiyama founded Tokyo-based street fashion brand FPAR (Forty Percent Against Rights) in 1996 to subvert the media and fashion industries for his own messages. The first of two collaborations with Nike SB, the shoe displays the message 'Don't follow me' as a call for the wearer to find their own path in life. Shown bottom right is the 2018 Dunk Low Mid 'White Widow' by serial SB collaborator Todd Bratrud – who also went on to design the 2020 Dunk High 'GDP' and the 2021 Dunk High 'Strawberry'. Shown below is the Dunk Low 'Brand Logo Sample' from 2017. For the SB Dunk's 15th anniversary, Sandy Bodecker (the man behind Nike SB from the beginning, who sadly passed away in 2018) unveiled this all-over design featuring iterations of Nike's iconic logo lock-ups.

174   Sneakers

Striped Box Era
Jan 2020 — Mar 2023

The Striped Box era again saw a collaboration with Medicom, resulting in the hairy leather upper of the Dunk Low 'Medicom Toy' from 2020 (below left). The following year saw the release of the 2021 Dunk Low 'Street Hawker' (below middle), featuring watercolour paintings created by artist Jason Deng that represented six different regional dishes from six Chinese cities. Again from 2021, Japanese artist Verdy collaborated with SB (for a second time) through his skateboarding and punk-inspired Wasted Youth label. The Dunk Low 'Wasted Youth' (below right) featured black denim and leather patchwork upper with metallic D-rings and jagged white and red stitching – a reference to the DIY punk aesthetic.

Shown bottom is the Dunk High Pro SB 'Faust', a 2022 collaboration with New York-based graffiti artist Faust. The shoe features a black premium textured leather and suede upper, with Faust's signature handstyle embroidered in both black and metallic gold. Also released from this box era was the 2020 Dunk Low 'Strangelove' and Dunk Low 'Cliver' (both designed by artist and skateboarder Sean Cliver (see pages 152-153), the 2020 Ben & Jerry's-themed Dunk Low 'Chunky Dunky', the 2021 Dunk Low 'Parra '21' (see page 230) and Dunk Low 'Neckface' (see page 51).

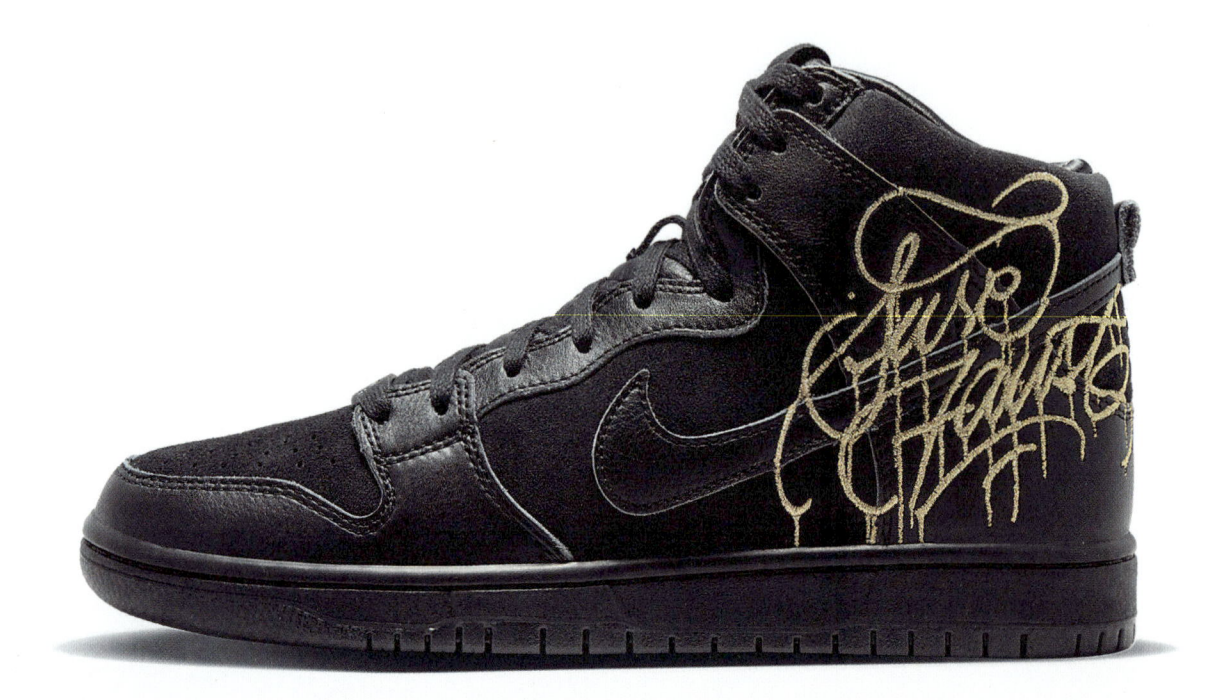

Sail Box Era
Mar 2023—

Born and raised in Northern Arizona's Diné Bikéyah (Navajo Nation), artist and skateboarder Di'Orr Greenwood celebrated her indigenous heritage with the Dunk High Pro SB 'Decon' (shown top right) in 2024. The Dunk Low 'There' (middle right) is a collaboration with Californian artist, skateboarder and musician Jeffrey Cheung. After founding Unity (a skateboard company/community/printing press) in 2017, Cheung now runs There Skateboards, a collective dedicated to supporting queer and trans skateboarders of colour (QTPOC). Using Cheung's 'ultra humanized' artwork as the foundation, the shoe blends unique materials with custom artwork throughout the design – including a two-tone hairy suede, co-branded tongue and heel artwork, and engraved dubraes. Shown below is SB's third collaboration with Japanese artist and designer, Verdy – the 2024 Dunk Low 'Verdy' was transformed with the use of furry fabric inspired by Verdy's popular 'Visty' plush doll character. Also released from this box era was the 2024 Dunk Low 'FUTURA LABORATORIES' (see page 122).

Sne

Sneak & Art

Art & Makers

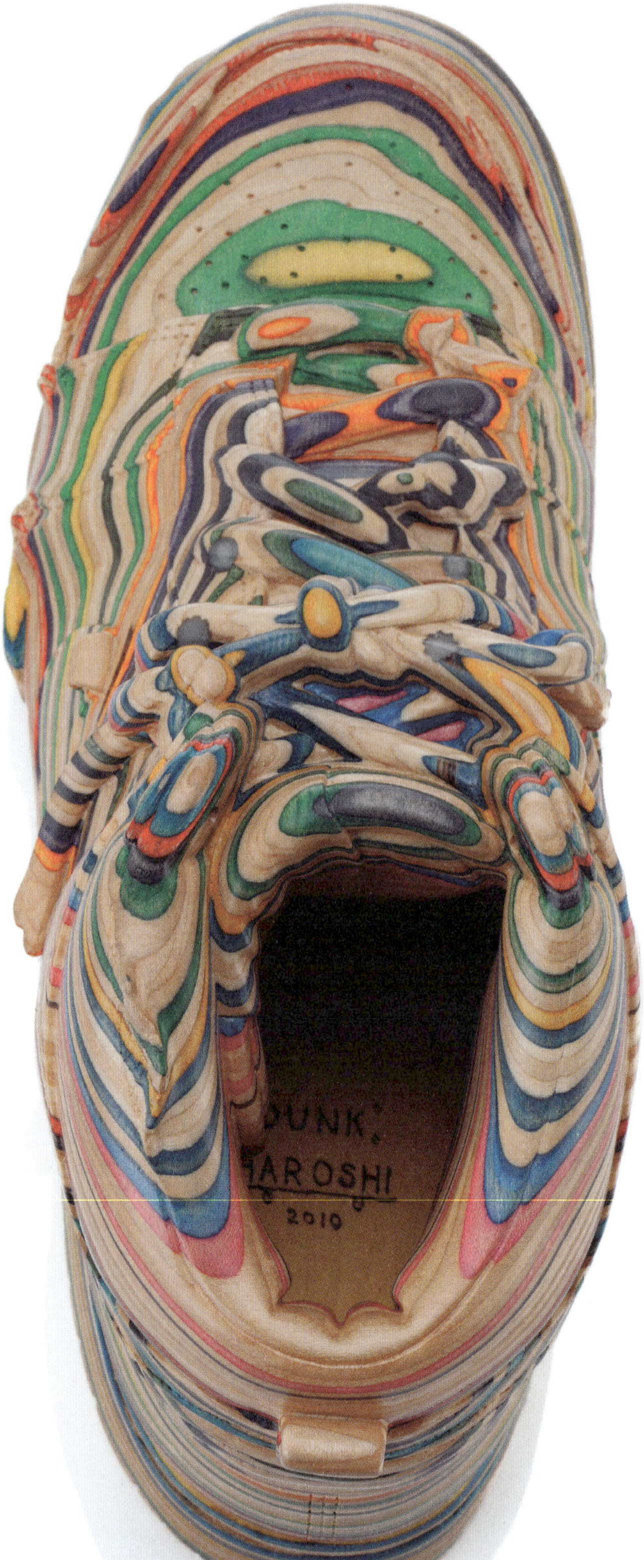
DUNK
HAROSHI
2010

Haroshi

This pair of Nike Dunks are sculptures made by Haroshi, a Japanese artist who's made his name creating art from recycled skateboards. The shoes were created from old skateboard decks that had been used by Nike pro riders including Paul Rodriguez, Lance Mountain, Eric Koston, Cory Kennedy, Justin Brock and many more.

    Commissioned by then CEO of Nike, Mark Parker, the Dunks were modelled on Haroshi's own sneakers, with every detail faithfully replicated. 'I didn't believe the email from him [Mark Parker] at the time,' says Haroshi, 'so I said I wanted to make 'used Dunks' from the used boards of Nike SB pro skaters. I thought that if he is fake, he can't make my order. Surprisingly, one month later, the boards arrived at my studio.' It took three months to carve the Dunks, and even the inside of the shoes has been meticulously sculpted. There are also two hidden messages within the shoes; 'Kick x Kick', which references the fact that the curvature of the skateboard decks match that of the Dunks, and 'Sole in Soul', which can only be revealed using an X-ray scan.

The concept of I Have Pop™ was conceived in 2003 by JUSE, a graffiti artist disillusioned by the medium's conservative nature. His idea was to create a different perspective on particular elements of pop culture through a series of street art projects. These projects could be either a tribute or a criticism, but the meaning was deliberately left open to the observer. 'The items themselves and the location create the context. Not everyone will be able to understand what is being communicated, but the people who it is intended for will get it,' explains JUSE.

By 2004, I Have Pop™ had turned into a reality. For the first project release, JUSE created a series of life-size concrete Nike Dunk sneakers and secretly placed them in front of some of the world's most high-profile sneaker boutiques. Without knowing where these concrete sneakers had come from, some of the stores took them inside and put them on display. Word of the mysterious project travelled quickly and one year later all was publicly revealed, sparking a huge response. JUSE is responsible for each project, from plans to production, and personally travels to all destinations for each project's execution and documentation. 'In the course of these projects my frequent-flyer status went from nothing to gold, and my bank account the other way around.'

I Have Pop™

Art   181

In 2004, between the months of June and November, Netherlands-based artist JUSE secretly made ten pairs of concrete Nike Dunks and placed them in front of various streetwear stores in North America and Europe. Each pair of Dunks was numbered, and encased within the concrete itself was a card detailing the release date. After the last pair was placed, the moulds were destroyed to ensure exclusivity. 'The desired response was to have people wondering what they were and who was behind them. I wanted to create a sense of want, just like Nike does with their limited edition shoes. I also wanted people to question the limited edition phenomenon.'

The stores were selected based on their involvement with popular street culture and included UNDFTD (Los Angeles and Santa Monica), Richard Kidd (Vancouver), Nort (New York and Berlin), 90 Square Meters (Amsterdam), Solebox (Berlin), Huf (San Francisco) and Dave's Quality Meat (New York).

182 ● Art

Commissioned in 2006 by Nike for its Festival of Air exhibition in Niketown, London, this piece was created as a tribute to the subcultures that adopted the Nike Air Max 90 and the streets on which it is used. Entitled *The Streets*, the idea was to make the base of the piece the focal point, rather than the shoes and legs on top of it. The piece also highlights the contrast between the heavy surface materials used on the street and the lightness of the air in the sole of the shoe. The shoes and legs are made from solid concrete, while the air bubble was created using clear polyurethane resin. The base is made from various pavement and surface materials such as asphalt, bricks, cobblestones and concrete.

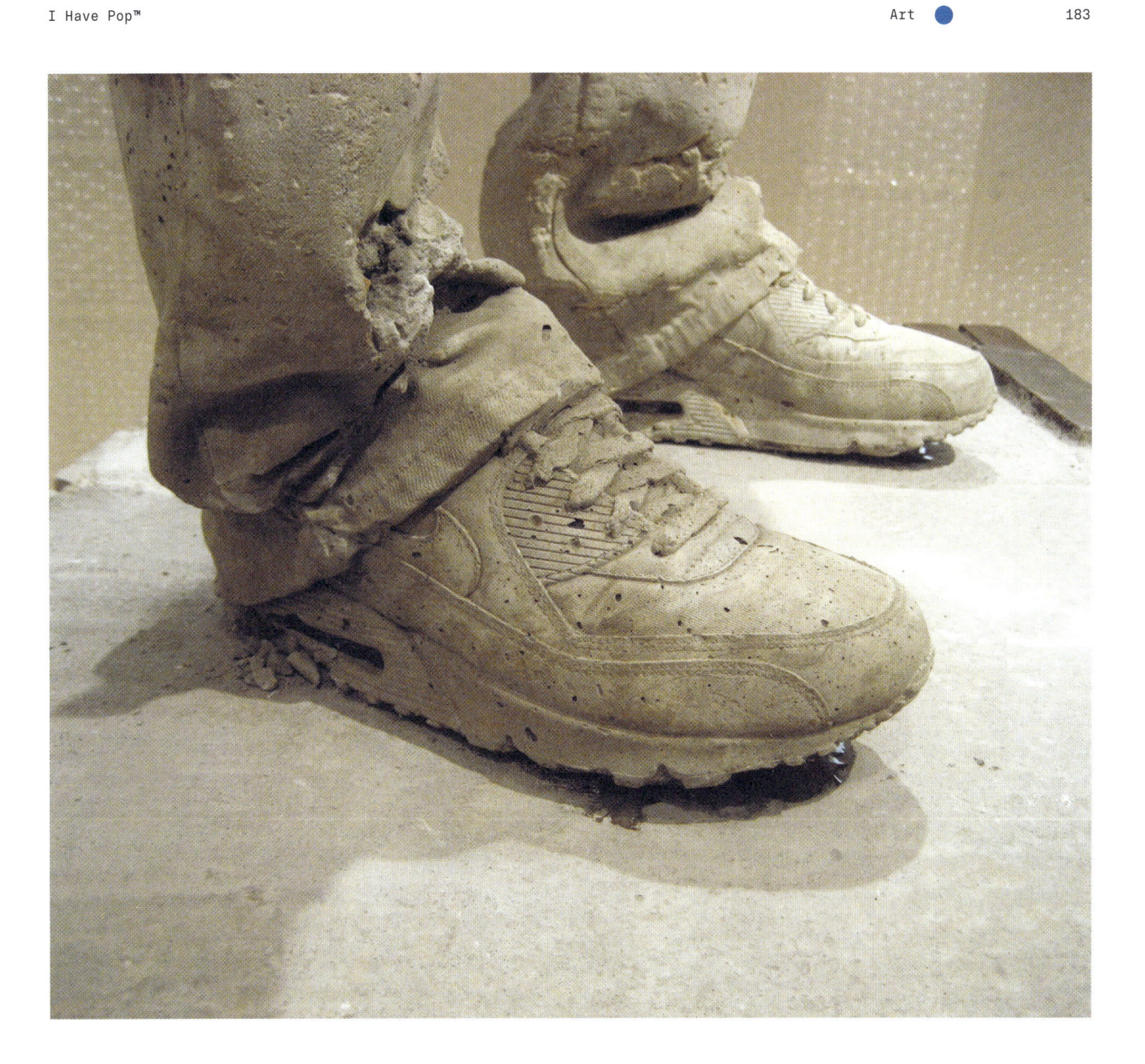

I Have Pop™ · Art

184 • Art

I Have Pop™ — Art — 185

Produced in collaboration with Solebox for the 2006 Berlin and Barcelona exhibition, Untitled, I Have Pop™ came up with the idea of creating sneakers from the boxes they are packaged in. 'Because most of my projects have a critical note, I dubbed the project *Think Outside The Box*, hoping to spur people on to think a little further than the next cool pair of sneakers.'

90x90

In 2006, Ido de Voos (of Amsterdam-based store 90 Square Meters) teamed up with photographer Yamandu Roos and stylist Clyde Semmoh to create a concept and exhibition highlighting the diversity of people who wear the Nike Air Max 90 on the streets of Holland. They observed: 'The shoe lives among many different cultures and subcultures. It knows no colour, no race and no religion.' For the first stage of the project, Roos captured various Air Max 90 aficionados in a series of photographs (shown here). The images were then used as a starting point for a group of eight artists each to create their own interpretation of the shoe. Artists involved included Dutch graffiti legend Delta, JUSE from I Have Pop™, Riëlle Beekmans and Leon Perlot, Russell Maurice of Gasius, News, Pane, Woes van Haaften and Patty Bleumink.

For the exhibition, held at 90 Square Meters, the photographs and artwork were displayed together and a one-off Nike Air Max 90 iD shoe was created for each exhibit (both the artwork and the shoes were available to purchase on the opening night). Nike became involved during the creation of the exhibition, and the artwork from 90x90 eventually became part of Run on Air: Seven Cities (Seven Shoes), Seven Stories – a celebration of three decades of Nike research and development into air-cushioning technology. Run On Air was a creative project combining artists, illustrators, sculptors and filmmakers from Paris, Amsterdam, Berlin, Barcelona, London, Milan and Istanbul.

Art 187

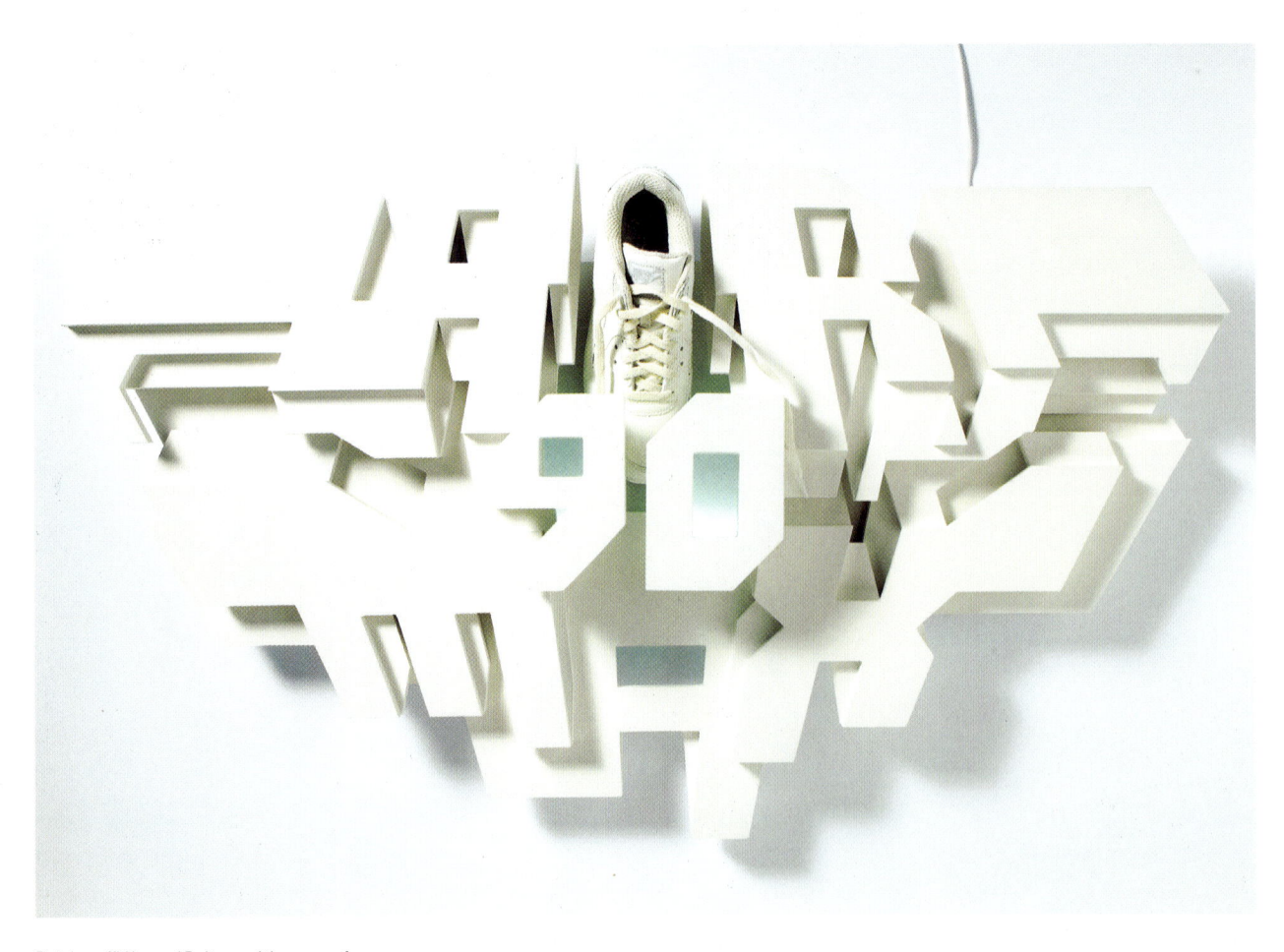

Dutch graffiti legend Delta used the name of the shoe and his 3D style to create this intricate typographic sculpture (above). Riëlle Beekmans and Leon Perlot interpreted the Air Max 90 in Delft Blue porcelain (opposite).

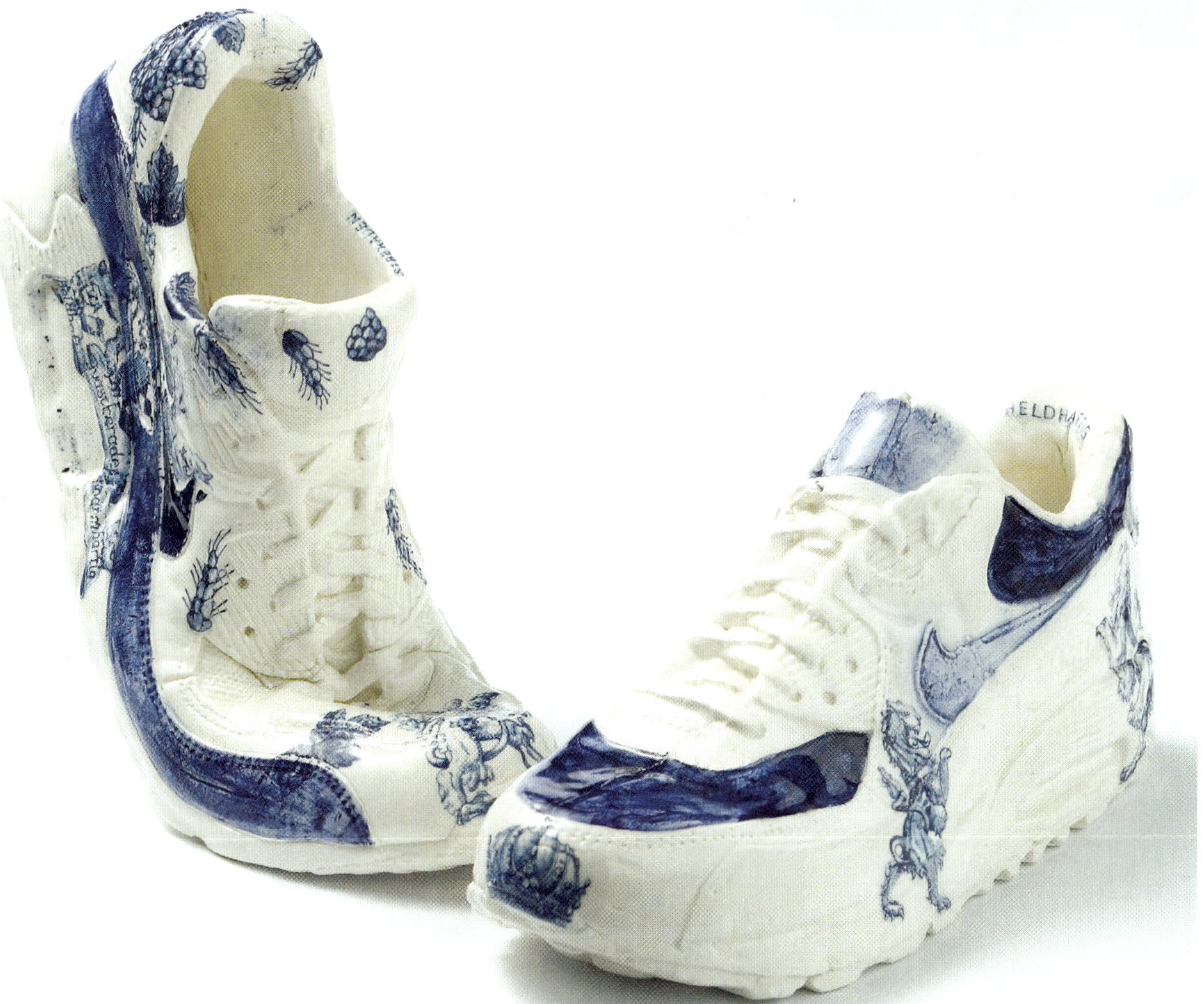

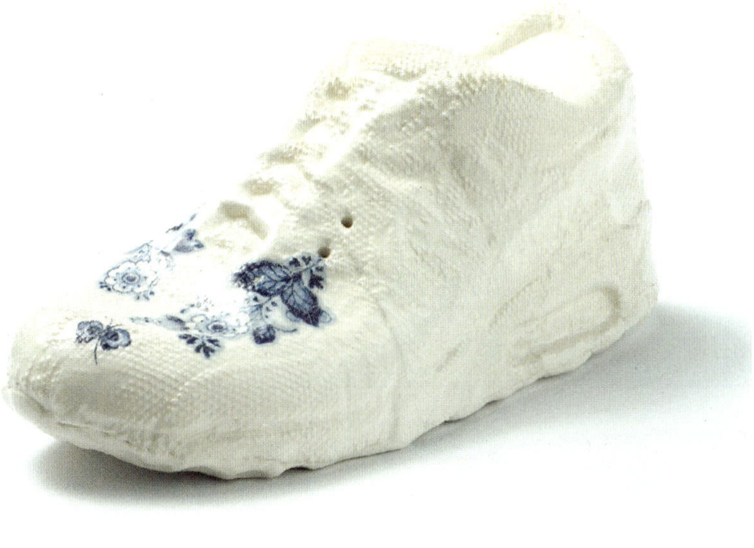

Art

JUSE, of I Have Pop™, took his inspiration from street football; the result is *Panna* (opposite top), a concrete table-football game. Entitled *Cavern Biosphere*, Russell Maurice took the ultimate symbol of Air Max and created a mini-city existing among the caverns of the Air Max 90 cushion bubble (opposite bottom). 'I like the idea of the nano-city, a tiny microcosmic biosphere existing in this minute encapsulated area of oxygen and space.'

For this piece entitled *Air Mix* (above), Woes van Haaften was inspired by mobility, sport and the urban lifestyle to reinterpret a classic Dutch symbol – the bike, adding Air Max 90 air bubbles to a bike wheel.

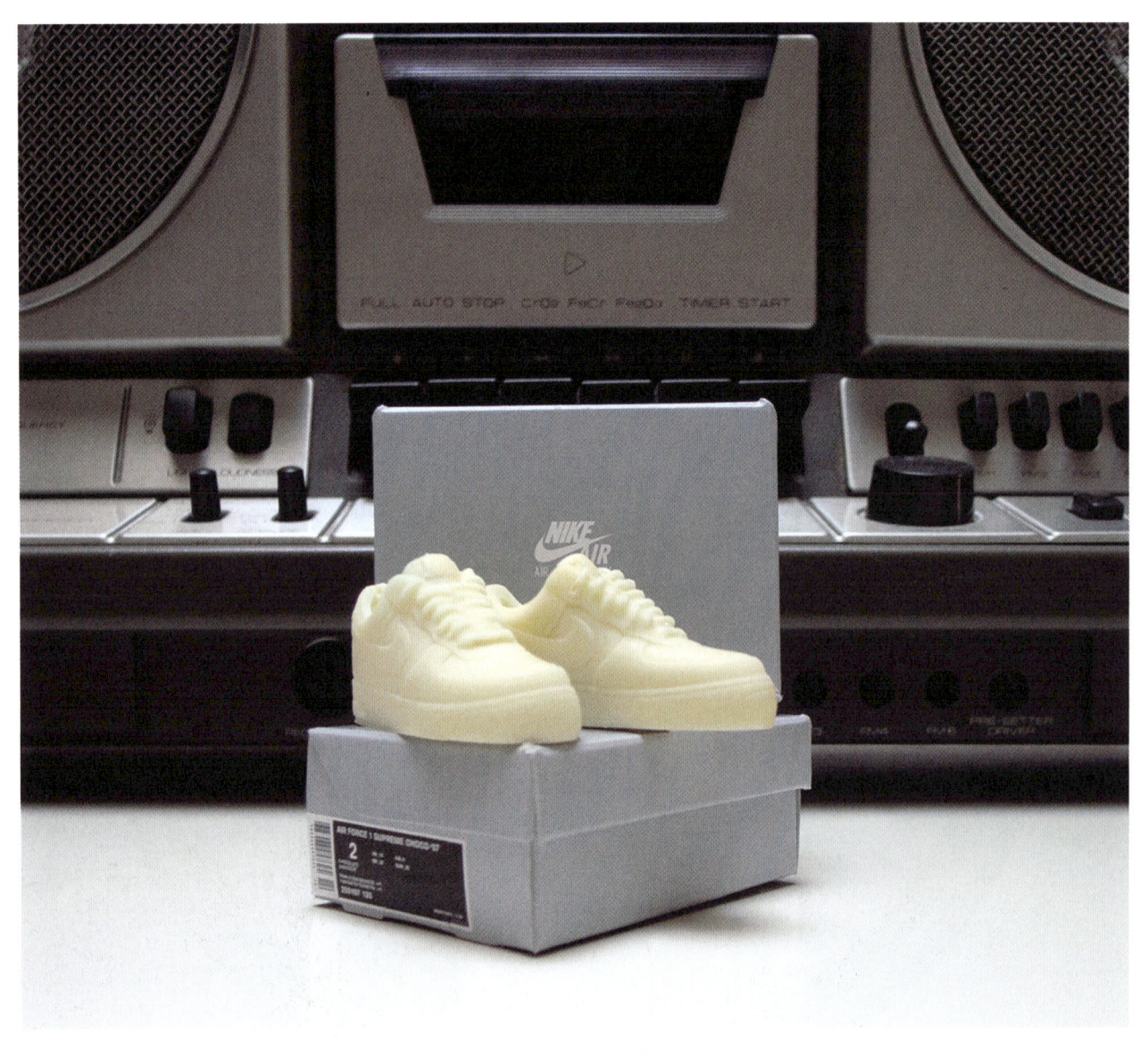

+41

As well as being the international dialling code for Switzerland, +41 is also the fashion and music brand of Swiss graphic design studio //DIY (see page 198). It was set up in 2001 by Laurence Jaccottet, Ivan Liechti and Philippe Cuendet after the three met while studying at ÉCAL (École cantonale d'art de Lausanne) in 1997. Their first collection was essentially made up of basic T-shirts used as vehicles to convey the group's visual and graphic style. Since then, more collections have been completed and +41 have had the opportunity to create some exclusive works for numerous brands and designers such as Nike, Apple, Etnies Plus and Colette. In 2003, +41 expanded its activity into the music business after it created a compilation of hip-hop remixes produced by member Cuendet (aka MPC) entitled, *Look Ma No Rappers*.

+41 created this Mini Choco AF1 (above) to celebrate the 25th anniversary of the Nike Air Force 1. Shown left are Mini Choco Sneakers from +41 in collaboration with Bastien Thibault from the Lausanne-based chocolaterie: Blondel. Production started with three different models: the Nike Dunk, Air Trainer and Blazer.

Before making these life-size chocolate sneakers, +41 got in touch with Bastien Thibault from Blondel chocolaterie. 'He liked the idea and told us it was possible,' explains Cuendet. 'After that we spoke with Nike Switzerland and they got involved and provided us with a pair of sneakers.' Swiss artist and model-maker Denis Biggler then made a plaster mould of the shoes, which was given to Thibault to be thermoformed. The initial result lacked detail, so Biggler suggested making a silicone mould that was far more precise.

194 ● Art

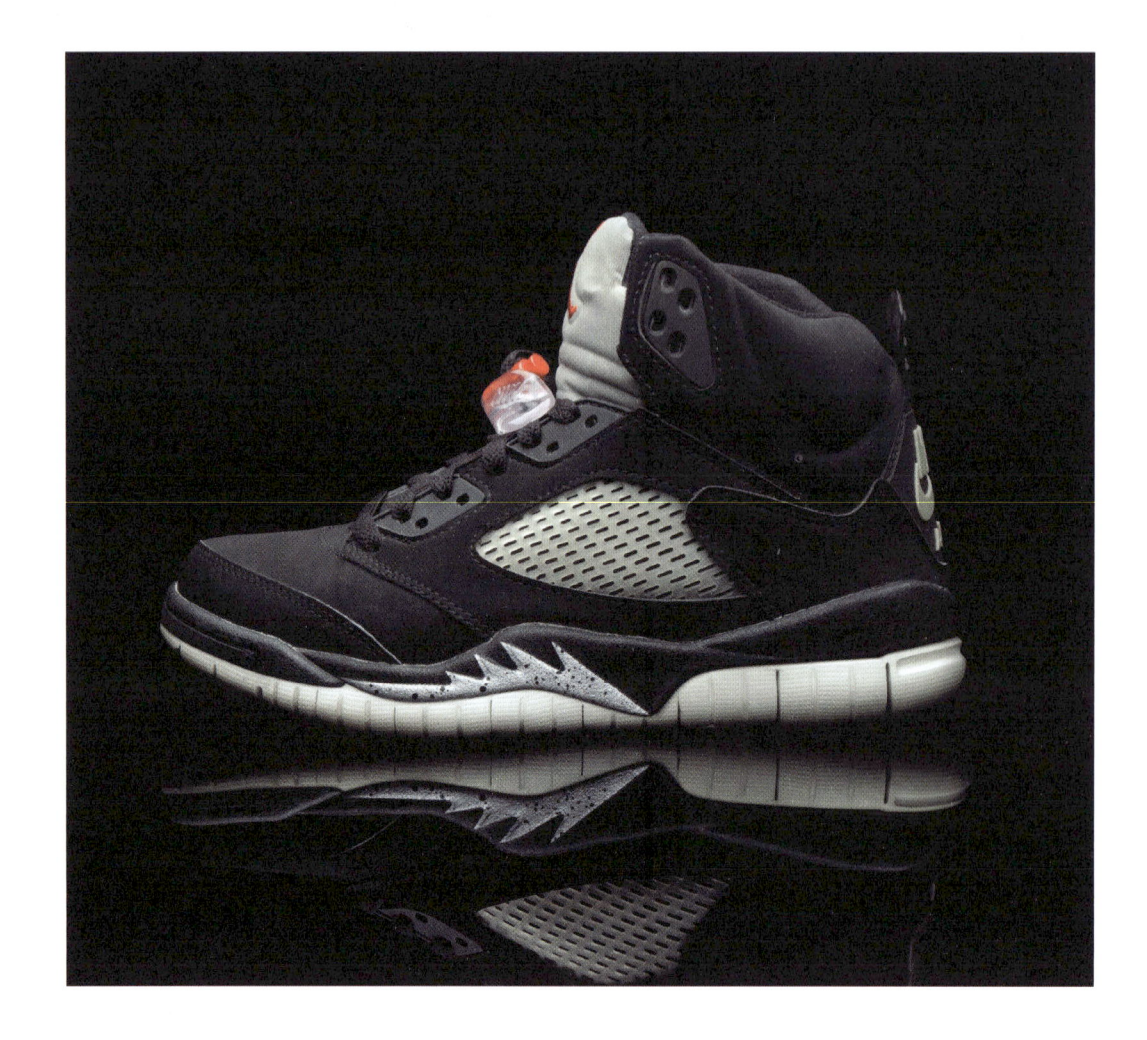

Think Free is the title of an artwork conceived by Philippe Cuendet for //DIY and +41 as a way to produce ultimate Nike iD (now Nike By You) sneakers. Existing shoe designs were mutated by combining elements from various sneakers. 'Three artefacts were conceived, as an unlikely triptych, hybrid but not altered; and respectful of a certain consistency that endows bastards with a pedigree.' Interestingly, since this project, Nike itself has been pushing the boundaries of its designs by creating a range of hybrid concepts such as the One Time Only Air Max 360 sneaker pack from 2006.

Starting with a Nike Air Max 180 iD, produced at the Nike Spirit Room in Berlin, Cuendet added a Nike Free Sole while keeping the 180 cushioning on the heel (opposite top). An Air Jordan 5 was then upgraded with elements of the Jordan 4 and mounted on a Nike Free sole (opposite bottom), and a Nike Air Trainer was combined with a Free sole and mesh panel from the Air Jordan 4 (above).

Produced in 2006, the +41 Nike iD Air Max was a numbered series of 41 pairs which each came in a drinks-straw style package, containing a pair of +41 Nike iD Air Max 1's, a +41 Air Max 1 artwork T-shirt and a pack of sticker eyes. By personalizing the sneakers with eyes, +41 had the intention of switching traditional roles: instead of people looking at the sneakers, it's the sneakers that look at you. Also, the shoe represents Nike's vision in terms of what they've accomplished: 'A revolutionary system that brought something new and crazy to sports technology,' explains +41, 'and definitively changed the game of the sneaker scene. The artwork +41 created represents these aspects with a glass of sparkling soda full of air bubbles, shoes and history… and when the air bubbles go through the straw, they turn into eyes.'

The shoes were only available at the Thomas I Punkt store in Hamburg, with all benefits going to a children's charity. There was a last chance to purchase a pair through the +41 Nike iD Air Max 1 Christie's auction in Zürich (the first time ever Christie's had auctioned a pair of sneakers), with proceeds going to the Schtifti Foundation, a Swiss charity promoting health for young people through freestyle sports. Five pairs were auctioned, with the highest price reaching EU€1,000.

Designed by +41 in collaboration with Swiss rapper Stress, only 15 pairs of the 'Stress' Nike iD Air Force 1s (below) were made. The shoe was designed in 2007 for A Journey of Force, a Zürich event to celebrate the 25th anniversary of the Nike Air Force 1.

+41 also collaborated with Etnies Plus for this release (bottom) in 2007. The project included two versions of the Welldon High model (one men's and one women's). The white (women's) shoe featured an overall print of various +41 illustrated icons. Only 289 pairs of the men's and 167 pairs of the women's shoes were available worldwide.

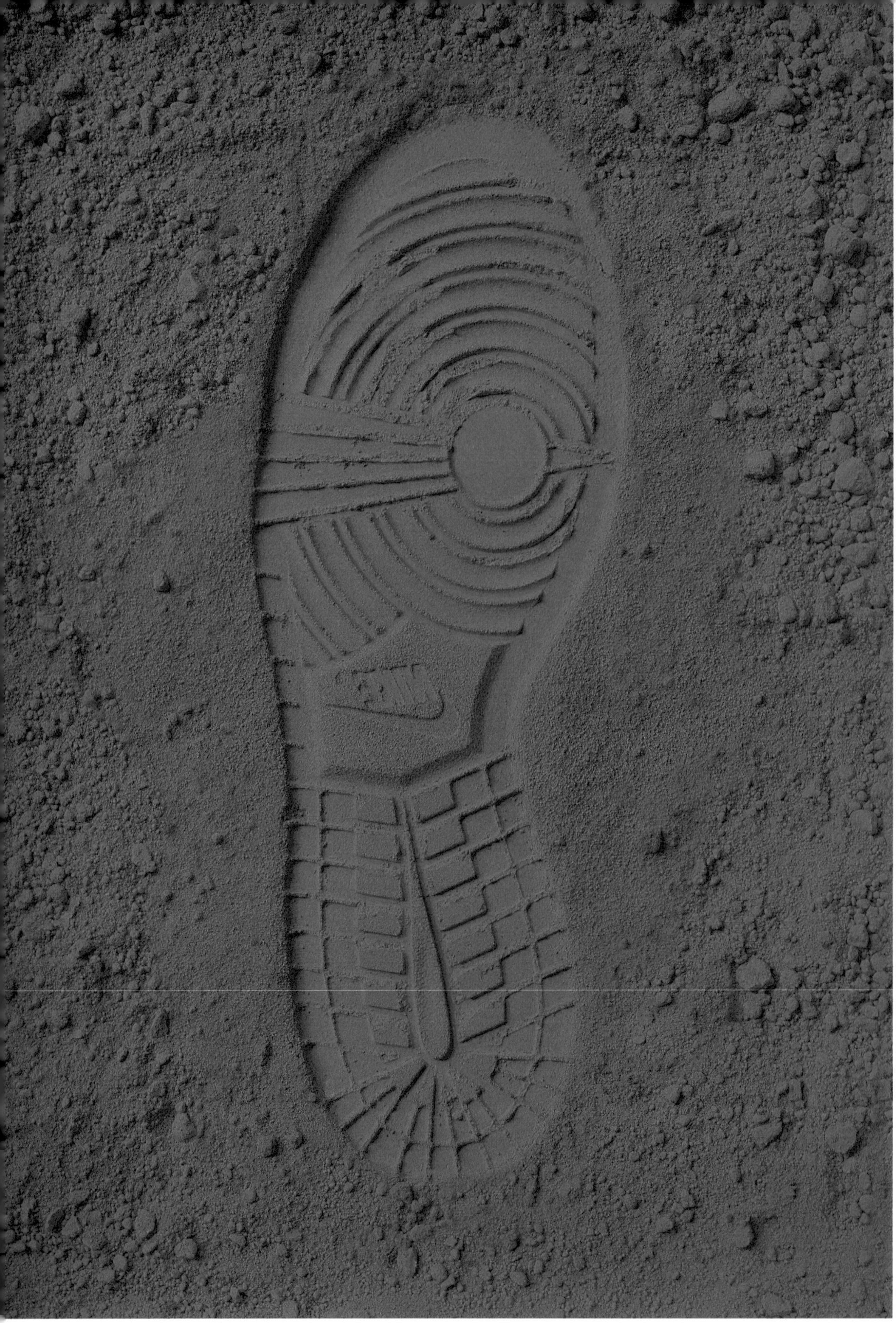

//DIY

Entitled *Footprint – Nike Klein's Blue Monochromes*, this beautiful photographic project is by Laurence Jaccottet, Ivan Liechti and Philippe Cuendet of Swiss graphic design studio //DIY (see page 192). Commissioned to create imagery for the Nike Switzerland showroom in Bassersdorf, //DIY responded by creating these iconic images of Nike sneaker soles pressed into blue pigment powder.

The pigment colour used is International Klein Blue (IKB), a deep blue hue first mixed by the French artist Yves Klein, and the immortalized imprints belong to a Nike Dunk, a Nike Air Max 1 and a Nike Lunar Wood (the images certainly have lunar connotations).

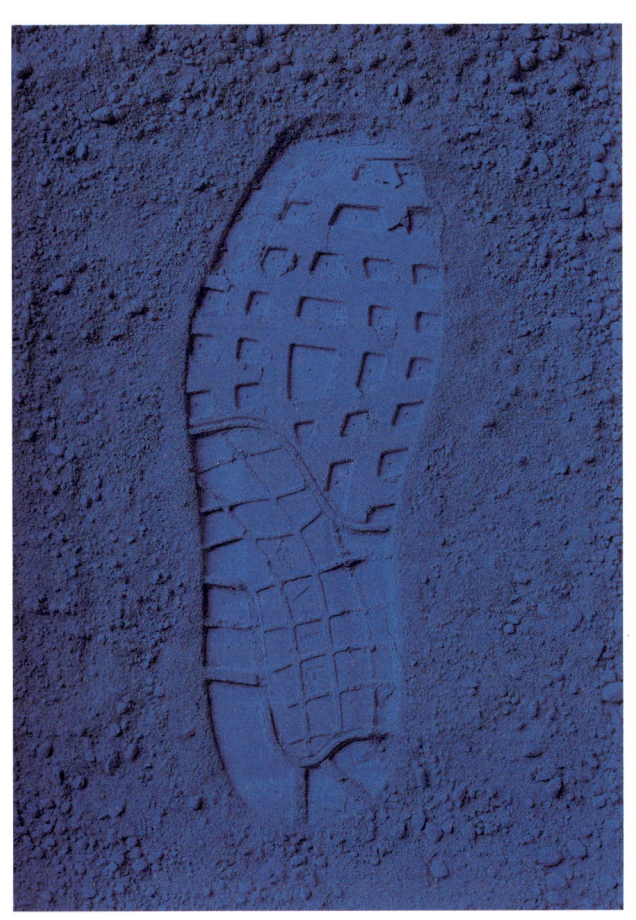

Dave White

Born in Liverpool, UK, in 1971, Dave White attended art school at the age of 16 and had his first solo exhibition by the time he was 18. Since then, he has exhibited worldwide and pioneered sneaker art with a unique body of work in 2002. 'I have explored sneakers as a vehicle for my painting as I find them incredible objects to look at. Whether it's the line, the silhouette, colour, shape, form or texture, I believe sneakers are some of the most beautiful things ever designed.' Being on the cover of *Creative Review* in 2003 helped bring his work to world attention, and projects with the likes of Nike soon followed. White is one of only a handful of artists to have his own signature Jordan releases.

White has pursued many subjects over the years, giving a lot of focus to environmental issues and highlighting endangered species with his signature expressive style, and supporting conservation charities globally. In 2016, White collaborated on a project with size? and Nike for the Air Max 95 'DW', depicting both the *Rabbit* and *Fox* artworks from his Albion Collection. Since creating the sneaker series, White's work has been coveted globally, featuring in the Phillips sneaker exhibition, Tongue + Chic, in New York, Hong Kong and Shanghai. His sneaker paintings have been installed at The Walker Museum, Liverpool and his Jordans displayed at the Bata Shoe Museum, Toronto, Canada.

Art

201

Art

Dave White

White is best known for his trademark sneaker paintings. 'The intent of my work has always been about capturing the character and essence of my subjects. I would say what I do is somewhere between Pop and Expressionism.'

In order to support its WINGS for the Future charitable program, Nike's Jordan Brand commissioned White in 2011 to create this Air Jordan 1 Retro, which features an NBA All-Star-inspired stars and stripes design. Limited to an extremely small run of just 23, hopeful collectors could bid to win a pair of the exclusive sneakers via a charity auction, with all proceeds going to the WINGS for the Future cause. Metallic gold paint covers both the upper and the midsole of the sneakers using White's signature style. The stars in the shoe's midfoot are another White trademark, and the stripes on the heel are made from his brush strokes, recreated and screen printed on to the leather.

An additional layer of paint was also added over the stripes by hand, to build up the thickness and replicate the texture of White's paintings – making each shoe unique. As a nod to the traditional surface White uses for his art, premium canvas was utilized for the tongue tag, and additional features include a label with White's signature behind the tongue. Extra attention was also given to the laces, which read 'WINGS for the Future', and even the shoebox was treated to White's interpretation of the Jordan Wings logo.

Dave White — Art — 205

Continuing his work for the WINGS for the Future project, White once again collaborated with Jordan Brand to create this signature Air Jordan 1 High 'DW'. Utilizing his trademark paint splatter and brush stroke techniques, the Air Jordan 1 High 'DW' this time featured the iconic Jordan black/sport red-white colourway, and utilizes elephant print on the forefoot lace strap. In addition to the sneakers, and to help commemorate the release, the pack also contained a T-shirt featuring White's interpretation of the Jordan Wings logo, a design which also featured on the shoe-box. A portion of all proceeds was donated to the WINGS for the Future program.

Art

In 2005, White worked on the Nike Wet Paint project (below), a collaboration with size? and Nike to help celebrate the 10th anniversary of the Air Max 95. A pack of neon and grey Air Max sneakers was released, paying homage to Sergio Lozano's original Air Max 95 colourway. The pack originally included an Air Max 1, Air Max 90, Air Max 95 and an Air Stab (which wasn't released until later). The AM1, AM90 and AM95 were released as a Hyperstrike set with a specially designed box, limited edition prints, stickers and a Tyvek jacket. Only 40 sets of each were released. The missing element from the original pack was the Air Stab. Five years on, and as part of their 10 Years of Obsession anniversary project, size? decided to give the shoe its release as the last silhouette in their ten-shoe collaboration series with Nike. Available exclusively through size?, the shoes were limited to 400 pairs worldwide.

Revisiting their relationship for a third time, size? and Dave White collaborated with Nike on the iconic Air Max 95 (opposite) in 2016. The two-shoe pack took inspiration from White's Albion Collection, which saw Britain's native species re-imagined in White's signature style. Focusing on the fox and the rabbit, the artwork adorns the no-sew paneling of the silhouette, drawing upon the many layers and elements from the paintings themselves. A rough hairy suede sits alongside a soft canvas on the upper whilst contrasting hits of pink and blue add an additional depth and coat to the story. Each pair also pays homage to the respective artwork by featuring the image on both the insole and the box.

Dave White   Art   207

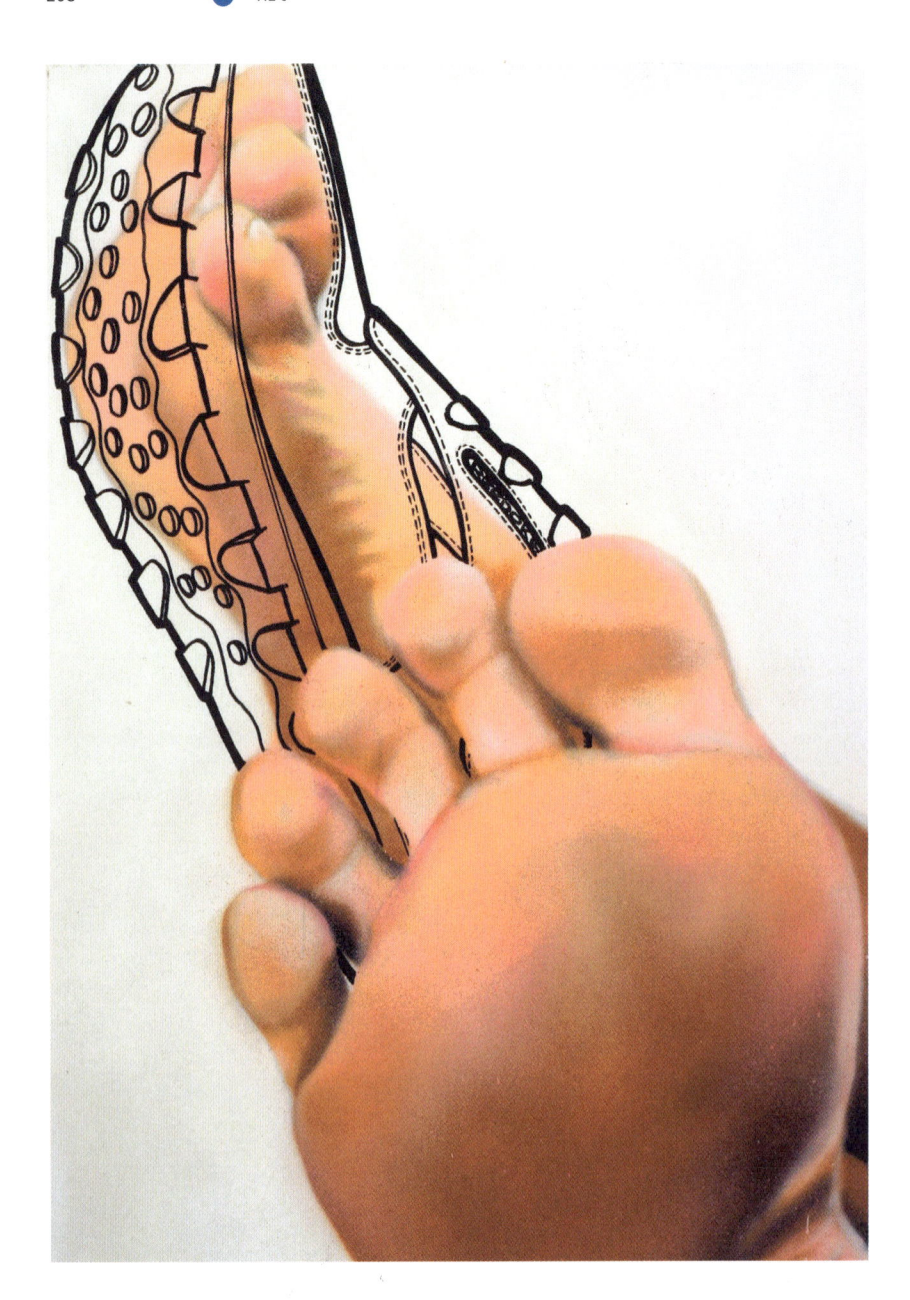

INSA

London-based graffiti artist INSA is probably most recognized for his Graffiti Fetish work, which explores the idea of graffiti/art as an obsession and uses the traditional fetishistic image of the high heel as a recurring motif. INSA first used this motif on a graffiti piece in which he spelled his name in heels. 'To me the high heel began to represent the ideas I was having about graffiti being an obsession, and it became a symbol of the graffiti fetish I was controlled by.'

Drawing parallels from the fetishistic nature of high heels, INSA's work also focuses on sneakers and sets out to explore the fetish many people, including INSA himself, have for these objects of desire. 'Heels are more of a sexual fetish, but sneakers are a consumer fetish – the only real satisfaction is to buy them and continue this by owning more and more. This fascinates me as in our society so many of our wants and needs are being replaced by consumerism.'

In the work shown here, entitled *Sneaker Fetish*, INSA displays his technical skills by using the relatively clumsy media of marker and spray paints to question his relationship with objects of consumer fetishism. 'Fetishism to me represents a desire inside us that is beyond our own control. I like exploring the key elements that signify these fetishes and applying them to other areas of desire in our lives, whether they be natural, like our need for creativity, or forced on to us, like consumerism.'

Art   209

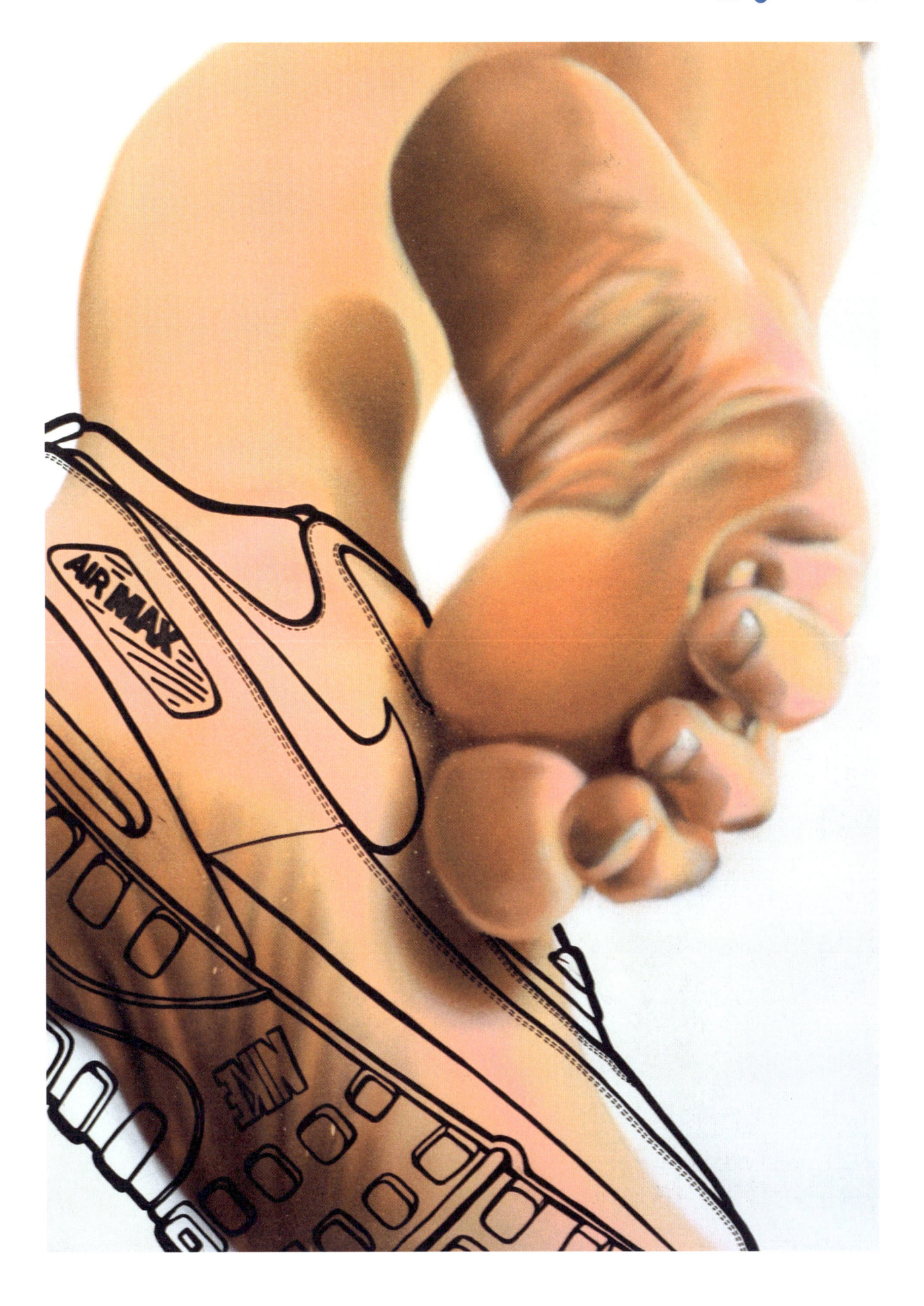

Art

INSA   Art   211

Created in 2005, the one-off custom-painted Dunk Ethel (opposite top), was named after INSA's graffiti partner and girlfriend. Shown beneath it is one of three pairs of custom-painted Dunks created in 2005 as a follow-up to the Dunk Ethel. Shown on this page are a pair of Air Max 90 sneakers, custom-made for the Festival of Air exhibition at Niketown London, 2006.

John Baldwin

In 2000, Lancashire-born artist John Baldwin created these paint-encrusted sneakers for an exhibition at Michael Naimski Gallery, London, in collaboration with adidas. Baldwin's art was applied directly to the shoes, which were then turned into photographic prints displaying the high colours and textural surfaces of the paint.

To capture the images, Baldwin used photographic microscopes at London's Tate Gallery's Department of Conservation, which allowed him to develop images that withstood great magnification, giving the prints a particularly intense quality. For the exhibition, the images were displayed alongside the original painted shoes.

Art

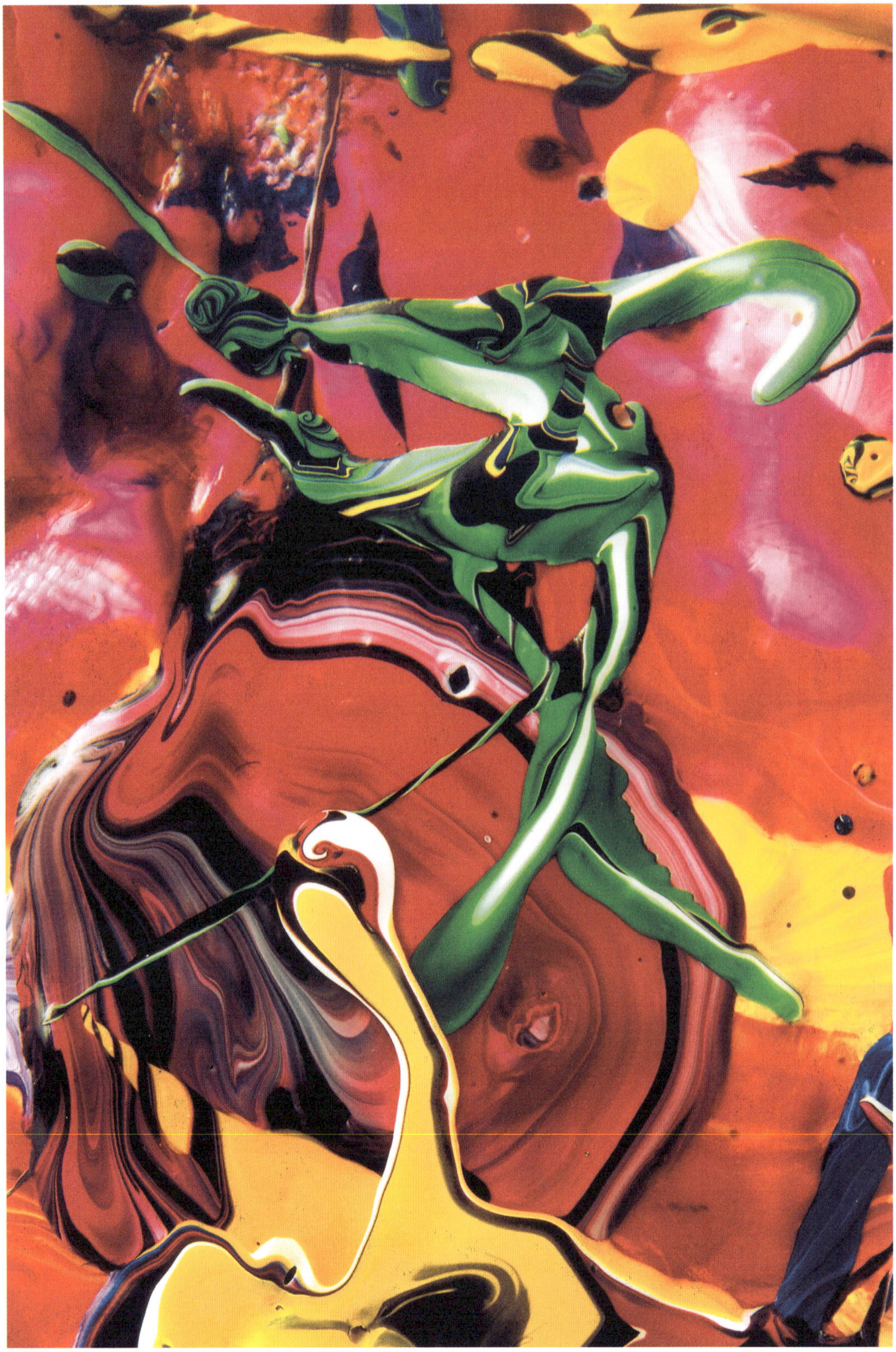

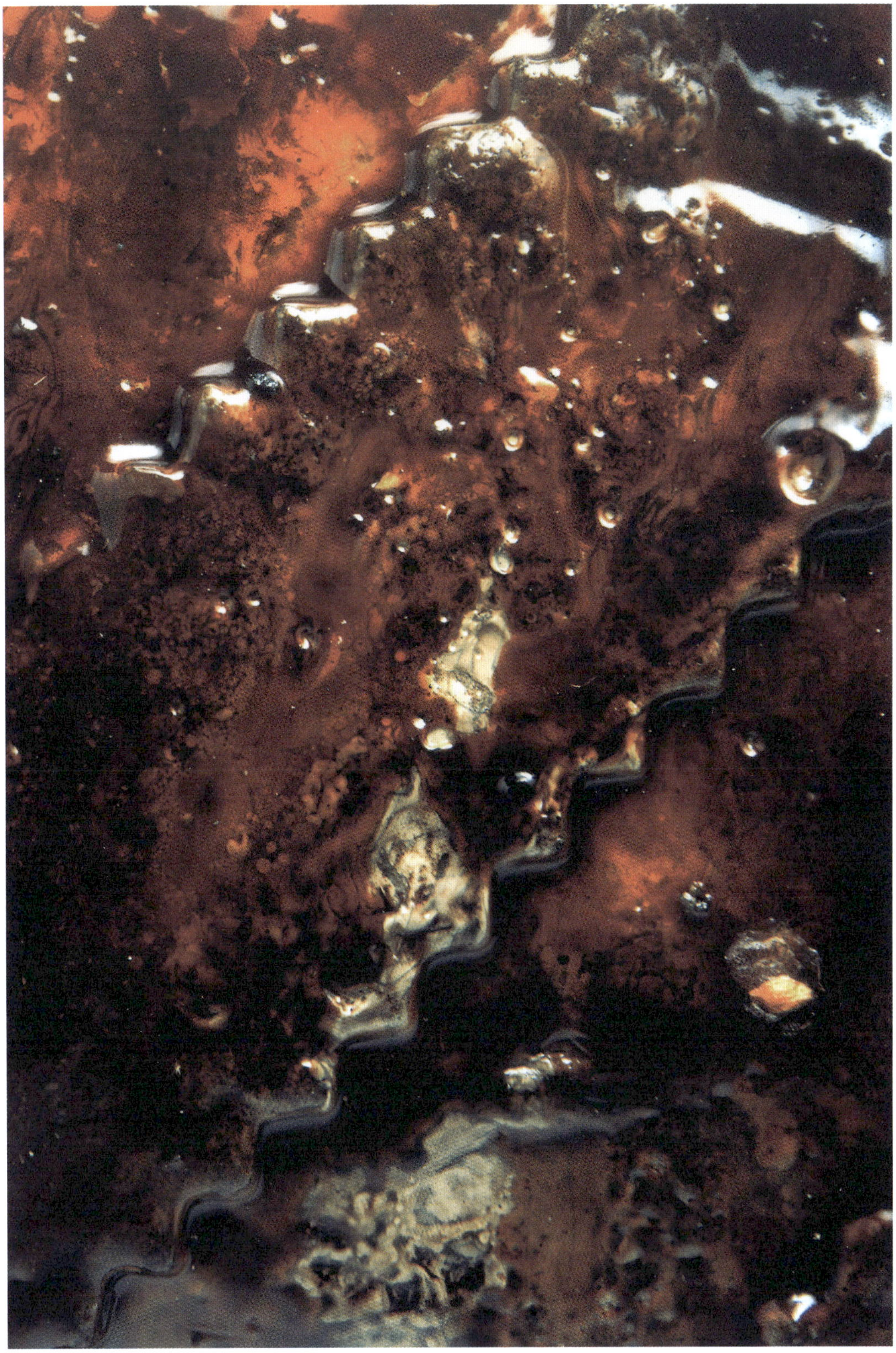

Steph Morris

Fuelled by an early fascination with sneakers, Manchester-based artist Steph Morris uses the traditional medium of pencil and paper to create hyperrealistic artworks, with footwear as her subject of choice. Capturing every stitch with incredible detail, each piece can take up to a staggering 350 hours to complete and requires intense concentration to ensure the form is as perfect as the original.

    Each shoe ranges in difficulty – from the smooth lines of the Air Jordan 1 'Dior', to the knitted upper of the Nike Air Vapormax (opposite) and the hairy cow-print leather of the Nike SB 'Chunky Dunky'. 'Sneakers can have all sorts of crazy textures that you don't really notice until you see them up close. There have been many times I've started creating a texture without knowing how to tackle it. When I worked on the Chunky Dunky, I'd never drawn hairy leather like that before. But it's the therapeutic process, married with a desire to perfect each texture, where I find the most joy.'

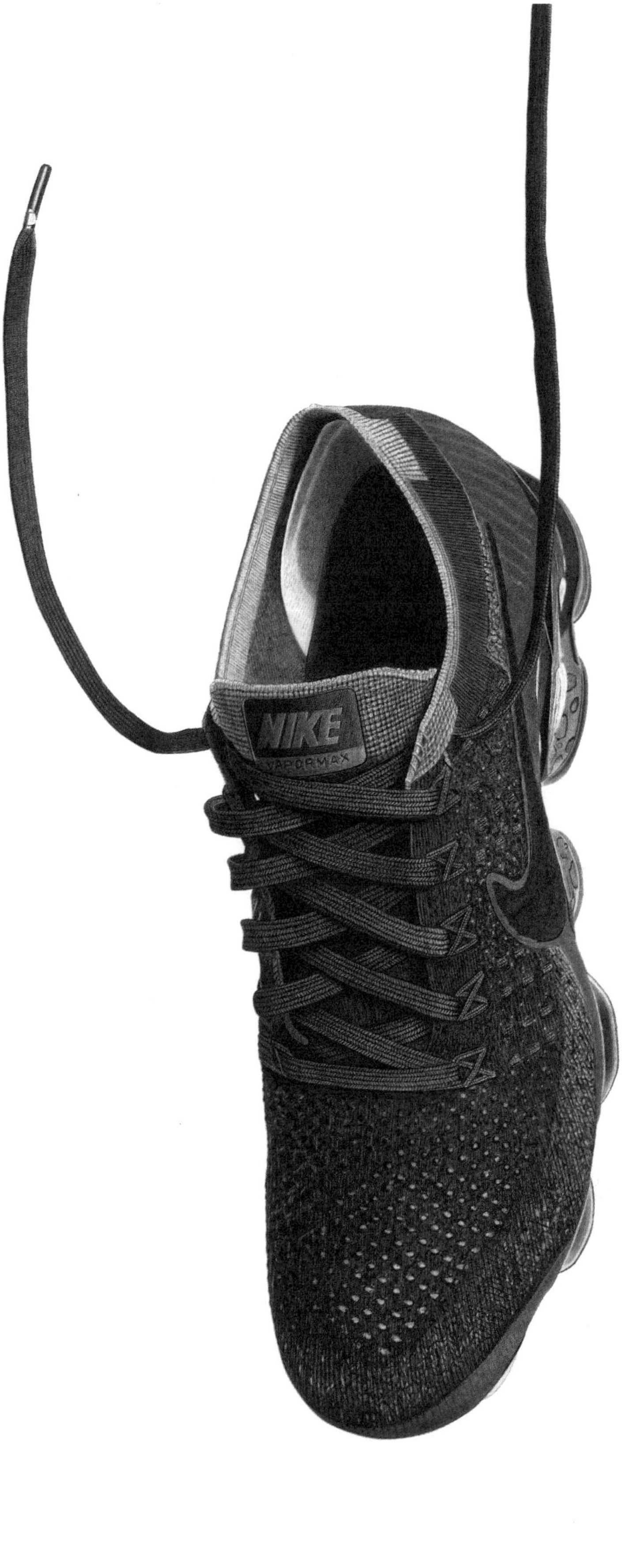
NIKE
VAPORMAX

Art

Steph Morris

Art

Steph Morris — Art — 221

Shown on pages 218–219 is a combination of four Nike Dunk Low SB collaborations: the Dunk Low 'Pigeon', Dunk Low 'What The Dunk', Dunk Low 'Black Pigeon' and Dunk Low 'Panda Pigeon'. Shown on this spread are the Off-White™ Air Jordan 1 'The Ten' (opposite) and Nike Dunk Low SB 'Paris' (above).

Toby Neilan

Drawing digital images with a fixed-width dot, UK-based graphic artist Toby Neilan produces visuals with a free, painterly aesthetic. His work generally falls into two main categories – fashion and architecture – and often includes the subject matter of sneakers (including the *Air 2 Zoom* project where he illustrated an A-Z of his favourite Nike sneakers, from the Air Max 1 and Dunk Low, to the Air Max Nitro and Kukini).

Shown here is a triptych of prints that focus on the colourways of the Nike HTM Flyknit as inspiration. First launched in 2012, Nike Flyknit was a groundbreaking design technology, with footwear created using a 'knitted' upper. Neilan's expressive style captures the essence of Flyknit perfectly, with intricate detailing and bold use of colour. 'As a keen runner, I was interested in the pared-down technology of the Flyknit range,' explains Neilan, 'especially the concept of barefoot running and how Nike has tackled the issue with the one-piece woven upper. As always with HTM collaborations, the colour palette adds an extra dimension.'

Art   223

Parra

Parra (aka Pieter Janssen) is an Amsterdam-based artist who is best known for his surreal bird-like characters and distinctive use of bold, flat colour. While his early work explored hand-drawn lettering, recent years have seen his work evolve into abstract interpretations of his core motifs. Working across large scale public sculpture, painting, drawing and textile work, Parra has exhibited his work in solo shows spanning Asia, the United States and Europe – his work is even in the public collection of the San Francisco Museum of Modern Art. Parra is also co-founder of cult apparel label ByParra and a member of music group Le Le and MICH.

Parra created this series of Nike Air Max illustrations for an editorial feature entitled Art And Science in the October 2006 issue of *Dazed & Confused* magazine. The back cover of the magazine featured Parra's rendering of an Air Max 360, complete with transparent air bubbles.

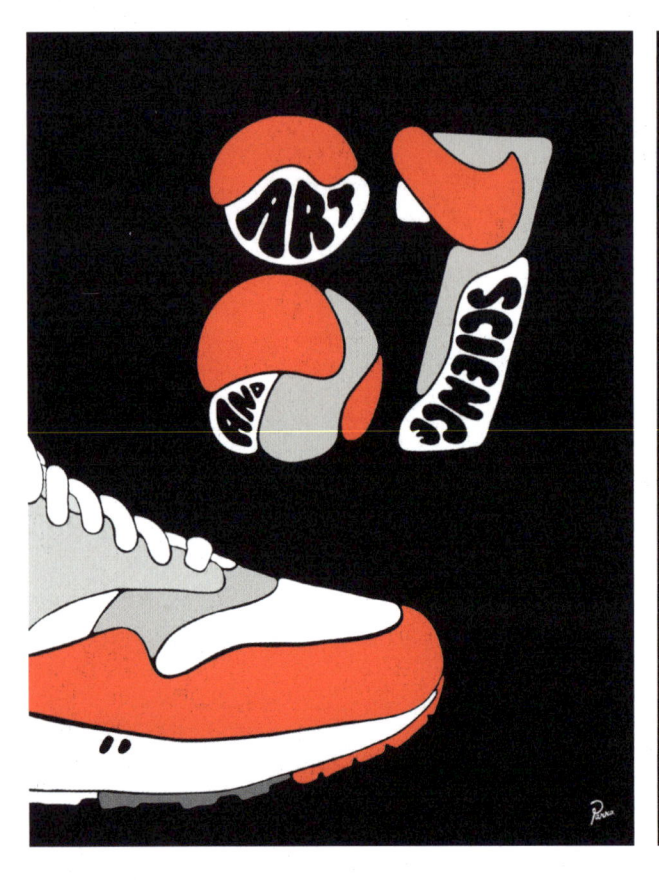

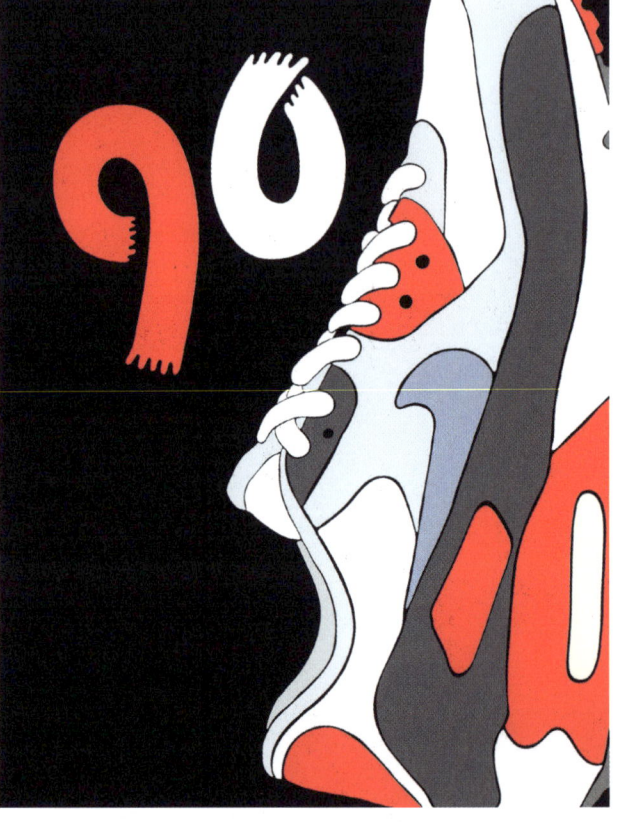

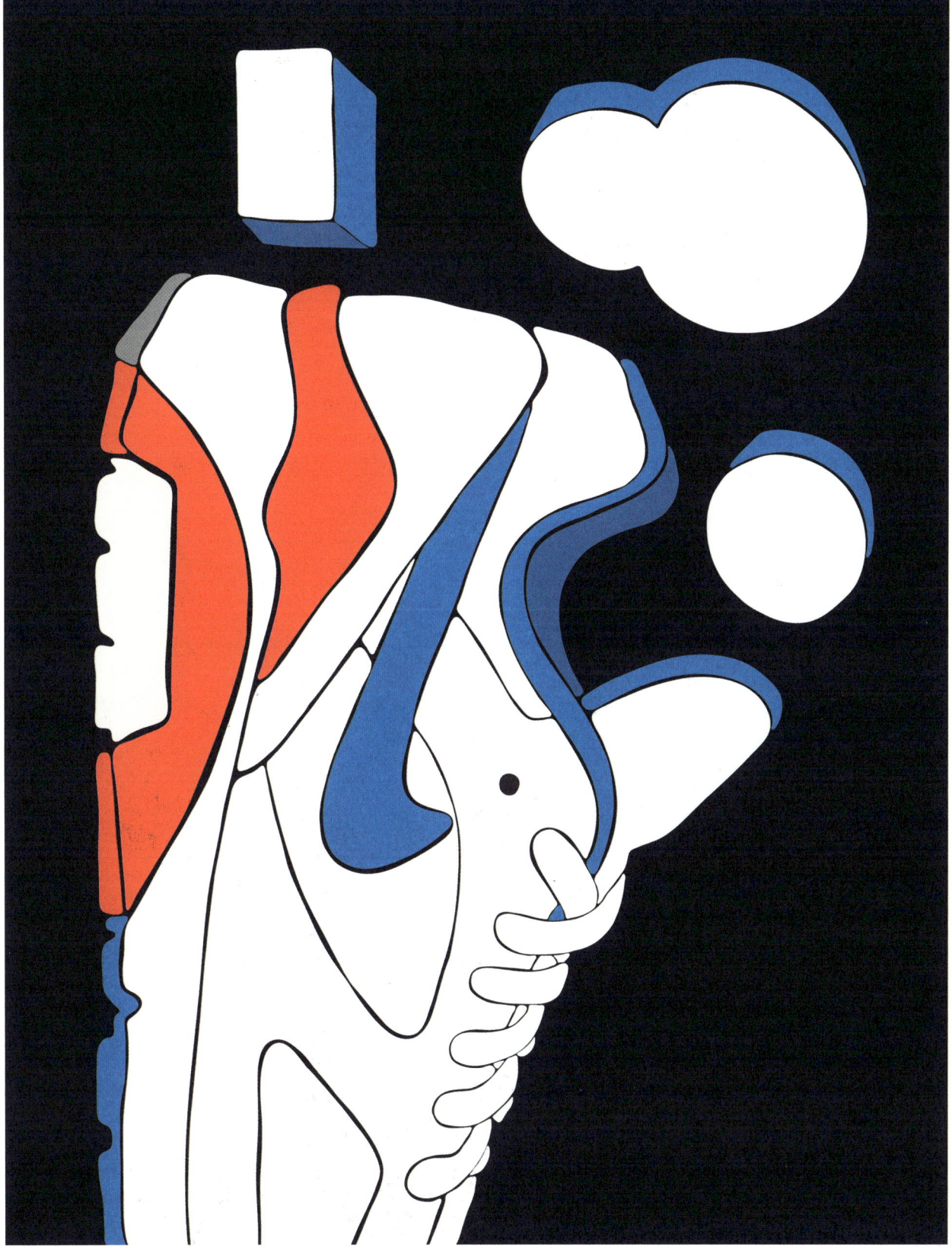

Art

Art

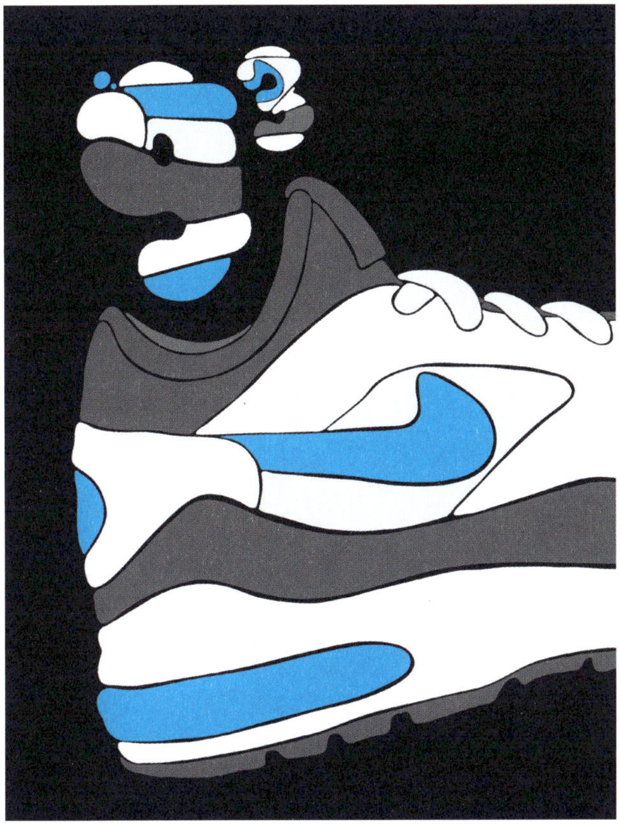

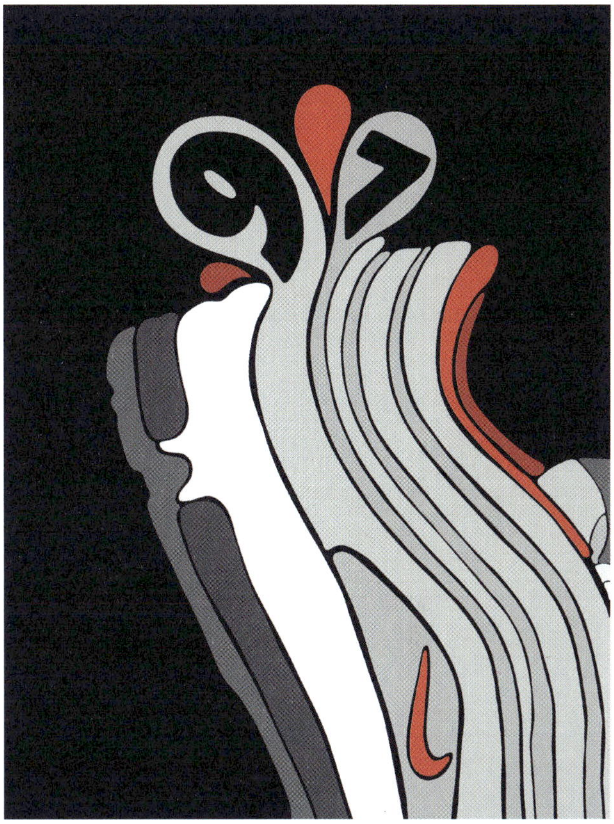

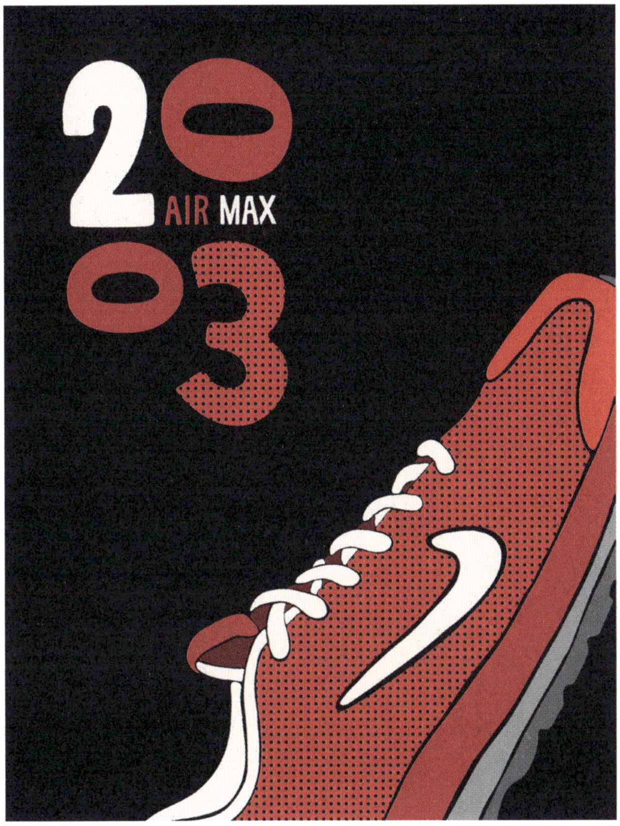
2003
AIR MAX

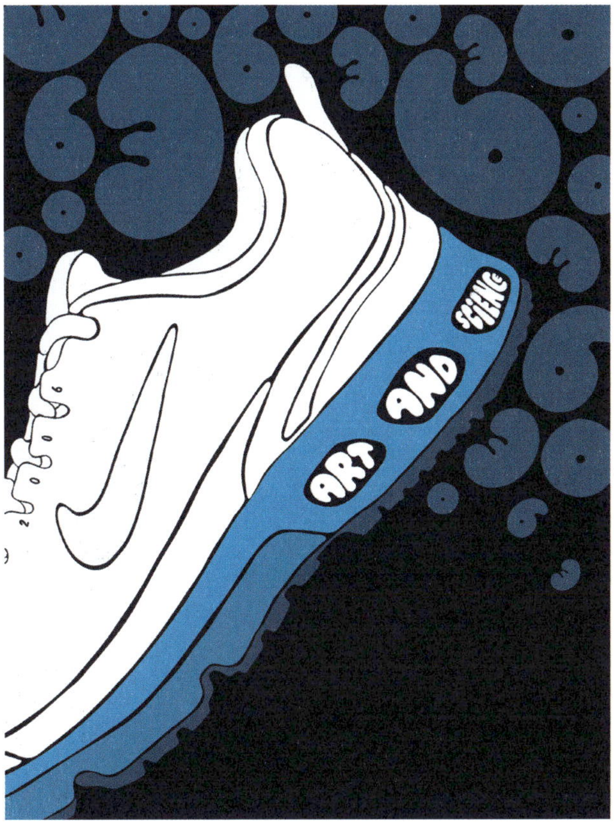
ART
AND

Parra is undoubtedly most famous in the sneaker world for his Air Max 1 Amsterdam collaboration with Nike in 2005. Created for Nike's Capital Series (see page 20), the first colourway was based on the corporate colour palette of Holland's Albert Heijn supermarket (initially Parra also wanted to create carrier bags for the release). The shoe was never produced as the supermarket chain changed its colour scheme to blue and white (from orange, blue and white).

Parra then changed the design to the now infamous 'Red Light District' colourway, featuring his iconic Air Max Girl illustration on the insole. Only 220 pairs of the Quickstrike shoe were released worldwide; 24 pairs of a Hyperstrike version, featuring Parra's embroidered signature, were also created.

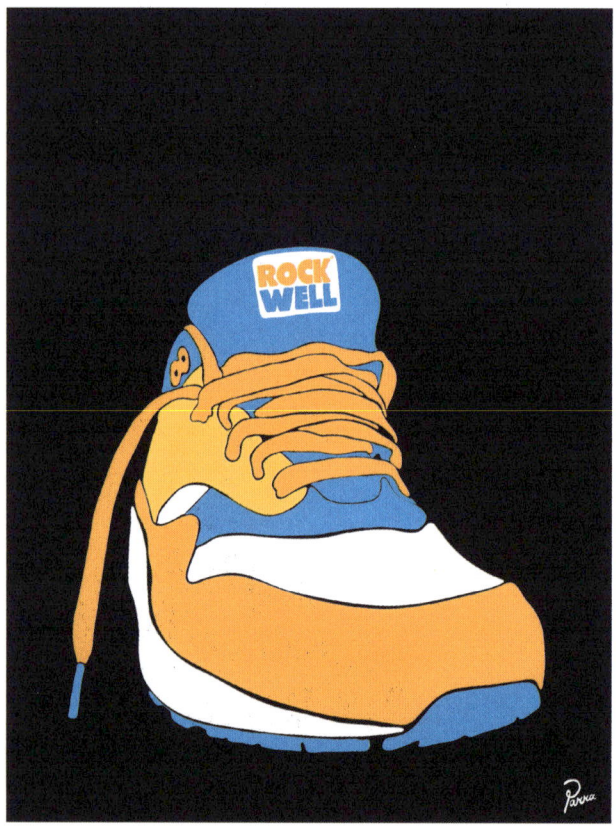

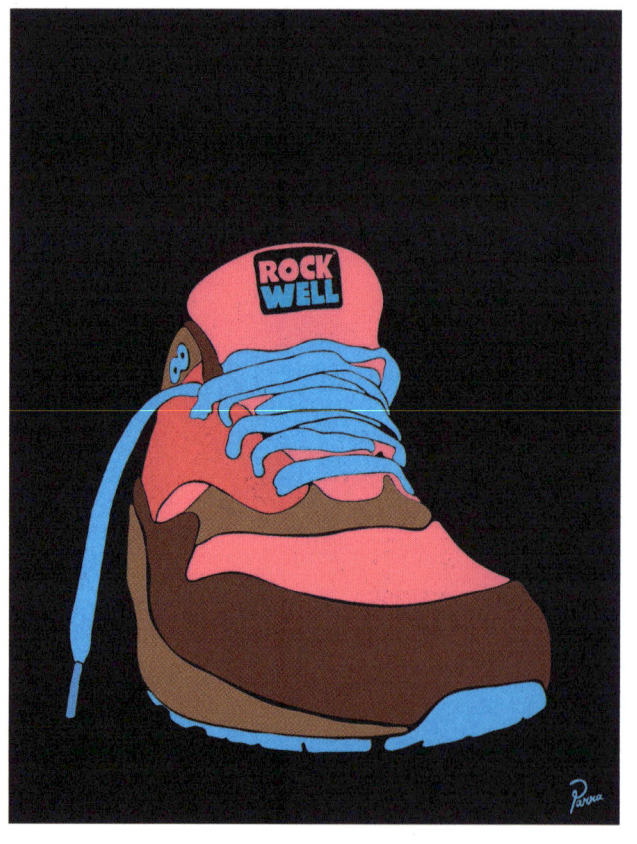

Following a 'fantasy sports' apparel collaboration with Nike Sportswear in 2009, Parra was given a last-minute opportunity to design a very limited edition Air Max 1, to be sold exclusively through Patta in Amsterdam (Parra's studio at the time was above the store). With only one day to deliver the design, the Nike Air Max 1 'Cherrywood' (above) was eventually released in 2010. The shoe features a rich burgundy suede, with asymmetric burgundy and blue Swooshes, satin insoles and tri-branded outsoles.

The next time Parra was to revisit the iconic Air Max 1 silhouette was in 2018. Inspired by the Dutch landscape and a love of pop culture, the Air Max 1 'Parra' (below left) was released alongside a Zoom Spiridon (below right) and a track jacket. The Friends & Family edition of the Air Max 1 is shown on page 295 – with pink and purple striping around the mudguard. This edition also features a cloud graphic in place of the Swoosh logo.

Art

With Parra's roots firmly planted in skateboarding (he was a sponsored amateur from the early 1990s until the early 2000s), a collaboration with Nike SB was almost inevitable. The pair first teamed up in 2019, for a Parra Dunk SB and Parra Blazer SB release. Following that, it was actually the postponement of skateboarding's debut at the 2021 Summer Olympics in Tokyo that brought the Nike SB Dunk Low Pro 'Abstract Art' sneaker (below) to fruition.

Parra's original idea of designing a shoe to coordinate with the Federation Kits he was developing for the Games was able to become a reality thanks to the added window of opportunity. Furthering his abstracted landscape-inspired design, Parra created a weaving pattern of shape and colour that extended to fully cover the insoles of the shoes. A Friends & Family iteration of the shoe was also created using asymmetrical colour blocking to give each shoe a unique feel.

In addition to his work with Nike, Parra has collaborated with a number of other sneaker brands including Etnies, Converse, ASICS and Vans. The wavy panelled Half Cab (above), was released in 2024.

Julien Rademaker

Amsterdam-based Jules David Design was founded in 2005 by Julien Rademaker. Inspired by his favourite sneakers, Rademaker created these prints to highlight their shapes, textures and colours. 'I think some of these shoes are a work of art,' says Rademaker, 'a unique piece of design perfectly shaped and beautifully composed. I wanted to play with that idea and change the composition into a new abstract form by using the parts of the shoe I liked the most.' Nothing is added to the imagery of the original shoes; elements of the existing designs are simply emphasized to turn them into beautiful abstract kaleidoscopic patterns.

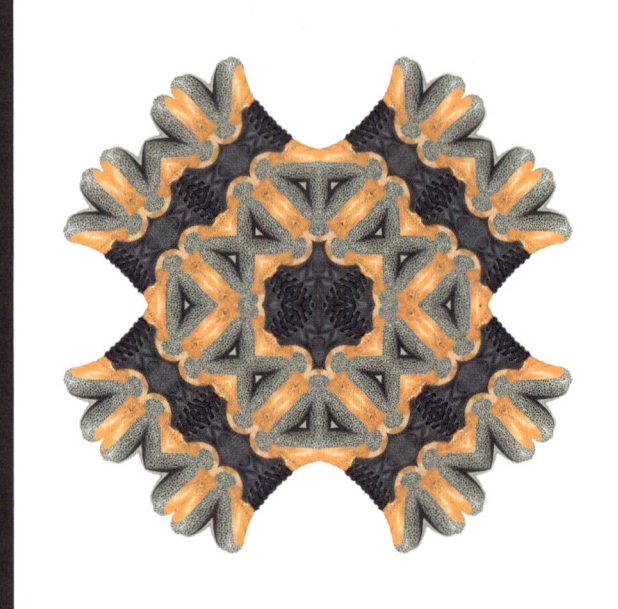

Art

Art

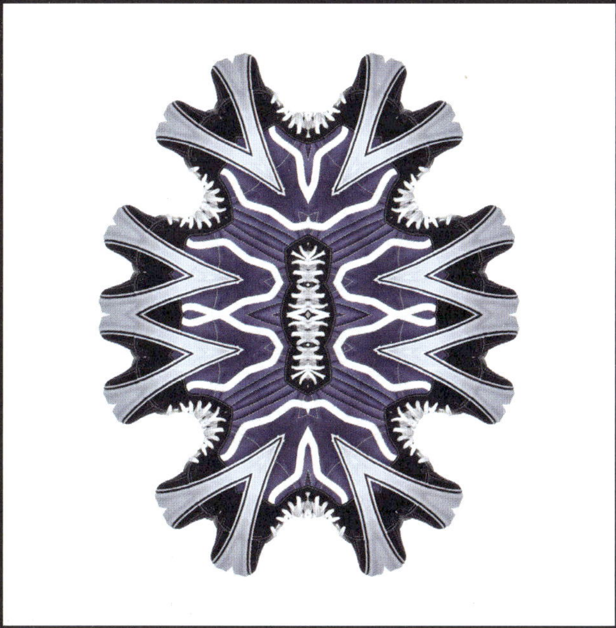
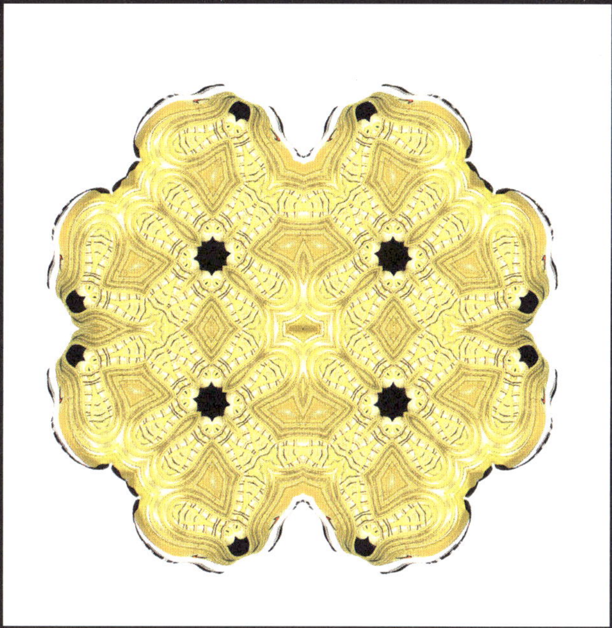
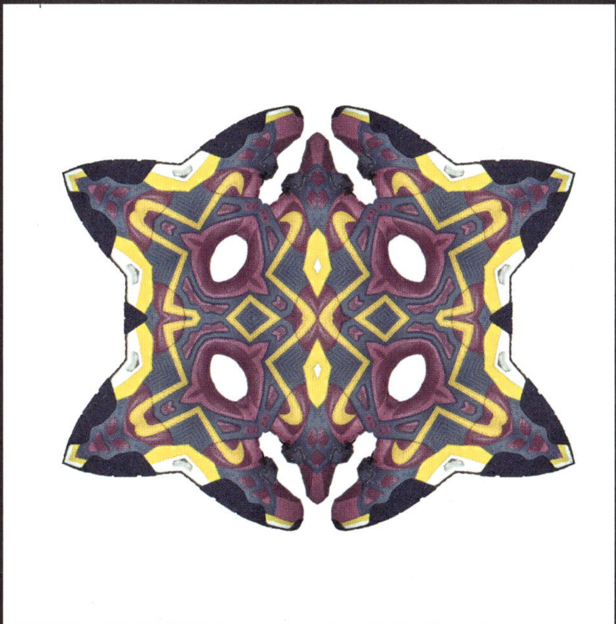
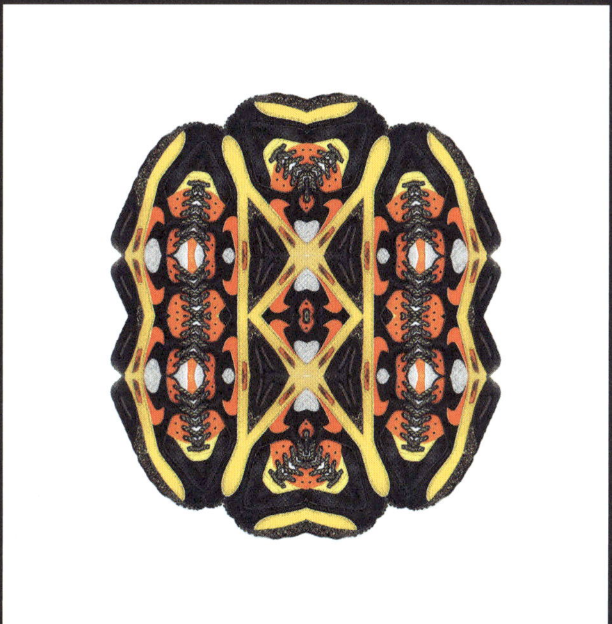

Art

UK-based LORENZ.OG, real name Lorenzo Federici, has a client list that includes Virgil Abloh (see page 88), Lil Yachty, Drake and Salehe Bembury. Federici's work is all about colour, and he uses the term 'Patented Colorschemes' to refer to the vibrant colourways he creates. 'It was how Virgil [Abloh] described my work during our first proper conversation together. His words, thoughts and ideas were always gold.'

Although sneaker customization is a large part of his work, Federici doesn't actually categorize himself as a sneaker customizer. Instead, his focus is to enhance existing products through his colourful and nature-inspired design language. 'When I was 19, I landed an internship with Nike and that definitely influenced my desire to move into colour design. My approach tries to add value in places overlooked by the industry, focusing on the smaller details. I love it when I can truly add value to something that already has immense value on its own – especially silhouettes that have multiple materials, such as the Nike Air Max 95 Comme des Garçon.'

LORENZ.OG

The Nike Air Max 95 'Summerhouse OG' (above) was designed in collaboration with Netflix and celebrated the final chapter of British crime drama television series, *Top Boy*. Each of the 30 pairs created came housed within a special box that included a map of London (with the names of actors and directors who worked on the series) on the base. Shown opposite is a detail of the Nike Air Max 95 'Genesis'.

238 • Art

Shown on this page is a trio of Nike Air Max 95 Comme des Garçon (above), the Salomon ACS Pro 'Dusk' (below left) and the New Balance 860v2 'Dusk' (below right). Shown opposite is the Nike Air Max Sunder 'Dusk'.

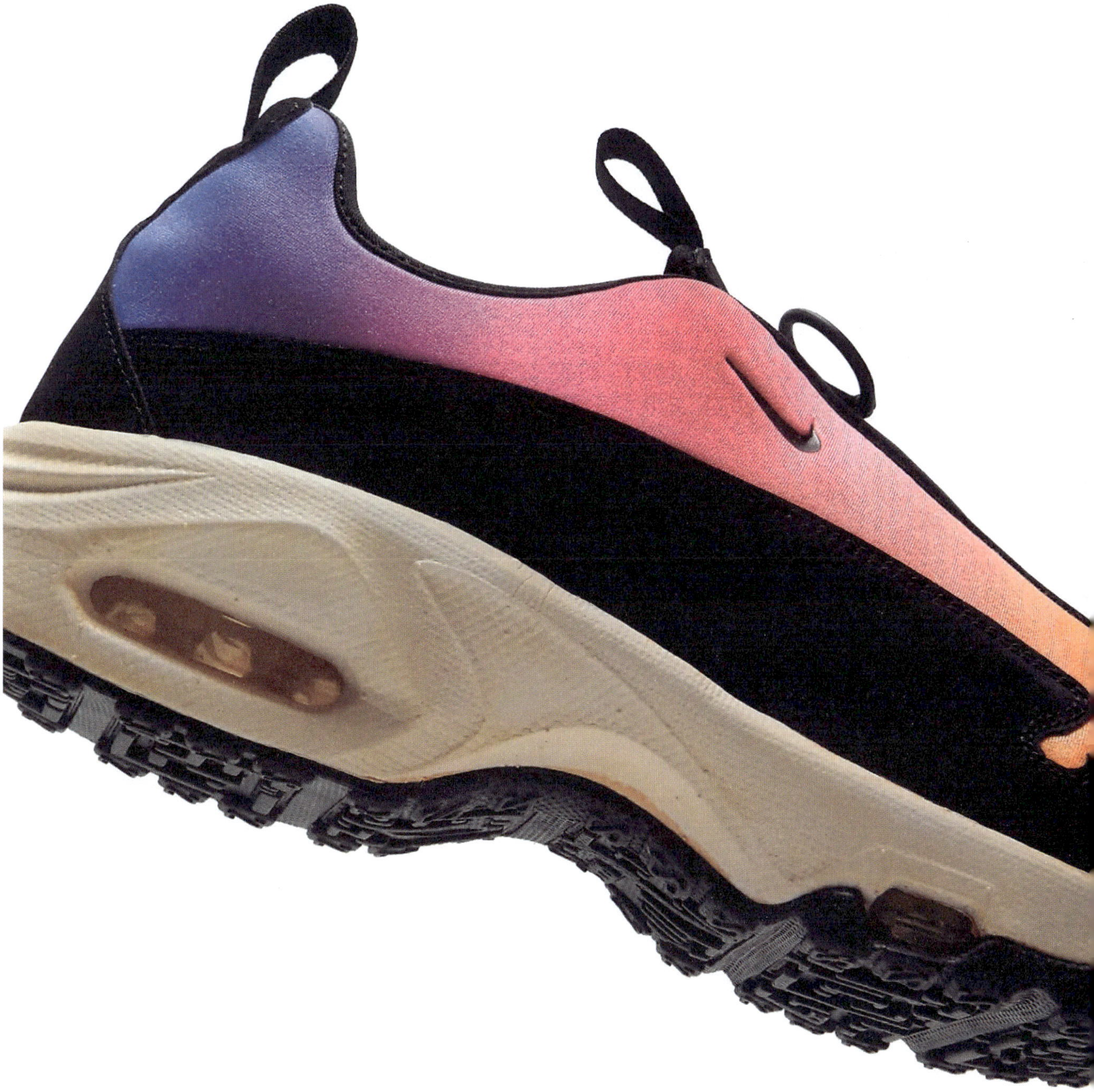

Art

Shown opposite is a trio of Nike Air Max 97 Off-White™ sneakers. On this page, clockwise from top left, is the Air Jordan 4 Off-White™ 'Dusk', Nike Air Force 1 Off-White™ 'Solis' (conceived to be gifted to Virgil Abloh), Nike Air Max 90 Off-White™ 'Menta' and Air Jordan 5 Off-White™ 'Dusk'.

Studio Hagel

Founded by Mathieu Hagelaars in 2015, Studio Hagel has established a reputation as the world's leading experimental footwear design studio. Based in Amsterdam, the studio designs and develops footwear for brands such as Valentino, ASICS and Off-White™.

Shortly after its inception, the studio quickly learned that actually making its shoe concepts, rather than simply drawing them, was a far more productive way to work. With this creative process seeming to always happen at the start of the week, the Makersmonday initiative was formed – a no-rules day of experimentation that serves as a 'visual playground' for future projects and inspiration. Various experiments from the initiative are shown on this spread.

Intent on showing the full potential of the studio's experimental approach, 2022 saw Hagel release its very own footwear collection, starting with the Hagel Shroud (see overleaf) – a shoe inspired by a Makersmonday Nike Cortez experiment in 2018, itself influenced by car covers/shrouds. The following year saw the release of the Hagel Tent, a shoe inspired by 'the cozy feeling of camping in the outdoors while still looking like you're ready to attend a Paris Fashion Week show', says Hagelaars.

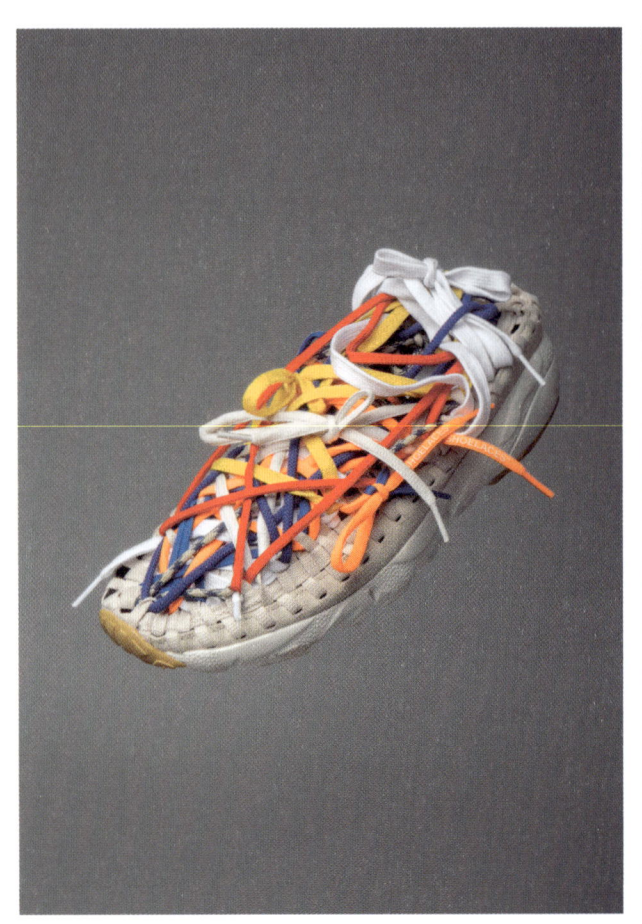

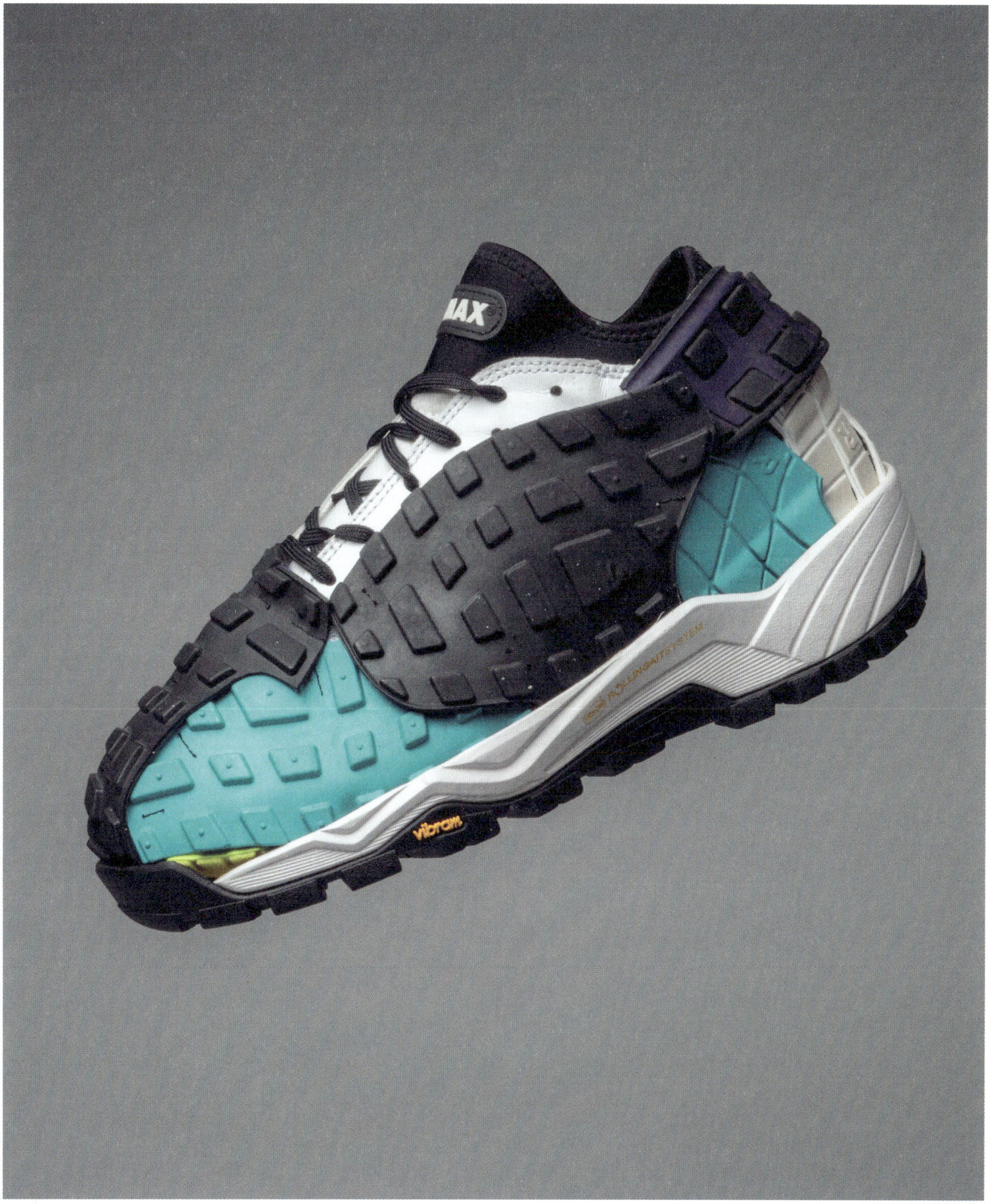
vibram

244 • Art

Studio Hagel · Art · 245

Shown opposite is the Hagel Shroud in RTE Mango and Ice White. Hagel also made a car cover to promote the release of the Shroud silhouette. Shown on this page is the Hagel Tent in Dark Black.

MSCHF

Brooklyn-based art collective MSCHF has a mission to subvert consumer culture – and the corporate entities that feed it – through the use of art, fashion, technology and capitalism. The collective has courted controversy since its inception in 2018, with projects such as the Jesus and Satan shoes (see pages 248–249), and the Wavy Baby release – all of which were the subject of now-settled law suits.

Although the impossible-to-pigeon-hole art collective isn't exclusively tied to footwear, its shoe releases create huge amounts of publicity. Probably best known for their Big Red Boots – oversized, cartoon-inspired boots that were released in 2023, MSCHF also released the controversial AC.1 boot in 2022 – inspired by the aesthetic of a medical boot. From the outset, MSCHF has shunned regular brand collaborations and the idea of simply choosing a colourway – opting instead to pursue its subversive (and often humorous) take on both the sneaker industry and wider culture of consumerism.

Art   247

Following the release of the Jesus and Satan shoes (see overleaf), the TAP3 (opposite, top left) was released in 2022. Inspired by the shape of the Nike Air Force 1, and as a reaction to the AF1's many imitators, the shoe is covered in MSCHF-branded tape, censoring the shoe's form. The Gobstomper (opposite, top right) was released in 2022 and took its inspiration from gobstopper sweets – its multi-coloured layers can be exposed through wearing. The impossible-looking BWD (opposite, bottom left) from 2023 is a shoe that can be worn backwards. Perhaps MSCHF's most controversial shoe, the 2022 Wavy Baby (opposite, bottom right) drew obvious, and very much intended, references to the Vans Old Skool silhouette. A collaboration with American rapper Tyga, the Wavy Baby was the focus of a now-settled lawsuit from Vans, who considered the shoe damaging to its intellectual property rights.

In 2024, MSCHF used its distorted Super Normal silhouette (above) as the base for a collaboration with technology-focused fashion brand, ACRONYM. The Super Normal 'ACRONYM AG' featured lateral slash detailing, revealing an embossed acid green leather under-layer, a water-resistant zip and a metal lace buckle. MSCHF's first legitimate brand collaboration was the Reebok Pump Omni Zone IX in 2023 (below). Produced in two colourways, the shoe was rebuilt to house nine functional pumps.

The Jesus Shoes (above) was a custom sneaker project released in 2019. Using what MSCHF described as a 'censored 1997 air bubble shoe' as the starting point, the shoes were modified to contain 60cc of holy water, directly sourced from the River Jordan, in the air bubble. This reference to the Biblical tale of Jesus walking on water is further alluded to by 'MT. 14:25' stitched on the front of the shoes which is the particular passage in the Bible that recounts the story (US$1,425 was also the retail price). The religious theme continued with a crucifix dubrae and frankincense-scented insoles.

The follow up to the Jesus Shoes, the Satan Shoes (below) were released in 2021 and endorsed by American rapper Lil Nas X. The custom sneakers feature a host of satanic references and, most controversially, contained 60cc of red ink and one drop of human blood (donated by the MSCHF team) in the air bubble. Individually numbered from 1 to 666, the shoes featured a pentagram dubrae and biblical reference to 'Luke 10:18' (in which Jesus says he saw Satan fall from heaven like lightning) on the front (US$1,018 was also the retail price). The completely sold out shoes sparked a now-settled lawsuit from Nike, the result being that MSCHF had to post a voluntary recall where people could return, and be refunded for, the shoes if they wanted.

Nash Money

London-based sneaker customizer Alex Nash, aka Nash Money, experiments with construction and deconstruction rather than simply applying painted patterns or colourways. He is best known for his Nike customizations, where he applies a moccasin-style stitch to the toe and adds other features like embroidery and coloured stitching. 'It's all done with one leather needle and the iron tips of my fingers – well they feel like iron now anyway,' says Nash. Always thinking about new projects, not just towards sneaker customization but design in general, one of Nash's customs saw him create a bike seat using an Atmos Nike Free Trail 5.0 shoe. In Nash's own words, 'I always have constant pressure to improve my skills and push the boundaries with every custom I make.'

The Bush Walkers project (above) is a classic example of Nash's destroy-and-rebuild approach to customization. Starting with one of his favorite sneaker silhouettes, the Nike Air Max BW, Nash added his signature moccasin stitch, deck shoe interlacing, brass hiking hooks, and contrasting autumnal-themed colour palette. The name, Bush Walkers came from a conversation with Simon 'Woody' Wood, editor-in-chief of Australia-based *Sneaker Freaker* magazine, and is a hiking-inspired play on the BW in the shoe's orginal name (which actually stands for Big Window). Shown below are the 'Bel Air Max' from Nash's 2006 Afro Centricity Pack (originally commissioned by Nike for their Festival of Air celebrations in 2006), and a Visvim FBT skilfully combined (using hand stitching) with a Nike Air Max 360.

Commissioned by Intercity in 2011, Nash created these fully functional sneaker speakers as part of the Inspired Ingenuity project from Havana Club. 'I chose the Nike Air Force 1 as the starting point,' explains Nash, 'because the outsole has such a flat sole to sink the speaker cone into. The fact that the AF1 is probably one of the world's most recognizable and iconic sneakers, was a plus.' The creation process was a steep learning curve for Nash, who hadn't anticipated quite how much work would be involved. 'I've always had to tackle problems and learn new skills or techniques with most of my customs/designs, but I never thought electronics and carpentry would be among them.'

Later that year, Nash worked on a second sneaker speaker project, this time as part of a four-way collaboration also involving Puma, MF Doom and *Sneaker Freaker* magazine. Based around a huge promotional Puma Suede shoe, the speaker included lights, ignition keys, touch pads and graphic equalizers. The speaker was eventually gifted to MF Doom.

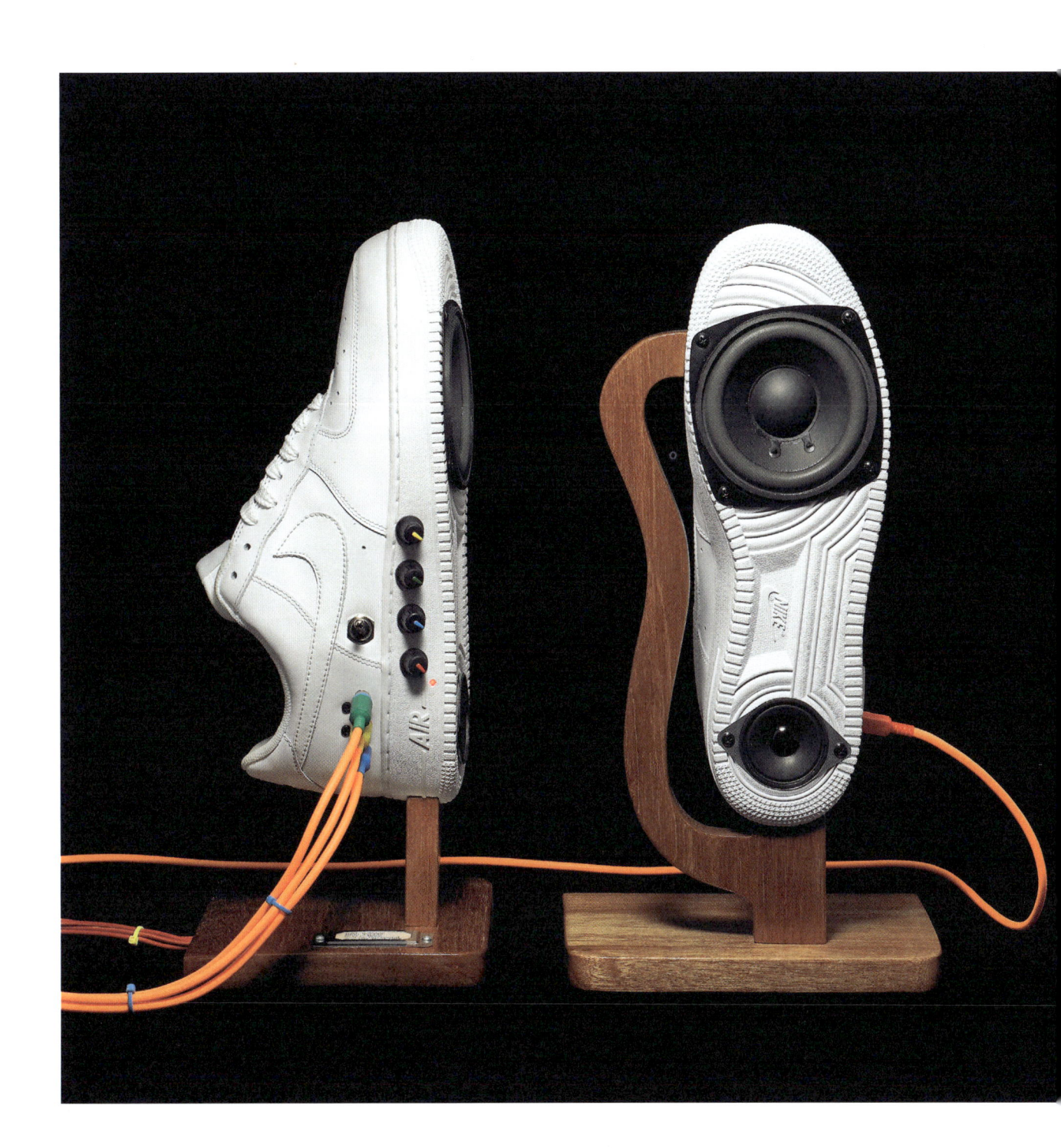

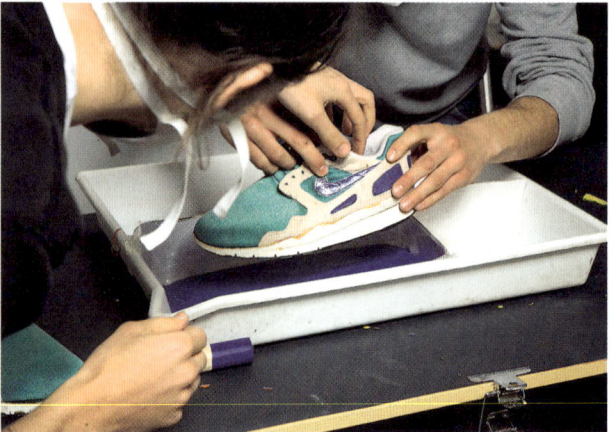

Cemal Okten & Martin Price

Originally part of the NIKE78 project created by Paul Jenkins (where select creatives were asked to challenge the function of a pair of Nike sneakers), Nike Fix by Cemal Okten and Martin Price was a project which aimed to repair well-worn sneakers using liquid rubber – an alternative take on the culture of sneaker customization. As Okten explains: 'At the end of their life, a pair of shoes have become extensions of the individual; inevitable wear and tear create a perfectly suited shoe for how the individual runs, walks, kicks a ball, skateboards or rides a bike. Nike Fix is a project which aims to repair and refresh these well-loved shoes using colourful liquid rubber; giving them a new lease of life and a fresh new look.'

Lady Brown

Korean-based Lady Brown is a fabric artist who aims to convey emotion through her running stitch technique. Producing artworks ranging from basketball inspired rugs to fabric-clad stools, Lady Brown also oversees the figure costume design at Coolrain Studio (see page 254).

    The shoes shown here are part of a collaboration with custom sneaker artist Steven Kim (of Korean custom brand fe:rker). Lady Brown's fabric with its free-flowing, irregular stitching, is contrasted with Kim's precision construction and sewing. The Nike Air Max 1 from the collection (bottom right) was gifted to, and worn by, the silhouette's original designer, Tinker Hatfield.

Coolrain Lee

Inspired by anime, and after pursuing a career in animation, Seoul-based toy artist and creative director Coolrain Lee started making collectible 12" figures in 2004. Since launching his Monsterz Crew collection that same year, Lee has worked on numerous projects with brands such as Nike, NBA, Reebok, Puma, Cinelli and Converse.

A key aspect of Lee's figures are the highly-detailed sneakers he creates, which both adorn the feet of his creations and function as works of art in their own right. Each sneaker can take up to two weeks to create, depending on complexity, with the basic construction process being very similar to that of the full-size counterparts. 'At first, I'll make a 3D model of the outsole,' explains Lee, 'then I'll put masking tape on a shoe tree to draw out the sneaker pattern. Finally, I'll find a material similar to the actual shoe, then cut and combine the patterns.'

Art 255

Art

Shown opposite is a selection of highly detailed 12" figures, with custom outfits, from Lee's OG Series – cartoon-inspired representations of industry leaders from the worlds of fashion, music and sneaker culture. Clockwise from top left are *MRBAILEY*, *Lil Yachty*, *Virgil Abloh* and *Salehe Bembury*. It took Lee over four weeks to make MRBAILEY's Takashi Murakami 'Dobtobus'-inspired custom sneaker replicas (top left).

Shown above is a collaboration with art and fashion-focused Korean sneaker brand Seven Eight Under. The X-1 embodies the concept of the space explorers from Lee's ongoing Astro Series and reflects the 'innocent longing for space' from his childhood. The upper is made using Tyvek®, with a detachable pocket, and the midsole displays the footprints of an astronaut taking their first steps on the moon.

Michael Lau

Hong Kong artist and toy and toy designer Michael Lau is widely credited as the pioneer of the urban toy movement. His highly collectible figures form ever-growing urban tribes, such as the Gardeners and Crazy Children, and are famed for their reflections of global street culture.

In 2004, Lau designed 100 sneaker-based figures for an exhibition in his own Hong Kong gallery. Based on the Nike Air Force 1, the Mr. Shoe (Sample) character is a hard-edged and roughly sculpted creation that was created to reflect Lau's design philosophy; that although there is one mould, each shoe takes on its own personality and chooses its own audience. Lau hand-painted each figure, taking inspiration from his favourite design and pop culture references, including fashion brand Hermès, Stanley Kubrick's cinematic masterpiece, *A Clockwork Orange*, and the work of contemporary artist Damien Hirst.

Art

259

260   Art

Michael Lau   Art   261

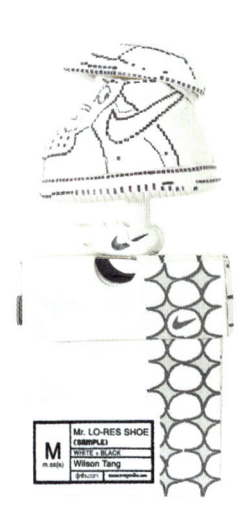

After a second show in Tokyo, fashion label Maharishi brought the Mr. Shoe touring exhibition to the UK in 2005. Held at the DPMHI gallery in Soho, the exhibition featured all of Lau's Mr. Shoe pieces alongside one-off customized figures created by a range of leading designers and creatives, including Ben Drury, Eley Kishimoto, Zoltar and Lupe Fiasco.

262   Art

In 2002, Lau teamed up with designers FibreOps and Nike for the release of a limited edition Nike Wildwood sneaker. Limited to only 60 pairs worldwide, the shoes have 'FibreOps' embroidered on one shoe and 'Michael Lau' on the other. As part of the release, Lau created this limited edition Boy-D figure (part of Lau's Crazy Children series). The character has a pixelated face and is wearing a Nike shirt and hat – and is even sporting a miniature pair of the Nike Wildwood FibreOps shoes. The figure was limited to 540 pieces, comes with a Crazy Children pig (in one of two colours) and is packaged in a pixelated box. The version shown here is the Maharishi variant, limited to just 100 pieces.

Michael Lau

In 2006, Lau collaborated with Nike SB for the release of this wood-grain Dunk Low. Released in Hong Kong only, the shoe was limited to an edition of 106. Each pair came with a wooden box and a Michael Lau NY Fat wood-grain figure. Shown here is the Friends & Family version of the shoe created for Lau, featuring a number of differences including a detailed wood-grain midsole instead of the solid brown midsole on the Tier Zero release.

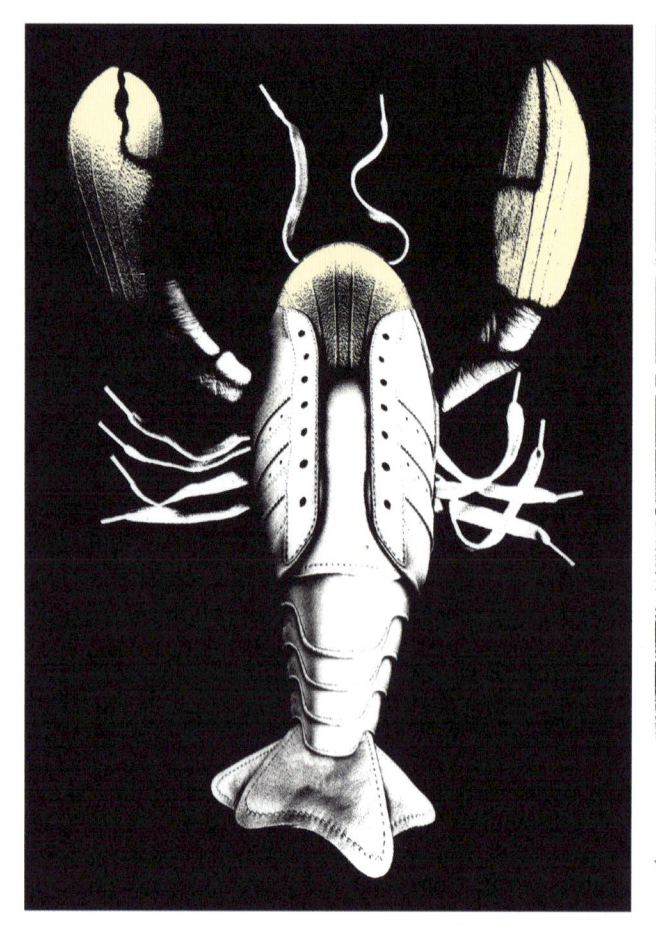

Mark James

Mark James is a multi-disciplinary artist and graphic designer based in Cardiff, Wales. Working across multiple creative platforms including video, photography, illustration and animation, James adapts his work to a variety of styles. His conceptual work is inspired by a mix of popular culture and social commentary, gaining him a reputation for being both humorous and controversial. Shown above (with detail on the right) is *The Lobstar*, a two-colour, limited edition screenprint that pays homage to three design icons; the adidas Superstar, Andy Warhol's 1982 print, *Lobster*, and Mother Nature's very own creation.

CardBoy, shown below, was created and designed by James as an answer to the dilemma of 'what to do with the box?'. When opened, the packaging of this mini-figure transforms into the head of the character. 'I've always designed characters, and collected a few, but the idea of actually making my own figure was something I'd always wanted to do. The cost of getting something made wasn't an option at the time, so I started developing cardboard figures.' CardBoy Sneakers was the second in the CardBoy series and paid homage to classic sneaker boxes. It featured eight characters (each one came with its own accessories) and is blind-box packaged with a chase figure. A limited edition pack was also released containing all eight characters, with the packaging turning into a 200 per cent scale figure.

Nike SB
Three Be@rbrick
Project

In 2006, Nike SB teamed up with Japanese toy manufacturer Medicom to produce these Be@rbrick figures as part of the Nike SB Three Bears Pack – a trio of sneakers including a (baby bear) Dunk Low, a (mummy bear) Dunk Mid and a (daddy bear) Dunk High. All three of these unique shoes were manufactured using faux fur. Each Be@rbrick figure, which featured a rendering of a Dunk toecap on its body, was produced in the same colourway as its respecitve sneaker: the smallest Be@rbrick is the same colourway as the Dunk Low; the medium size matches the Dunk Mid; and the largest Be@rbrick corresponds to the Dunk High.

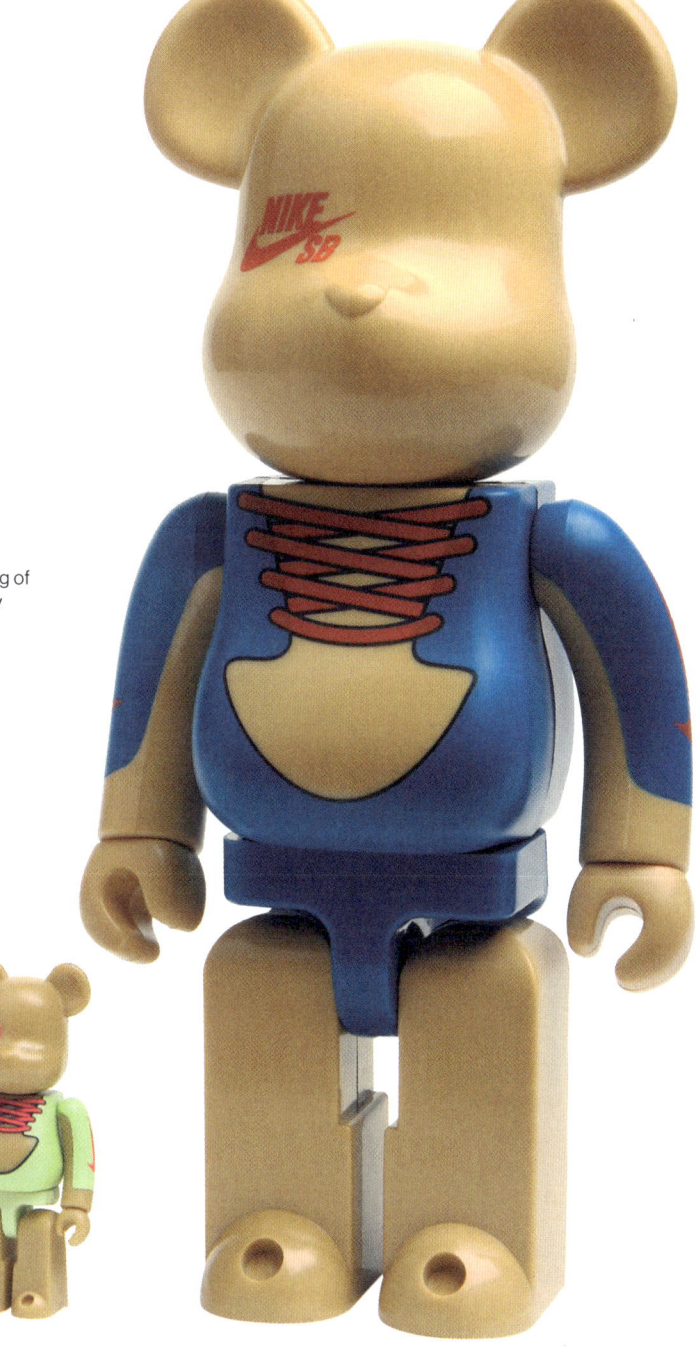

Nike Transformers

For the release of the *Transformers* movie in 2007, Takara Tomy worked with Nike Japan to produce these shape-changing sneakers. Based on the Nike Free 7.0, the fully transforming sneaker figures were available to buy in the guises of Convoy (the Japanese name for Optimus Prime), commander of the Autobots, and Megatron, the leader of the Decepticons. An alternate version of Convoy with a marine colourway was also released. At approximately 13cm in length, the models have real laces connected to the top of the shoe, and each character is also wearing a miniature pair of Nike Free 7.0 sneakers.

Art

Vinti Andrews

Vinti Andrews is a London-based fashion designer, whose work cross-references various cultures, including the UK's rich historic past. In 2006, Andrews was invited to participate in the Festival of Air, an event held at London's Niketown celebrating three decades of Nike Air Max. The brief was to represent the history of the Air Max sneaker within British youth street culture. 'We chose the Air Max 95 model as it meant a lot to me – it was a groundbreaking design that totally stood out. I used to hang around Portobello Road market and was one of the first wearing the green neon colourway – you just couldn't get hold of them.'

The idea of choosing to make the dog figures came from the British phenomenon of 'one man and his dog'. 'We added a twist to this idea by choosing the pit bull species to give our project bite and to represent the aggressiveness and strength of Nike. Also, the only dogs where I live seem to be hybrid pit bull breeds – it wouldn't sit right if we made Nike poodles!' Andrews selected the sneakers according to colour, design and, most importantly, the cultural significance of the models and how they reflect changing times.

Art

.SWOOSH

Inspired by the global interest in NFTs and the idea that digital creations can have lasting value to serious collectors, Nike launched its .SWOOSH initiative in 2022, a web3-enabled platform that aims to foster an inclusive digital community and experience – while also being a home for Nike virtual creations. Starting life as a beta, the platform was set up to allow Nike Members to learn about, collect and eventually help co-create interactive digital objects such as virtual shoes or apparel.

Gradually growing the platform throughout its initial year, 2023 saw the launch of the first .SWOOSH digital footwear collection, the Our Force 1 (OF1). The OF1 collection was co-curated by the .SWOOSH community and launched in two digital 'boxes', the Classic Remix box and the New Wave box. Each was priced at US$19.82 (a reference to 1982, the year the Air Force 1 was first released) and contained a digital Our Force 1 version of the Air Force 1. Owners could open their box, if desired, to discover which iconic digital version of the Air Force 1 it contained – to learn its unique features, unlocking utilities for special access to physical products or experiences, and even download a 3D file of their virtual creation in order to customize it further.

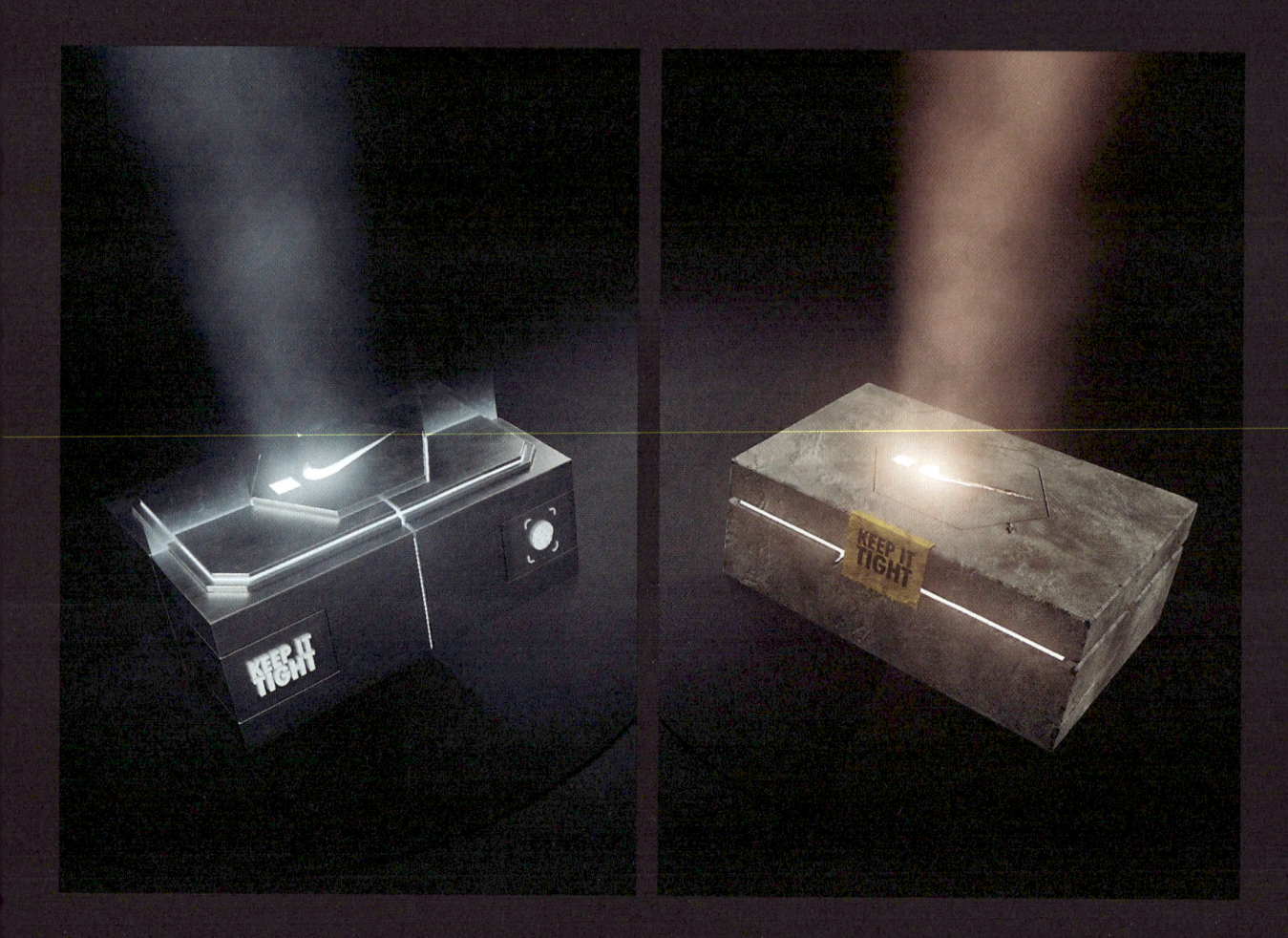

Art   271

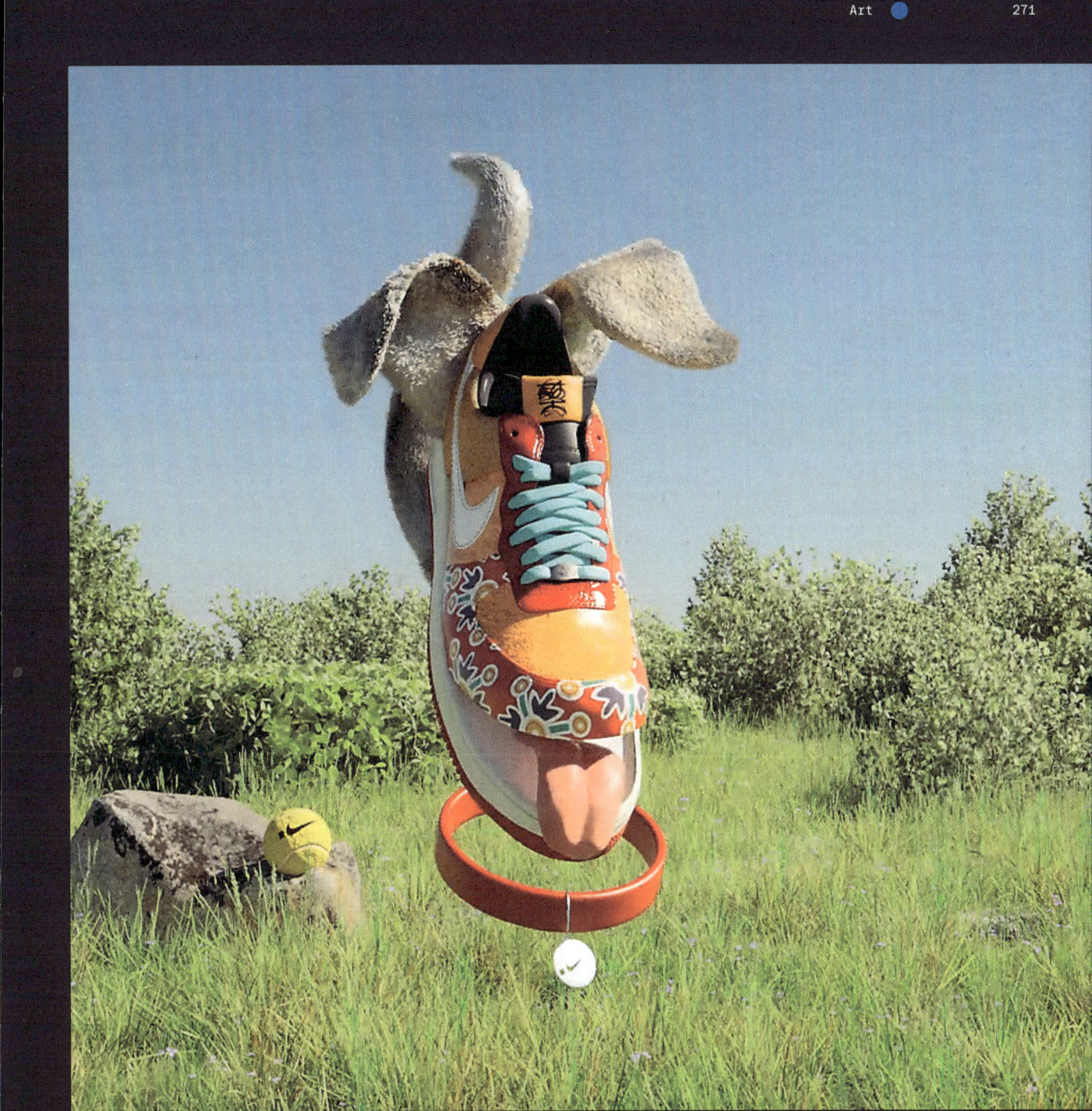

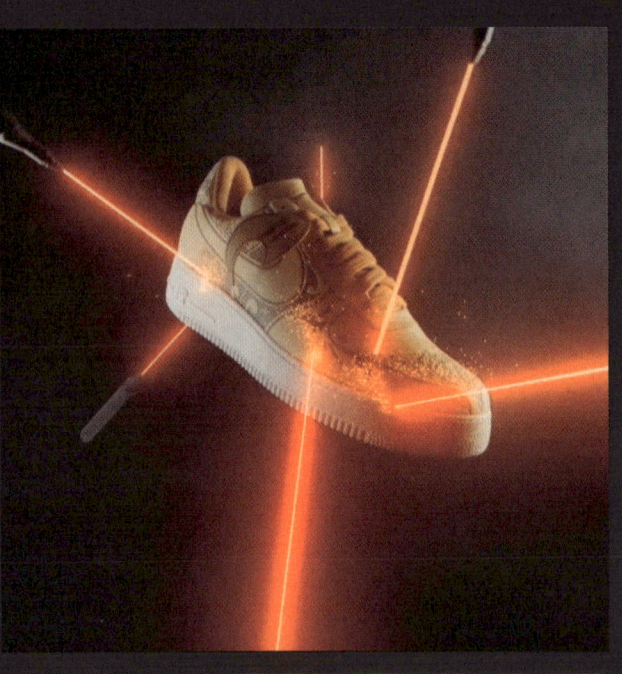

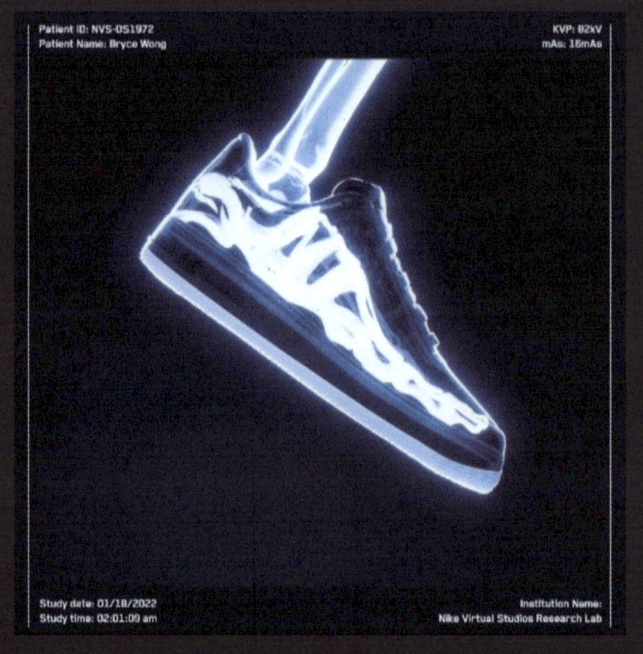

Art

Shown this page, clockwise from top left, are the Nike Air Force 1 'Laser', Air Force 1 'Invisible', Air Force 1 'Skeleton' and Air Force 1 'Crocodile Lux' – all brought to digital life as part of the .SWOOSH OF1 collection.

404 Error
The requested upper
was not found. Try again.

404 Error
The requested upper
was not found. Try again.

RTFKT

Founded in 2020 by Benoit Pagotto, Chris Le and Steven Vasilev, RTFKT (pronounced 'artefact') created digital and physical products that combined the worlds of fashion and gaming. Using in-game engines, NFTs, blockchain authentication and augmented reality, RTFKT created one-of-a-kind experiences and 'phygital' products – including sneakers. A forward-thinking Nike acquired RTFKT in 2021, a move that led to a succession of co-branded projects.

    The Nike Air Force 1 Collection, shown here, was a digital and physical ten-shoe project that included two shoe designs by Japanese artist Takashi Murakami – the 'Murakami Drip' (edition of 4,182), top, and the 'Murakami DNA' (edition of 167), above. Each pair in the collection was limited to a specific quantity and eligible NFT holders were able to redeem their digital Air Force 1s for limited made-to-order physical versions at a special 'forging' event, lasting for a limited time. While the silhouette remained generally faithful to Bruce Kilgore's original design, the medial Swoosh was replaced with the RTFKT logo. The sneakers also featured a laboratory equipment-inspired dubrae and, in order to prove authenticity, were equipped with the RTFKT WM NFC chip.

Art • 275

This page, clockwise from top left, features the 'Reptile' (edition of 399), 'Alien' (edition of 60), 'Human' (edition of 1,986), 'Robot' (edition of 1,126), 'Demon' (edition of 1,031) and 'Undead' (edition of 190). The collection also included the 'Angel' (edition of 1,327) and 'Genesis' (edition of 1,776).

276 ● Art

The Nike Dunk Genesis project started life as a purely digital concept, but evolved into a brand new physical design of the classic Nike Dunk silhouette. First released in 2024, the digital collectible is powered by 'Skin Vial Tech' which enables collectors to evolve and change the 'skins' of their digital sneakers. The initial forging event for the project featured three colourways; the 'OG' edition (top), the 'Void' edition (above) and the 'Clone X' edition, each with unique textures and storytelling. The physical incarnations also had removable parts that allowed collectors to customize their shoes. 1,000 pairs of the 'Void' edition (total quantity 11,394) were sold through Nike SNKRS.

In 2021, RTFKT collaborated with Jeff Staple (see page 104) on three unique NFTs. The 'Metapigeon K-Minus' (left) was listed at US$500 and included a virtual and physical version of the sneaker. With only 100 editions available, the 'Metapigeon MK' (top left) was a purple-themed digital and physical sneaker listed at US$2021. Finally, the digital-only 'Metapigeon' itself (above) was limited to 100 editions and priced at US$1.

The Cryptokicks iRL was the first native Web 3 sneaker, combining decades of Nike Sneaker innovation with RTFKT's vision to merge the digital and physical. Part-inspired by Tinker Hatfield's Air Mag, the Cryptokicks iRL featured auto-lacing, enhanced lighting, haptic feedback, gesture control, walk detection, app connectivity, AI/ML algorithms and wireless charging via the RTFKT Powerdeck. Created in four different colourways, the release was limited to 19,000 pairs, with the colourway split determined by the collectors themselves. As with the Air Force 1 and Dunk Genesis collections, the Cryptokicks iRL were sold as NFTs that could then be redeemed for physical counterparts through a forging event.

Freedom of Creation

The Electric Tiger Land campaign was created in 2008 by Amsterdam-based advertising agency StrawberryFrog, as part of Onitsuka Tiger's Made of Japan brand strategy. The *Electric Light Shoe*, the focus of the campaign, pays homage to the ambience and energy of Japan. Designed by Dutch agency Freedom of Creation (FOC), the one meter long sculpture featured a city within a shoe, incorporating elements from Tokyo's skyline including neon signage, various modes of transport, markets and vending machines. Many of the features were individually lit by one of 300 LED lights and there was also an iPod dock that enabled ambient sounds to be played through hidden speakers.

The incredibly detailed shoe was created by FOC designers Janne Kyttanen and Mads Thomsen using rapid-prototyping technology – a type of three dimensional printing which uses successive layers of liquid, powder or sheet material to build a 3D model. The shoe was then shot by Japanese photographer Satoshi Minakawa. In addition, StrawberryFrog also produced seven 70cm-long sculptures (two for Germany and one each for France, UK, Korea, Australia and Japan), as well as 15 smaller 40cm-long versions, to be displayed in stores worldwide.

Art   279

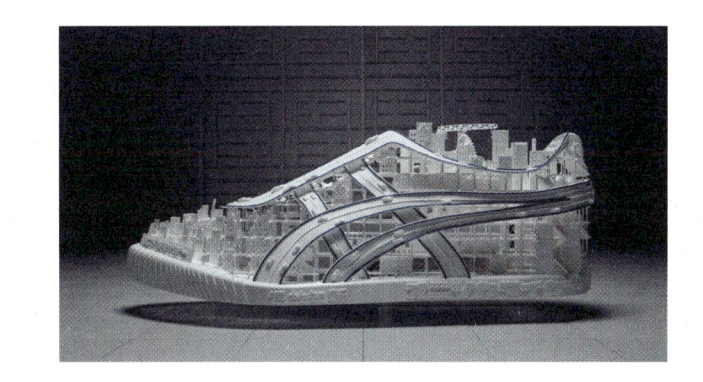

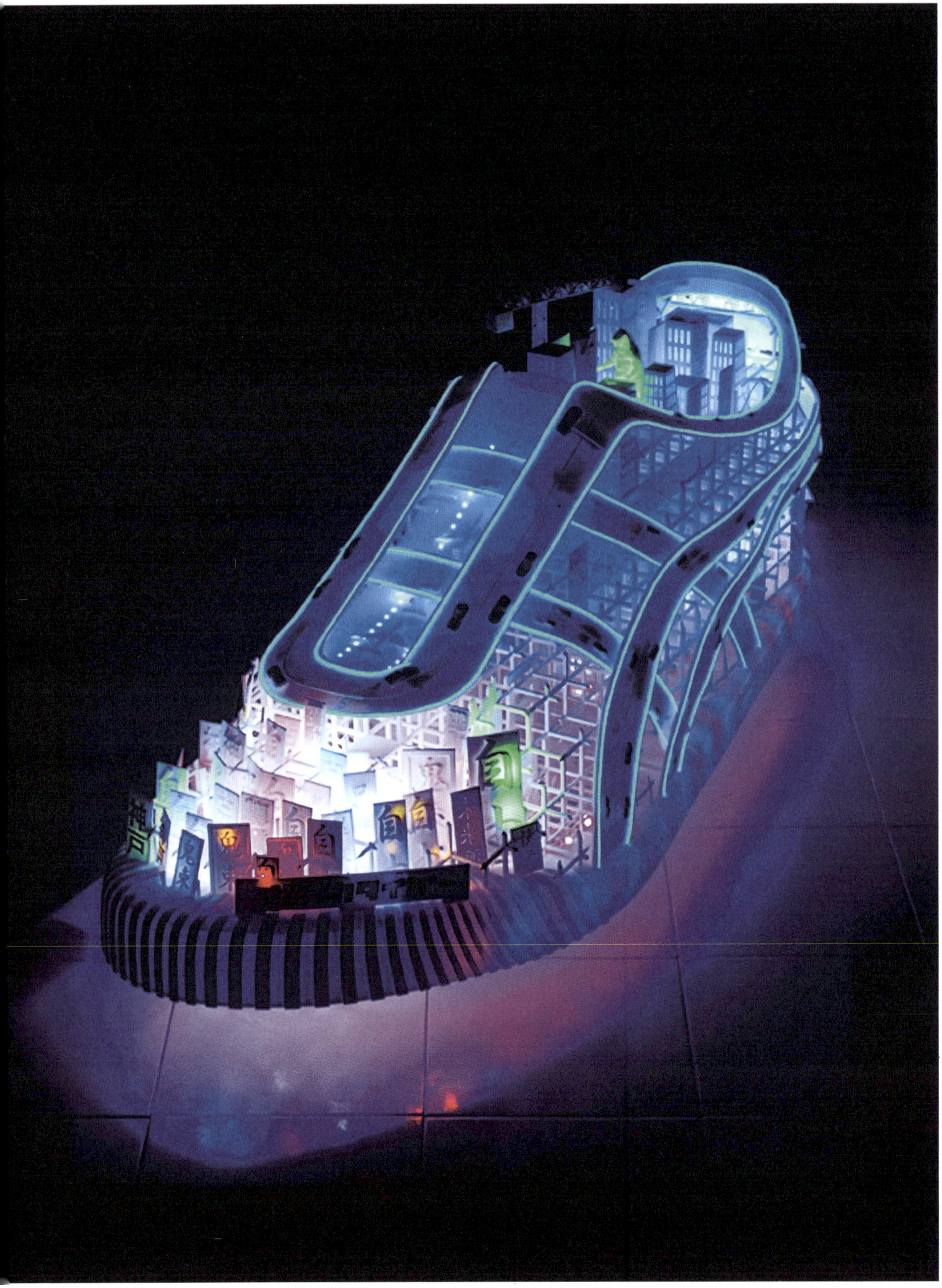

Freedom of Creation

Art

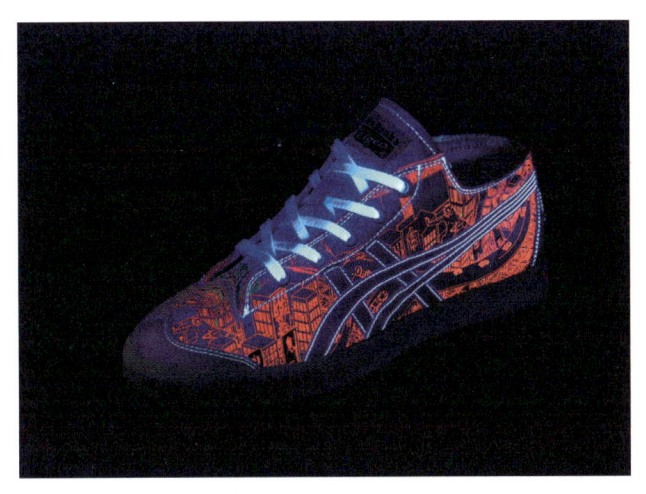

281

Advertising is usually inspired by product, but in this case a special rendering of the *Electric Light Shoe* model was created for three limited edition Onitsuka Tiger shoes. The Sunotore 72 models (above) incorporate reflective and light-emitting materials in their design. T-shirts using light-reflective inks were also produced as part of the project.

Jethro Haynes

Jethro Haynes is a London-based illustrator, designer and model-maker whose work uses a diverse selection of artistic approaches including textile prints, photographs, hand-drawn posters and paintings. Inspired by the world, his imagination and his love of model-making, Haynes built up a fertile working relationship with London-based Pointer Footwear (no longer trading), creating art pieces and advertising for the company. He would start with the shoes themselves: 'They are the blank canvas, and different shoes lend themselves to different styles of landscape; for example, a mountainous environment is more appropriate for a high-top sneaker.' Working in conjunction with design studio Hudson-Powell, Haynes created the dioramas to roughly 1:500 scale, as the starting point is always a UK size 8 shoe. They are extremely time-consuming to make, as a large number of the parts have to be handcrafted or sourced from a local model shop. 'We always manage to make everything really difficult for ourselves,' says Haynes, 'by having ideas that, once spoken of, can't be overlooked.'

Art   283

Sibalom (above) is the first in a series of dioramas created for Pointer Footwear. It's a depiction of a beautiful, almost untouched rainforest, which has begun to be cut down. 'Little do the loggers know that they have disturbed an ancient and sacred place containing a giant flower-beast.' The second of the Pointer Footwear dioramas is *Jahra* (left). 'There is an oil refinery owned and operated by Black Sun Industries. A helicopter from the refinery has crashed into the pipeline, causing an oil spill which has manifested itself as a huge oil monster about to attack the refinery.' *Doomsday Asteroid 2004 MN4* (opposite) is set in space. 'Humans are trying to destroy the asteroid before it reaches Earth, but inside the rock lies a beast with other ideas.'

Rosie Lee

London-based creative agency Rosie Lee took the original design inspiration of three iconic sneakers and used it to create this trio of conceptual CGI sculptures. The Air Max 1 (right) pays tribute to the inside-out-structure of the Centre Pompidou – one of Tinker Hatfield's principal references for the design of the Air Max 1 back in 1987. The construction closely resembles the inside-out-structure of the original building, designed by Renzo Piano and Richard Rogers in 1977.

The Air Max 90, originally created by Hatfield in 1990, was as eagerly adopted by crate-diggers as it was by runners so, as a nod to its music-related heritage, Rosie Lee chose to rebuild the iconic silhouette using speaker stacks (below). Finally, the Air Max 95 (bottom) was rebuilt as an anatomical model, referencing Sergio Lozano's radical and anatomy-inspired design from 1995.

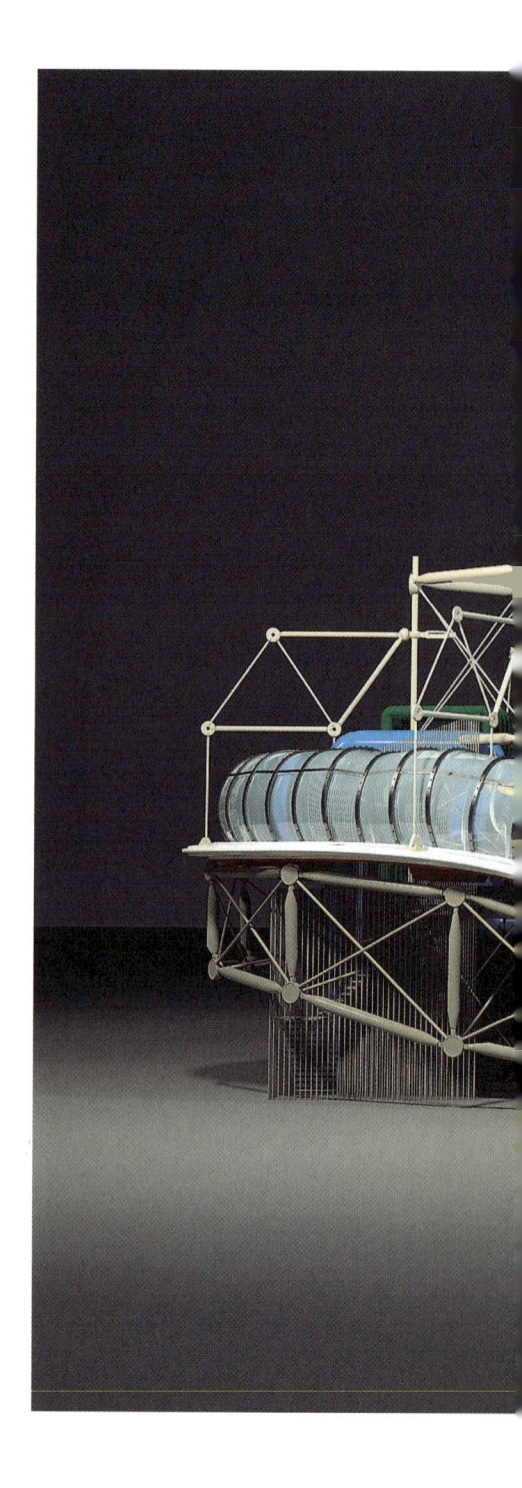

Art   ●   285

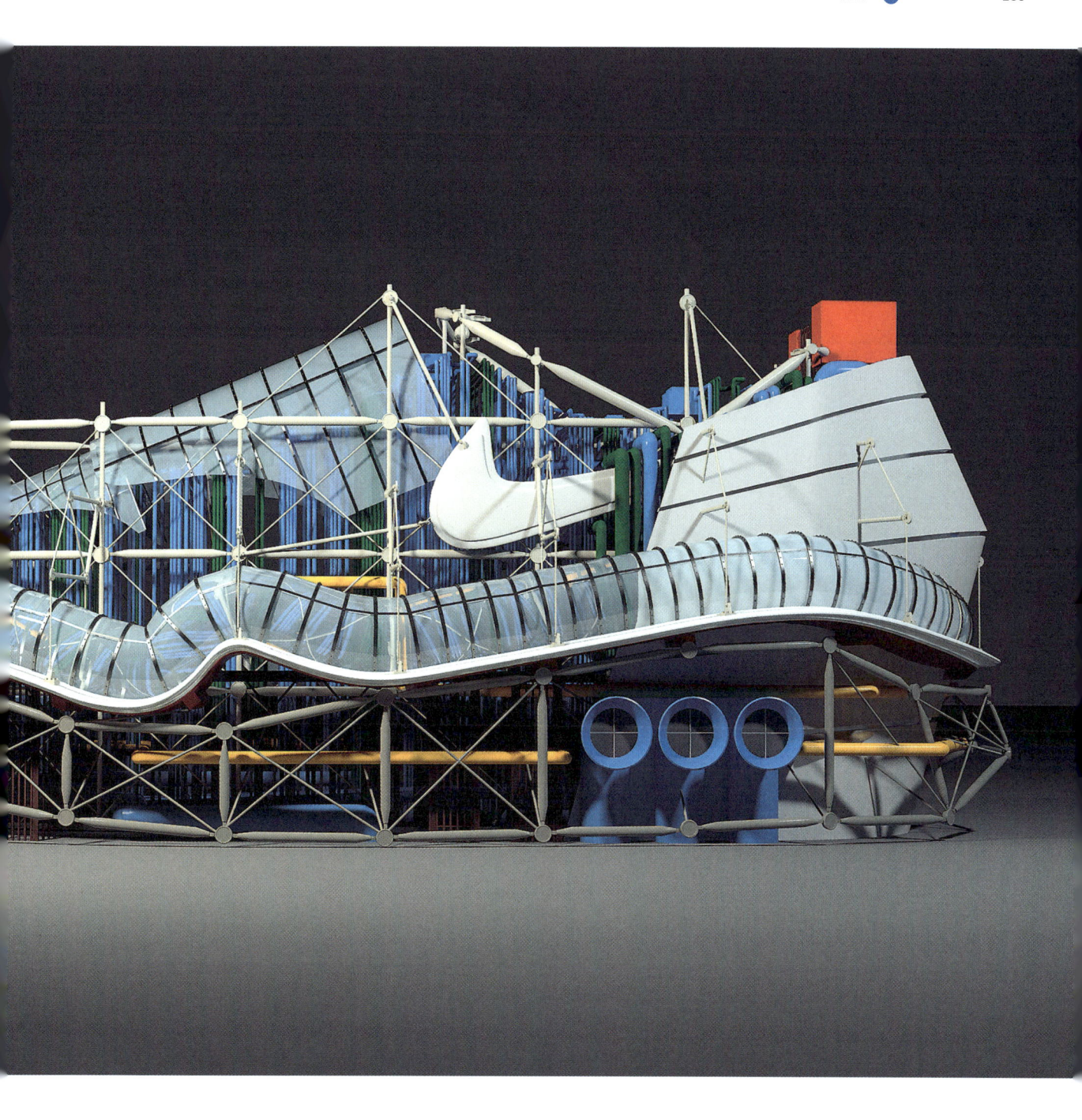

Art

Diva Eisaku Kito

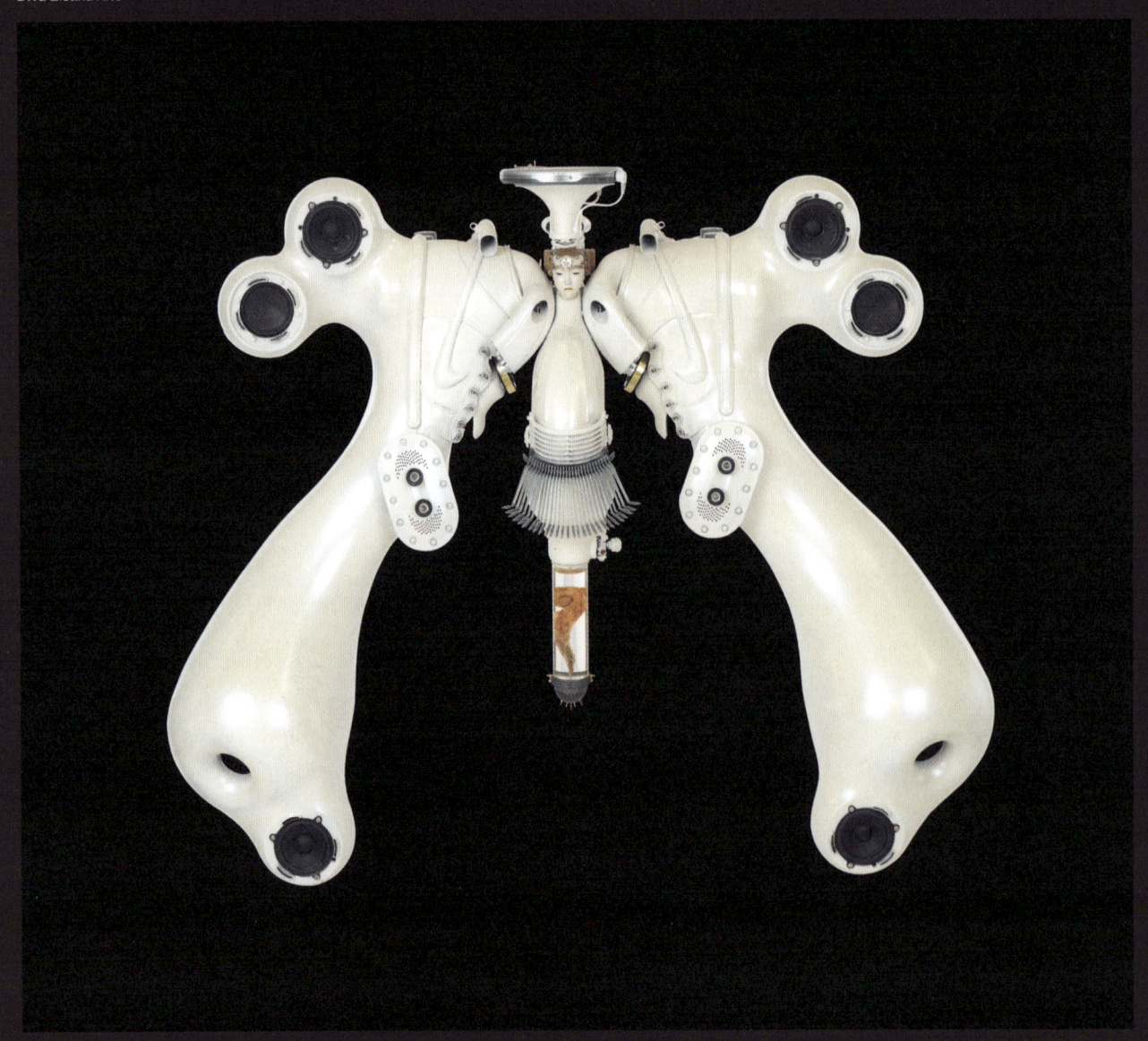

White Dunk: Evolution of an Icon

How does an object and what it represents inspire you? What form would that inspiration take using your imagination and creative skills as an artist? What paths would different creative minds take from the same starting point? These are the questions that Nike's Mark Parker asked a diverse group of Japanese artists, including animators, illustrators, toy-makers, graphic designers, model-makers and comic writers. Each was given the brief to respond to an unlikely source of inspiration; a white Nike Dunk basketball shoe (left).

The exhibition White Dunk: Evolution of an Icon took its name directly from the point of reference. In American basketball, towards the end of the 1970s, an exciting new technique had emerged on the court, popularly known as the slam-dunk. Nike began designing sports shoes that they hoped would become synonymous with this phenomenon and, inspired by their already successful Air Jordan and Air Force, Nike debuted the Dunk in 1985. The White Dunk exhibition opened in Paris in 2003, before moving to Tokyo in 2004 (with the exterior of the venue designed to look like a Nike Dunk SB silver box) and finally to Los Angeles in 2005.

Art 287

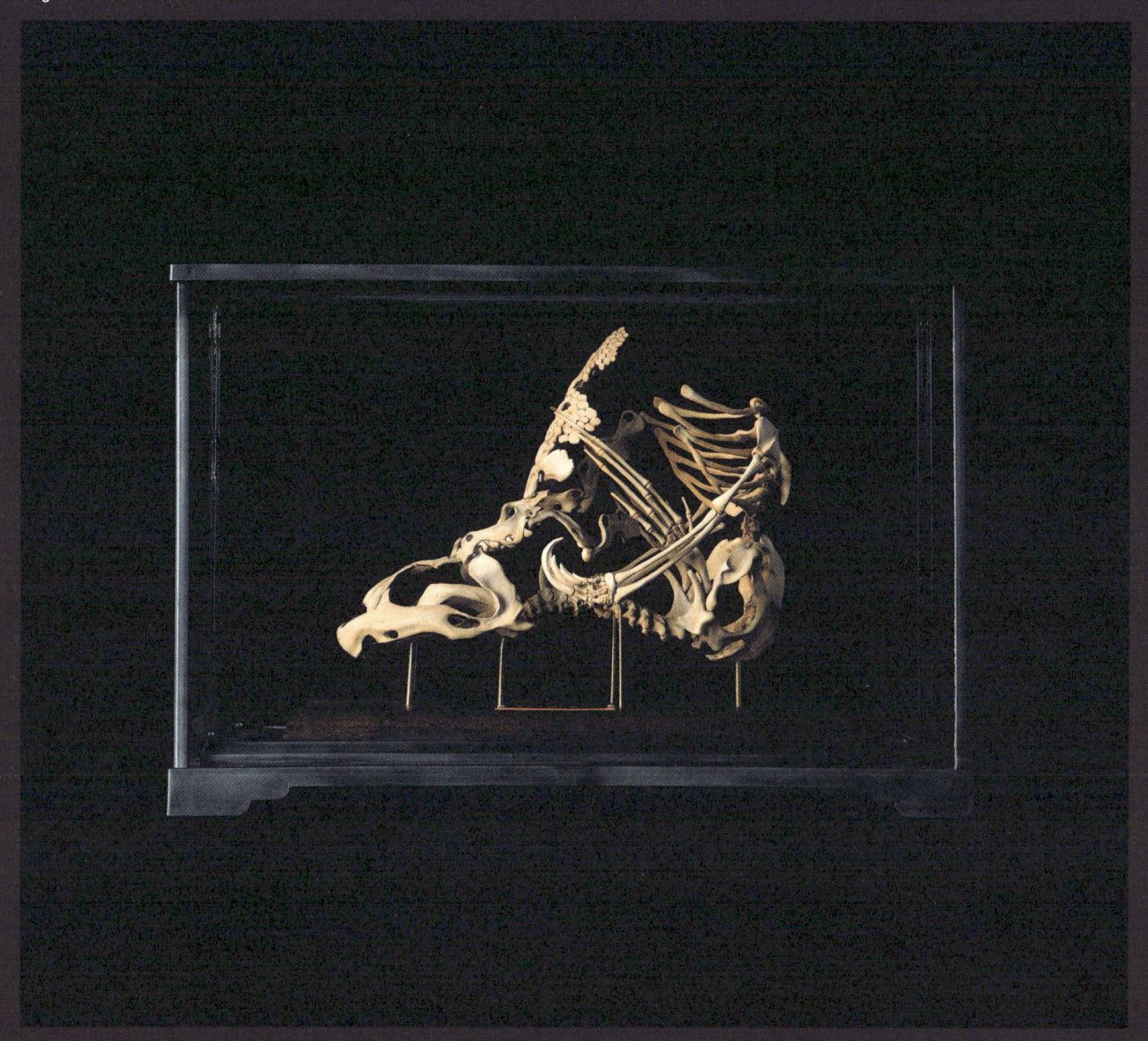

Original Piece Jun Goshima

Nikeman Keiichi Sato

Double Dunk Masakazu Katsura

My Double Dunk Junichi Taniguchi

Untitled Hitoshi Yoneda

Fireball Kow Yokoyama

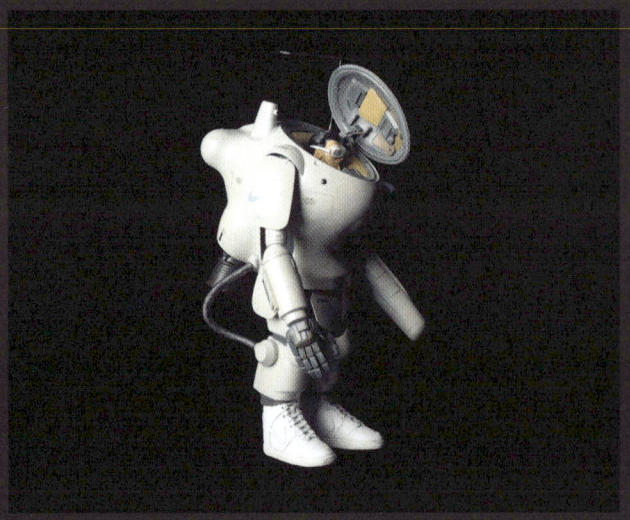

White Dunk — Art — 289

Rakugaki Dunk Katsuya Terada

White Dunk EX Naoki Sato

Untitled Shinichi Yamashita

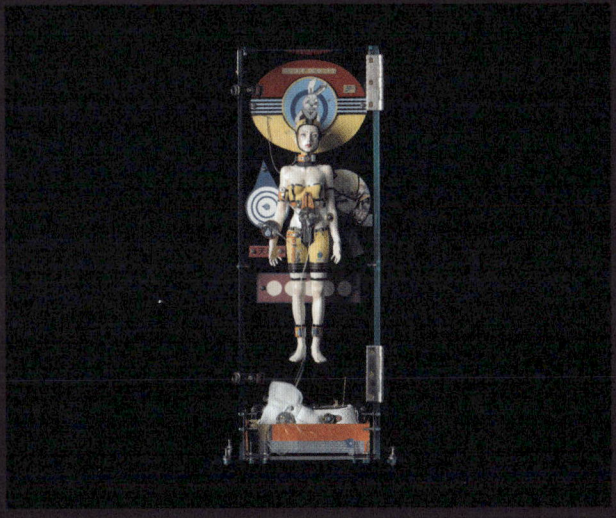

Vampire UV Yasushi Nirasawa

Defense!! Yoshikazu Yasuhiko

White Dunk   Art   291

My White Dunk Atsushi Kamijyo

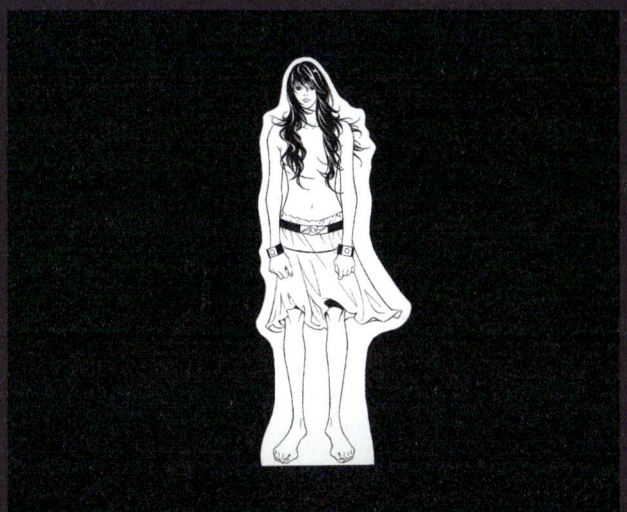

Untitled Eiji Nakayama

Untitled Yuji Oniki

Untitled Yukio Fujioka

Dunk Move Haruo Suekichi

Nike Goddess Hajime Sorayama

Let's Dunk Yasuhito Udagawa

Nike Robot Shuji Yonezawa

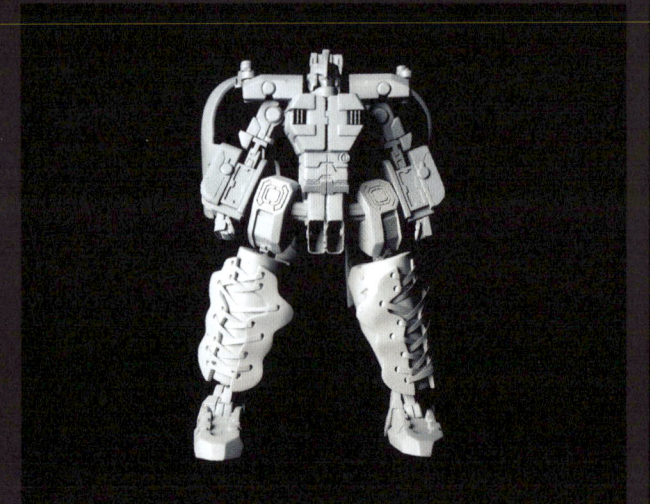

Farmer Takayuki Takeya

Path to the Sky Kenji Ando

Untitled Yukihiro Suzuki

Nick Glackin

Manchester-based photographer Nick Glackin, aka Glackster, has taken the concept of footwear photography to a whole new, and much smaller, level. The idea for Glackin's miniature scenes started in 2013 when he entered a Nike competition (held in conjunction with sneaker store size?) to showcase Air Max in a creative way. Inspired by architectural 1:76 scale model figures, Glackin's idea was to show just how 'big' Air Max was in the UK. Since then, Glackin has created numerous sneaker-based dioramas that focus around the scale figures, or 'microdudes', including the elderly lead protagonists of Harold and Maud. Each scene is inspired directly by the design of the starring shoe, and can take weeks to complete. Shown here, from left to right, are scenes featuring the Patta Nike Air Max 1 'Monarch' (2021), the Nike Air Max 1 City Pack 'Amsterdam' (2020) and Parra Nike Air Max 1 'Red Light District' (2005) and the Parra Nike Air Max 1 Friends & Family (2018).

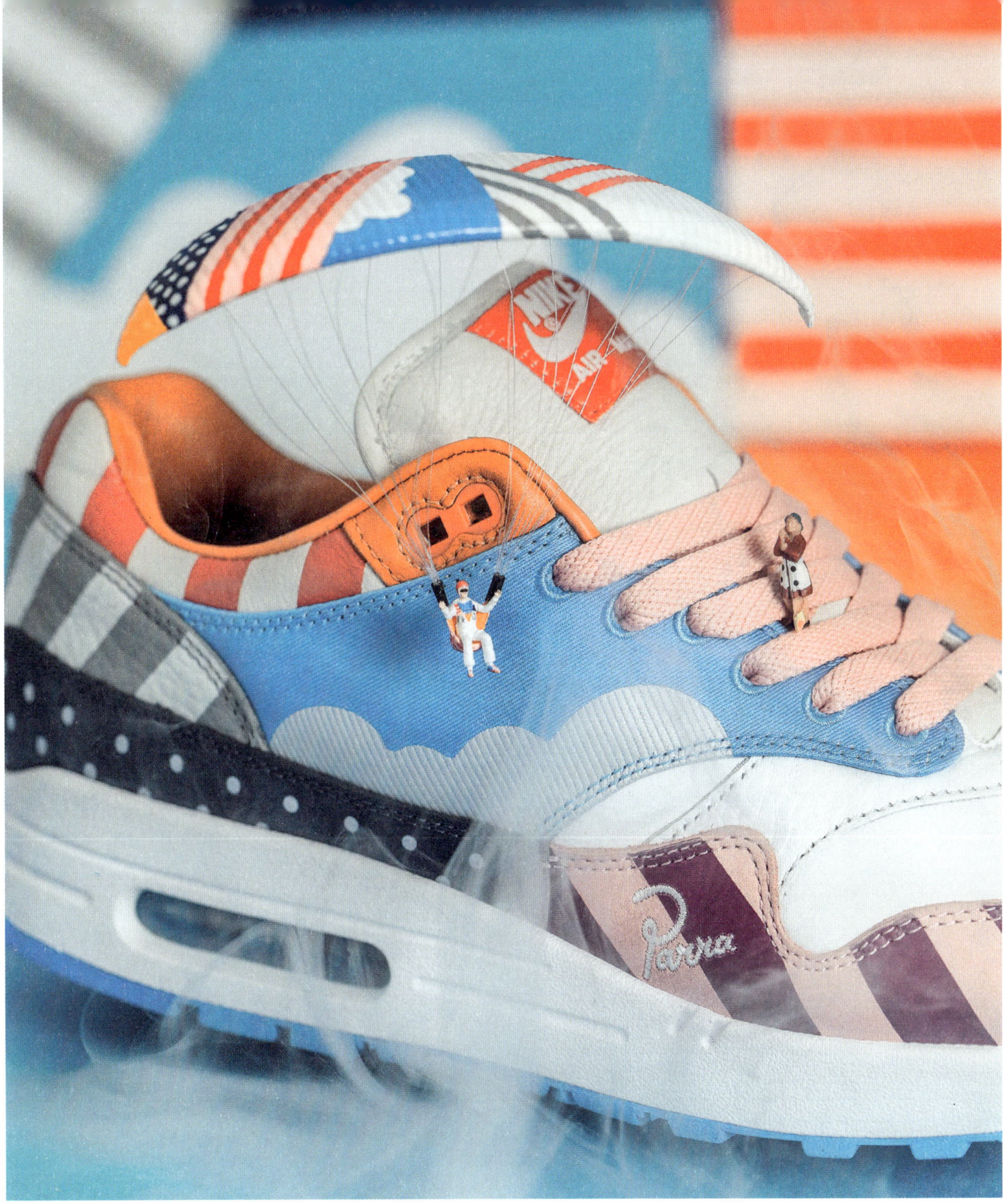
Parra

"Off-White™ for NIKE
"NIKE ZOOM FLY"
Beaverton, Oregon USA
NIKE
OFF-WHITE C/O NIKE
C. 2017 "ZIP TIE"
"MICRODU ES"" "FAM"
D
"SHOELACES"

Nick Glackin   Art   297

Miniature scenes featuring the Virgil Abloh Nike Zoom Fly SP 'The Ten' from 2017 (opposite), the Nike Dunk Low Pro SB 'Civilist' from 2020 (below left), the Nike Air Max 97 'London Summer Of Love' from 2019 (below, top right) and the Staple New Balance 575 'White Pigeon' from 2009 (below, bottom right).

Gary Baseman

Los Angeles-based Gary Baseman is an award-winning toy designer, illustrator, artist and Emmy award-winning director. Baseman's work is highly influenced by Japanese culture and he is probably best known for his toys (including Dunces, Fire Water Bunnies and Egg Qees), many of which feature in this creation. Part of Onitsuka Tiger's Made Of Japan campaign, this 150cm-long shoe sculpture is based on the Fabre 74. It is made from Baseman's toys plus Japanese objects such as sushi, origami, lucky cats, noodles and chopsticks, with koi carp used to make the Onitsuka Tiger stripes.

Art   299

Art & Sole
Screenprint Series

Since the publication of the original edition of *Art & Sole* in 2008, Intercity commissioned a series of sneaker-inspired screenprints created by leading artists and designers from around the globe. Each print was limited to an edition of 50 and was signed, numbered and emboss-stamped for authenticity. Commissioned artists included James Jarvis (*Sole Inspector*, below left), Kustaa Saksi, Ben Drury (*The City*, below middle), Jiro Bevis (see page 13), Geneviève Gauckler, Darcel Dissapoints (*Never Knot*, below right), and Mark Ward.

    The last in the series of artworks was by Rob Flowers, a UK-based illustrator whose distinctive style is defined by bold colour, playful forms and eccentric characters. From aglets to outsoles, his print entitled *Anatomy of a Sneaker* (opposite) brings to life the various elements that make up a pair of sneakers – a fitting and informative way to sign off a book about the relationship between art and sneakers.

AGLET
INSOLE
FOXING
TRIM
FOXING
OUTSOLE
COLLAR
LACES
FOXING
EYELET
HEEL PATCH
1/4 PANEL
EYESTAY
HEEL COUNTER
ORNAMENT
UPPERS
VAMP
TOE BOX
AIR UNIT
MIDSOLE

Index

Page numbers in italics refer to illustrations

Abe, Chitose 63, 141
Abloh, Virgil 17, 88, 120, 236, 241, *256*, 257
Adams, Cey 70, 74
adidas 16, 17, 34, 38, 40, 64, 67, 76, 77
 adicolor 17, *17*, 68, *68*, 70–75, 159
 Anniversary Series 156, *159*
 Daniel Arsham shoes 22, *23*
 IRAK NY 19, *19*
 Originals Skateboarding 154, *154*, 155, *155*
 Silverbirch SPZL 161, *161*
 Spezial Pulsebeat SPZL 16, *16*
 Stan Smiths 70, *71*, *73*, *75*, 165, *165*
 Superskate Low 110, *110*
 Superstar 154, 156, *156–9*, 160, *160*, 165, *165*
 Superstar II *71*, *73*, 75
 ZX750 35, *35*
Also Known As (AKA) 78, *78–9*
Ando, Kenji *293*
Andrews, Vinti 268
Arigato, Axel 64, 65, *65*
Arizumi, James 171
Armstrong, Lance 119
Arsham, Daniel 22, *23*
ASICS 55, *55*, 144, 145, *145*, 231, 242
Aspen, Gary 161

Baldwin, John 212–15
Bankhead, Will 36
Baseman, Gary 146, 298–9
Basquiat, Jean-Michel 142, 164
Bathing Ape, A 39, 58
Beastie Boys, the 64
Beekmans, Riëlle 186, 188
Bembury, Salehe 236, *256*, 257
Benedikt, Allen 78
Betts, B. J. 67
Bevis, Jiro 12, 300
Biggler, Denis 193
Bleumink, Patty 186
Bloc, Alex *see* LX One
Blondel chocolaterie 192, 193
Bodé, Mark 112
Bodé, Vaughn 112, *112*, *113*
Bodecker, Sandy 173
Bratrud, Todd 171, *172*, 173
Brinkers, Erwin 135
Bryden, Steve 40
Budnitz, Paul 146, 148
Buffet, Bernard 169
Busenitz, Dennis 77

Campbell, Thomas 56
CES 117
Chen, Edison 14, 94
Cheung, Jeffrey 175
Chocolate Skateboards 168
Claw Money 115, *115*
Cliver, Sean 150, *150–53*, 168, 174
Closky, Claude 72
CLOT 34, 38, 94, *94–5*, 141
Converse 38, 64, 111, 116, 135, 231
 Chuck Taylor All Star 38, 120, 136, 137
Coq Sportif, Le 144, 145, *145*
Coolrain Studio 253, 254
Costello, Craig (KR) 41
Crooked Tongues 64, 67–9, *73*, 74
 Confederation of Villainy *66–7*, 67
Crude Oil 78
Cuendet, Philippe 192, 193, 195, 199
Cummins, Kevin 18

Dalton, Jess 65
David (Jules) Design 232
DC Shoes 56, *56*, *57*, 58, 99
Delta 166, *167*, 186, 188
Deng, Jason 174
Desmond, Mike 98
Dissapoints, Darcel 300
Dixon Goulden, Leon 40
//DIY 192, 195, 199
Dizmology 117
Donnelly, Brian *see* KAWS

Drury, Ben 21, 36–7, 38, 118, 261, 300
Dungen, Danny van den 135

Eblen, Thomas *see* McCoy, Blondey
ESPO (Steve Powers) 92, *92–3*
Etnies 197, 231
Evolution of an Icon (exhibition) 169, 286
Ewok 117
Experimental Jetset 135, *135*

Factory Records 16, 18
Fafi *72*, 74
Fairey, Shepard 56, *57*, 117
Faust 174
Federici, Lorenzo *see* LORENZ.OG
Fiasco, Lupe 261
FibreOps 262
Flores, David *133*
Flowers, Rob 300
Forbes, Reese 168
FPAR 173
Franklin, Josh *see* Stash
Freedom of Creation 278–81
Friedman, Matty 63
Frost, Phil 56
Fujioka, Yukio *291*
Fujishiro, Shigeki 34
Fujiwara, Hiroshi 138–41
FUTURA (Lenny McGurr) 21, 26, 117, 118–23, 169, 170, 175

Gander, Ryan 35
Garcia, Bobbito 159
Gasius (Russell Maurice) 20, *20*, 186
Gauckler, Geneviève 300
Gee, Huck 146
Georges, Stephan 'Maze' 98, *100*
Gesner, Eli Morgan 168
Giant, Mike 110, *110*
Glackin, Nick 294–7
Glover, Donald 64
Goldie 161
Gonzales, Mark (Gonz) 64, 76–7
Goshima, Jun *287*
Gravis Art collective 166–7
Green, Doze 117
Greenwood, Di'Orr 175
Gubin, Illya Goldman 65

Haaften, Woes van 186, 191
Haçienda, The 18, *18*
Hagelaars, Mathieu 242
Haring, Keith *72*
Haroshi *178*, 179, *179*
Harrington, Steven 32
Hatfield, Tinker 99, 138, 253, 284
Hayashi, Taka 48–9, *132*
Haynes, Jethro 282–3
Haze, Eric 64, 114, *114*
Hecox, Evan 56, 154, 155
Hirata, Hideaki *290*
Hirst, Damien 136
Hoka, Merrell 24, 26, *26*
Hook, Peter 18
Horvath, David 146
Howell, Andy 56

I Have Pop 180–85
INSA 208–11
Intercity 6–7, 12, 251, 300
Ip, Billy 94
IRAK NY 19, *19*

Jaccottet, Laurence 192, 199
Jackson, Johanna 56
James, Mark 264
James, Todd *132*
Janssen, Pieter *see* Parra
Jarvis, James 40, 300
Jarvis, Shaniqwa 137
Jenkins, Paul 252
Jeremyville 116, *116*
JUSE 180–81, 186, 191

Kamiya, Atsushi *291*
Katsura, Masakazu *287*
Kaupas, Natas 56, *57*, 168
KAWS (Brian Donnelly) *56*, 58–63, *132*
Kelly, Ben 18
Kidrobot 146–9
Kilgore, Bruce 274
Kim, Steven 253
Kinsey, Dave 56, *57*, 154, 155
Kirkum, Helen 28, *29–31*
Kishimoto, Eley 261
Kito, Eisaku *286*
Klein, Yves 199
KR *see* Costello, Craig
Krink 41
Krooked Skateboarding 76
Kuraishi, Kazuki 35
Kyttanen, Janne 278

Lady Brown *252*, 253
Lambie, Jim *72*
Lankin, Ari 74
Lau, Michael 168, 258–63
Lavelle, James 21, 36, 118
Law, Chris 64–5
Le, Chris 274
Lee, Coolrain 254–7
Leon, Michael 56
Leonard, Justin 159
Leyva, Jesse 114
Liechti, Ivan 192, 199
Limited Edt 55, *55*
LORENZ.OG 236–41
Lozano, Sergio 206, 284
Luedecke, Tom 78, 96, 98
Lundy, Chris 98, *100*
LX One (Alex Bloc) New Balance 1500 103, *103*
Lyons, Kevin 37, 38

McCoy, Blondey (Thomas Eblen) 160
McFetridge, Geoff 42–3, 45, 47, *132*, 168
McGurr, Lenny *see* FUTURA
Machado, Mark *see* Mister Cartoon
McLaughlin, Nicole 24, 26
McMorran, Matty 65
McMullen, Bill *71*, *73*, *75*, 147
Maeda, John 143
Maharishi 164, 261
Manchester United Football Club 16
Marok 166, *166*
Martin, Shantell 12, 14, *14*, *15*
Mastermind 34
Maurice, Russell 186, 191, *see* Gasius
Mdot 149
Medicom 168, 170, 174, 265
Methamphibian 56, *57*
MF Doom 251
Minakawa, Satoshi 278
Minami, Kenzo 142
Mister Cartoon (Mark Machado) 108–9
Morris, Steph 216–21
MŌTUG 117, *117*
Mr. A *see* Saraiva, André
MRBAILEY *256*, 257
Mr Sabotage (SBTG; Mark Ong) 54–5, 168
MSCHF 246–9
Mulder, Richard 168
Munoz, Tony *133*
Murakami, Takashi 274

Nakayama, Eiji *291*
Nash Money (Alex Nash) 250–51
Neckface 50, *51*, 168
Neighbourhood 34
Neilan, Toby 222–3
New Balance 55, 64, 67, 114, *238*
 New Balance 1500 103, *103*
News 186
Ng, Jeff *see* Staple, Jeff
Nicholson, Matthew 12
Nike 7, 12, 36, 38, 58, 67,114, 263, *263*
 Virgil Abloh's The Ten 88, *88–91*
 Air Footscape Woven 138, *138*, 139, *139*
 Air Force 1 41, 58, 88, *99*, *100*, 141

Index

Air Force 1 'Crocodile' 272
Air Force 1 '404'/'404 Error' 273
Air Force 1 Fukijama Turtle 101, *101*
Air Force 1 'Invisible' 272
Air Force 1 'Laser' 272
Air Force 1 'Pigeon Fury' 55, *55*
Air Force 1 'Skeleton' 272
Air Force 1 Off-White 'Solis' 241, *241*
Air Force 1 sneaker speakers 251, *251*
Air Jordan 1 'Dior' 216, *216*
Air Jordan 1 High 'DW' 205, *205*
Air Jordan 1 Low 140, *140*
Air Jordan 1 Off White 220, 221
Air Jordan 1 Retro 204, *204*
Air Jordan 3s 101, *101*
Air Jordan 4 Off-White 'Dusk' 241, *241*
Air Jordan 5 Off-White 'Dusk' 241, *241*
Air Max 1 36, *36*, 37, 146, *146*, 162, *162*, 206, 253, *253*, 284
Air Max 1 'Cherrywood' 229, *229*
Air Max 1 'Parra' 229, *229*
Air Max 1 'Red Light District' 228, *228*
Air Max 90 'Tongue N' Cheek' 36, *36*
Air Max 90 58, 88, 162, *162*, 182, 186, 188, 191, 206, 211, *211*, 284
Air Max 90 Current 36, *36*, 58
Air Max 90 Current 'Silent Listener' 36, *36*
Air Max 90 Off-White 'Menta' 241, *241*
Air Max 95 206, *207*, 268, 284
Air Max 95 Comme des Garçons 236, 238, *238*
Air Max 95 'DW' 200
Air Max 95 'Genesis' *236*, 237
Air Max 95 'Summerhouse OG' 237, *237*
Air Max 97 88
Air Max 97 Off-White *240*, 241
Air Max 360 37, *38*, 38, 195, 224
Air Max Sunder 'Dusk' 238, *239*
Air Stab 37, 39, *39*, 206
Air Talaria/Talaria Chukka 96, *96*, 97
Air Vapormax 216, *217*
Air Wildwood 262, *262*
Air Woven Boot 138, *139*
Air Zoom Spiridon 162, 229, *229*
Air Zoom Terra Tattoo 102, *102*
'Bel Air Max' 250, *250*
Claw Blazer 115, *115*
Cortez 12, 108, *108*
The Dunk 286
Dunk High Pro SB 'Brain Wreck' 172, *172*
Dunk High Pro SB 'Decon' 175, *175*
Dunk High Pro SB 'DUNKLE' 21, *21*, 36, 170
Dunk High Pro SB 'Ethel' *210*, 211
Dunk High Pro SB 'Faust' 174, *174*
Dunk High Pro SB 'FLOM' 118, *118*, 169
Dunk High Pro SB 'FPAR' 173, *173*
Dunk High Pro SB 'Gasparilla' 151, *151*
Dunk High Pro SB 'GDP' 173
Dunk High Pro SB 'Iron Maiden' 169
Dunk High Pro SB 'Krampus' 151, *151*
Dunk High Pro SB Premium 'F2T.50' 123, *123*
Dunk High Pro SB 'Send Help' 171, *171*
Dunk High Pro SB 'Skund Dunk' 172, *172*
Dunk High Pro SB 'Strawberry' 173
Dunk Low Pro SB 'Abstract Art' 230, *230*
Dunk Low Pro SB 'Black Pigeon' 105, *105*, 173, *219*, 221
Dunk Low Pro SB 'Bleached Aqua' 122, *122*
Dunk Low Pro SB 'Brand Logo Sample' 173, *173*
Dunk Low Pro SB 'Charity' 169
Dunk Low Pro SB 'Chocolate' 168, *168*
Dunk Low Pro SB 'Chunky Dunky' 174, *174*, 216
Dunk Low Pro SB 'Cliver' 153, *153*, 174
Dunk Low Pro SB 'Disposable' 151, *151*
Dunk Low Pro SB 'London' 169, *169*
Dunk Low Pro SB 'Medicom 1, 2 and 3' 170, *170*
Dunk Low Pro SB 'Medicom Toy' 174, *174*
Dunk Low Pro SB 'Neckface' 174
Dunk Low Pro SB 'NRF Edition' 104, *104*
Dunk Low Pro SB 'Panda Pigeon' 105, *105*, *219*, 221
Dunk Low Pro SB 'Paris' 168, 169, *169*, 221, *221*
Dunk Low Pro SB 'Parra'/'Parra 21' 173, 174
Dunk Low Pro SB 'Pigeon' 104, 105, *105*, 170, *218*, 221
Dunk Low Pro SB Premium 'SBTG' 54, *54*
Dunk Low Pro SB 'Pushead' 170, *170*
Dunk Low Pro SB 'Pushead II' 172, *172*

Dunk Low Pro SB 'Reese Denim' 168, *168*, 170
Dunk Low Pro SB 'SBTG', 54, 171
Dunk Low Pro SB 'Strangelove' *152*, 153, 174
Dunk Low Pro SB 'Street Hawker' 174, *174*
Dunk Low Pro SB 'There' 175, *175*
Dunk Low Pro SB 'Tokyo' 169, *169*
Dunk Low Pro SB 'Verdy' 175, *175*
Dunk Low Pro SB 'Wasted Youth' 174, *174*
Dunk Low Pro SB 'White Widow' 173, *173*
Dunk Low 'What the Dunk' 171, *171*, *218*, 221
Earth Day Collection 32, 33, *33*
HTM 138, 139, *139*, 222
Laser Project 98, *98–101*
Our Force 1 (OF1) 270, *271*
Three Be@rbrick Project 171, 265, *265*
Transformers 266, *266–7*
Vandal High 115, *115*
The Vault 168–75
Zoom Fly SP 88
90X90 186–91
Nirasawa, Yasushi *290*
Nishiyama, Tetsu 'Tet' 173
NYC Lase 117

Okamoto, Taro *74*
Okten, Cemal 252
Ong, Mark *see* Mr Sabotage
Oniki, Yuji *291*

Pagotto, Benoit 274
Pane 186
Parker, Mark 80, 138, 179, 286
Parra (Pieter Janssen) 168, 224–31
Patta 135
Perlot, Leon 186, 188
Philips, Chad 148
+41 9, 192–7
Poon, Kevin 94
Powers, Steve *see* ESPO
Price, Martin 252
Project Playground 159
Pucci, Emilio *73*
Puma 14, 24, 67
  Clyde 14, *14*, *15*
  Platform Strap 14, *15*
  Suede 14, *15*, 26, *26*, 251
  see also Bodé, Vaughn; Crooked Tongues
Pushead (Brian Schroeder) 170, 172

Quinones, Lee 156, 157

Rademaker, Julien 232–5
REBEL8 110
Reebok 24, 142, 143, 144
  Basquiat Reeboppers 164
  Club C Geo Mid 24, *25*
  I Am What I Am campaign 142, 164
  Instapump Fury 142, *142*, 144, 145, *145*
  Pump Omni Zone IX 241, *241*
  Ventilator Timetanium 143, *143*
  Zig Kinetica 'R58' 142
Rivellini, Tommaso 83
RMX EQT Support Runner 19
Roos, Yamandu 186
Rose, Aaron 45
Rosie Lee (agency) 163, 284–5
RTFKT 7, 274–7
Run On Air 186

Sacai 63
  LD Waffle 141, *141*
Sachs, Tom 83, *85*
  Nikecraft 82–7
Saksi, Kustaa 300
Salomon ACS Pro 'Dusk' *238*
Saraiva, André (Mr. A) 56, *57*, 165
Sato, Keiichi *287*
Sato, Naoki *289*
Scharf, Kenny 64
Schroeder, Brian *see* Pushead
Scott, Jeremy *72*
Scott, Travis 140
Semmoh, Clyde 186

Seven Eight Under 257
Sewell, Mark 166, *166*
SHFU 63
Sky High Farm 62, 63
Smith, Mark 98, *99*, 101, *101*
So, Eric 56
Solebox 185
Sorayama, Hajime *291*
SSUR 38, 56, *57*
Stallard, Rose 12
Stan Smiths *see* adidas
Staple, Jeff 7, 8, 104–7, 168
Stash (Josh Franklin) *123*, 123–9, *132*
Stolk, Marieke 135
StrawberryFrog 278
Stress (rapper) 197
Studio Hagel 242–5
Stüssy 38, 40, *40*
Suekichi, Haruo *291*
Suzuki, Yukihiro *293*
Swoosh 7, 270–73

Takahashi, Youichi 156
Takara Tomy/Tomy 266
Takeya, Takayuki *292*
Tamiya The Hornet radio controlled car 144, *144*
Taniguchi, Junichi *288*
Terada, Katsuya 102, *102*, *289*
There Skateboards 175
Thibault, Bastien 192, 193
Thomsen, Mads 278
Tiger, Onitsuka 278, 281, 298
Tilt 146, 149
TKID 170 117
Toofly 117
Transport for London 162–3

Ubiq 144, 145, *145*
Udagawa, Yasuhito *292*
Uniqlo 38, 40
UNKLE 21, 36
Unorthodox Styles (U Dox) 64, 67
Upper Playground 158

Valentino 242
Van Doren, Paul 49
Vans 24, 36, 38, 55, 58, 99, 231
  Authentic Pro S 150, *150*
  Half Cab 231, *231*
  Mid Skool and Old Skool 46, 47, 55, *55*, *132*, 150
  The Simpsons shoes 130–33
  Syndicate Authentic "S" 'Mister Cartoon' 109, *109*
  Vault by Vans 26, *27*, *46*, 47, 48, *48*, 52, *52–3*, 69
Vasilev, Steven 274
Verdy 174, 175
Voos, Ido de 186

Wang, Ruohan 33
Ward, Mark 40, 134, *134*, 300
Warhol, Andy 103, 156, 157
Watanabe, Jun 144
West, Kanye 94
White, Dave 200–7
White, Dondi 111
White, Michael 111
White Dunk: Evolution of an Icon 286–93
Wieden + Kennedy 80, *80–81*
Williams, Pharrell 92, 108
Williams, Robert 52
Williamson, Russell 64, *see* Unorthodox Styles
Wood, Simon 'Woody' 250
Wood, Wood 72

Y-3 18
Yachty, Lil 236, *256*, 257
Yamamoto, Yohji 18
Yamashita, Shinichi *289*
Yasuhiko, Yoshikazu *290*
Yokoyama, Hitomi 37, 38, 39
Yokoyama, Kow *288*
Yoneda, Hitoshi *288*
Yonezawa, Shuji *292*

Zoltar 261

Acknowledgements

Dedicated to Stan and Sukhi.

Special thanks to Trystan Thompson and Radley Cook at Intercity, Gavin Lucas, Chris Law, Steph Morris, Michiko Horie, Thomas Rampino, Ethan Stiles, Jason Pullyblank and Jo Rogers.

Images throughout this book were kindly supplied by brands and the artists and designers that have collaborated with them.

Intercity would also like to give thanks to those people behind the scenes who helped make this project happen, including Mark Bodé, Thomas Peiser, Chloe Longstaff, Robeson Mueller, Charlie Morgan, Jason Bass, Joanna Sieghart, Merryl Spence, Louisa Hammond, Karmen Wjinberg, Pat Lo, Jose Cabaco, Helen Sweeney-Dougan, Alison Day, Gary Aspden, Michael Klein, Jess Weinstein, Lauren Kauffman, Kristina Helb, Matt Ting, Brian Lynn, Shirley Schlatka, Allie Emery, Jason Thome, Keith Gulla, Nick Street, Victoria Barrio, Chris Overholser, August Benzien, Eladio Correa, Ashton Maxfield, Cristina Kown, Ashley Roberts, Daniel Glover, Helen Crossley, Barbara Normile, Penny Keen, Gareth Skewis, Peter Stitson, Rosina Budhani, Giorgio de Mitri, Manuel Maggio, Simon Porter, Joris Pol, Chris Love, Damian Loiselle, James Lavelle, Mubi Ali, Jesse Leyva, Jill Meisner, Drieke Leenknegt, Nate Tobecksen, Jason Badden, Mark Rhodes, Leo Sandino-Taylor, Acyde, Sebastian Palmer, Natsuhiko Kubota, Jun Shigenobu, Kasei JJ Lin, Masahiko Yamazaki, Kojiro, John Benson, Mark Ward, Peter Glanvill, Donald Dinwiddie, Jo Lightfoot, the FBRS, Vern Molidor, Sam Quelch, Tom Skipp, Karl Cyprien, Aimee Gray, Alice Perenich, Iris Schultz, Emily Bryson, Ann-Marie James, Sarah Andelman, Diana De Sousa, Zhaxi Danzeng, Joan Koo, Becky Bowler, Catherine Acosta, Alison Marshall, George Pedrick, Kelly Bird, Brent Lichtenberger, Lim Xue Man Nicole, Young Ho Choi, Holly Ferguson, Mark Fleming, David Akin, Daphne Seybold, Kanae Sawaguchi, Marc Chamberlain, Matt Sleep, Asif Husain, Jaileen Rivera, Nicholas Schonberger, Kristen Nguyen, Jeff Staple, Abigail Kim, Mark Suroff, Sky Gellatly, Peter Brockman, Stevey Ryder, Nick Halkias, Mariana Teles, Matthew Jones, Chris White, James Measom, Chris Binns, Greg Burne, Stephen Tetreault, Lukas Bentel, Paul Jenkins, Chris Le, Zachary Rubenfeld, Elen Jones, Tina Persaud, Philip Contos, Jessica Todd, Helen Rochester and Katherine Pitt.

Thanks also to PSC Photography, Anna Purchall and Lee Hind for their help with photography.

Credits

Pages 16 and 160 photography by
Gary Watson and Nathan Damour
Pages 28-31 photography by Bernhard Deckert
Page 35 © Ryan Gander; Courtesy Ryan Gander Studio
Pages 58-63 photography by Brad Bridgers
Page 65, bottom left, photography by
Deo Suveera and Pamela Dimitrov
Page 65, top, courtsey of Axel Arigato
Pages 92-93 photography by Matthew Kuborn
Pages 96-97 photography by Ryan Unruh
Page 112 Cheech Wizard is © Mark Bodé 2008
Page 146, top left, photography by Stevey Ryder
Pages 208-211 photography by Emma Slater
Pages 258-263 all images courtesy of Maharishi
Pages 286-293 photography by Harry Peccinotti

First published in Great Britain in 2025 by Laurence King, an imprint of The Orion Publishing Group Ltd, Carmelite House, 50 Victoria Embankment, London EC4Y 0DZ

An Hachette UK Company

The authorised representative in the EEA is Hachette Ireland, 8 Castlecourt Centre, Castleknock Road, Castleknock, Dublin 15, D15 XTP3 , Republic of Ireland (email: info@hbgi.ie)

10 9 8 7 6 5 4 3 2 1

Text and design © 2025 Intercity
www.intercitystudio.com

Front cover pencil drawing by Steph Morris, featuring the Off-White™ Air Jordan 1 'The Ten' by Virgil Abloh
www.stephfmorris.com

Back cover sneaker collaborations include the adidas RMX EQT Support Runner by IRAK NY, Nike Blazer Low by Sacai & KAWS, NikeCraft Mars Yard 2.0 by Tom Sachs, Vans Half Cab by Parra, Nike SB Dunk Low Pro 'Bleached Aqua' by FUTURA LABORATORIES, Puma Suede by Shantell Martin, Nike Air Force 1 'Blue Pack' Hyperstrike by Stash, Converse Chuck Taylor All Star CX by Shaniqwa Jarvis and Reebok Instapump Fury by Jun Watanabe.

The moral right of Intercity to be identified as the author of this work has been asserted in accordance with the Copyright, Designs and Patents Act of 1988.

Copy editing and proofreading by Gavin Lucas

All rights reserved. No part of this publication may be reproduced, stored in a retrieval system, or transmitted in any form or by any means, electronic, mechanical, photocopying, recording, or otherwise, without the prior permission of both the copyright owner and the above publisher of this book.

A CIP catalogue record for this book is available from the British Library.

ISBN 978 1 39962 413 8

Origination by F1 Colour, London
Printed in Italy by L.E.G.O. S.p.A.

www.laurenceking.com
www.orionbooks.co.uk